W0019524

RAMBLINGS FROM REMNANTS

RAMBLINGS FROM REMNANTS

Brian Bex

Edited by Amy Christine Weismiller

ATHENA PRESS
LONDON

RAMBLINGS FROM REMNANTS

Copyright © Brian Bex 2006

All Rights Reserved

No part of this book may be reproduced in any form
by photocopying or by any electronic or mechanical means,
including information storage and retrieval systems,
without permission in writing from both the copyright
owner and the publisher of this book.

ISBN 1 84401 699 4

First Published 2006 by
ATHENA PRESS
Queen's House, 2 Holly Road
Twickenham TW1 4EG
United Kingdom

Printed for Athena Press

To the Remnant... and those who would be so

Regret for the past is a waste of spirit – draw your own conclusions upon proper examination and stand up for those conclusions regardless of who or what you may find impeding. We are all given a finite amount of spirit – why waste it on personal contentions and useless parleys of personality? In any war, whether it be a war of words or a war of bullets – the first casualty is truth.

As you begin these ramblings remember how you can recognize a pioneer... count the arrows in his back.

Brian Bex

OTHER BOOKS BY BRIAN BEX

The Individualist Declaration, 1968
The Decline and Fall of the American Republic, 1972
The Hidden Hand, 1975
Commonweal, 1977
United States: Aborted, 1986
The Vanishing Dinosaur (autobiography), 1989
Out of Bounds, 1992
A Question of Focus, 1996
The Teetor-totter Equation, 1997
Buckwheat and the Giant, 2001

BOOKS CONTRIBUTED TO BY BRIAN BEX

Nelson Grills, *The Road: Never the Inn* (biographical sketch), 1982
Sheila Suess Kennedy, *Pickin' Fights with Thunderstorms* (biography), 2005

CONTENTS

The Treasure of Wisdom is chiefly contained in Books[1]

The desirable treasure of wisdom, which all desire by an instinct of nature, infinitely surpasses all the riches of the world; in respect of which precious stones are worthless; in comparison with which silver is as clay and pure gold is as a little sand; at whose splendor the sun and moon are dark to look upon; compared with whose marvelous sweetness honey and manna are bitter to taste.

Where dost thou chiefly lie hidden, O most elect treasure, and where shall thirsting souls discover thee?

In books I find the dead as if they were alive; in books I foresee things to come; in books warlike affairs are set forth; from books come forth the laws of peace. All things are corrupted and decay in time; Saturn ceases not to devour the children that he generates; all the glory of the world would be buried in oblivion, **unless God had provided mortals with the remedy of books.**

TIKKUM[2]

---

[1] *Philobiblon* was written by Richard De Bury in A.D. 1344. It was the first work recorded about books.

[2] Hebrew, "To restore the world.'

PREFACE
A Great Conversation[1]

We have not seen our task as that of taking tourists on a visit to ancient ruins or to the quaint productions of primitive peoples. We have not thought of providing our readers with hours of relaxation or with an escape from the dreadful cares that are the lot of every man in the second half of the twentieth century after Christ. **We are as concerned as anybody else at the headlong plunge into the abyss that Western civilization seems to be taking. We believe that the voices that may recall the West to sanity are those which have taken part in the Great Conversation. We want them to be heard again – not because we want to go back to antiquity, or the Middle Ages, or the Renaissance, or the eighteenth century. We are quite aware that we do not live in any time but the present, and, distressing as the present is, we would not care to live in any other time if we could. We want the voices of the Great Conversation to be heard again because we think they may help us to learn to live better now.**

We believe that in the passage of time the neglect of these books in the twentieth century will be regarded as an aberration, and not, as it is sometimes called today, a sign of progress. We think that progress, and progress in education in particular, depends on the incorporation of the ideas and images included in this set in the daily lives of all of us, from childhood through old age. In this view the disappearance of great books from education and from the reading of adults constitutes a calamity. **In this view education in the West has been steadily deteriorating; the rising generation has been deprived of its birthright; the mess of pottage it has received in exchange has not been nutritious; adults have come to lead lives comparatively rich in material comforts and very poor in moral, intellectual, and spiritual tone.**

We do not think that these books will solve all our problems. We do not think that they are the only books worth reading. We think

[1] The original by Robert Maynard Hutchins, former president of the University of Chicago, appeared over half a century ago (1952). These excerpts are perhaps more relevant today than when they were written. The entire text of *The Great Conversation* is available through The Remnant Trust.

that these books shed some light on all our basic problems, and that it is folly to do without any light we can get. We think that these books show the origins of many of our most serious difficulties. We think that the spirit they represent and the habit of mind they teach are more necessary today than ever before. We think that the reader who does his best to understand these books will find himself led to read and helped to understand other books. We think that reading and understanding great books will give him a standard by which to judge all other books.

We believe that the reduction of the citizen to an object of propaganda, private and public, is one of the greatest dangers to democracy. A prevalent notion is that the great mass of the people cannot understand and cannot form an independent judgment upon any matter; they cannot be educated, in the sense of developing their intellectual powers, but they can be bamboozled. **The reiteration of slogans, the distortion of the news, the great storm of propaganda that beats upon the citizen twenty-four hours a day all his life long means either that democracy must fall prey to the loudest and most persistent propagandists or that the people must save themselves by strengthening their minds so that they can appraise the issue for themselves.**

Great books alone will not do the trick; for the people must have the information on which to base a judgment as well as the ability to make one. In order to understand inflation, for example, and to have an intelligent opinion as to what can be done about it, the economic facts in a given country at a given time have to be available. Great books cannot help us there. But they can help us to that grasp of history, politics, morals, and economics and to that habit of mind which are needed to form a valid judgment on the issue. Great books may even help us to know what information we should demand. If we knew what information to demand we might have a better chance of getting it.

Though we do not recommend great books as a panacea for our ills, we must admit that we have an exceedingly high opinion of them as an educational instrument. We think of them as the best educational instrument for young people and adults today. By this we do not mean that this particular set is the last word that can be said on the subject. We may have made errors of selection. We hope that this collection may some day be revised in the light of the criticism it will receive. But **the idea that liberal education is the education that everybody ought to have, and that the best way to a liberal education in the West is through the greatest works the West**

has produced, is still, in our view, the best educational idea there is...

Great books contain their own aids to reading; that is one reason why they are great. Since we hold that these works are intelligible to the ordinary man, we see no reason to interpose ourselves or anybody else between the author and the reader...

The tradition of the West is embodied in the Great Conversation that began in the dawn of history and that continues to the present day. Whatever the merits of other civilizations in other respects, no civilization is like that of the West in this respect. No other civilization can claim that its defining characteristic is a dialogue of this sort. No dialogue in any other civilization can compare with that of the West in the number of great works of the mind that have contributed to this dialogue. The goal toward which Western society moves is the Civilization of the Dialogue. **The spirit of Western civilization is the spirit of inquiry. Its dominant element is the *Logos*. Nothing is to remain undiscussed. Everybody is to speak his mind. No proposition is to be left unexamined. The exchange of ideas is held to be the path to the realization of the potentialities of the race.**

At a time when the West is most often represented by its friends as the sources of that technology for which the whole world yearns and by its enemies as the fountainhead of selfishness and greed, it is worth remarking that, though both elements can be found in the Great Conversation, the Western ideal is not one or the other strand in the Conversation, but the Conversation itself. It would be an exaggeration to say that Western civilization means these books. The exaggeration would lie in the omission of the plastic arts and music, which have quite as important a part in Western civilization as the great productions included in this set. But to the extent to which books can present the idea of a civilization, the idea of Western civilization is here presented.

These books are the means of understanding our society and ourselves. They contain the great ideas that dominate us without our knowing it. There is no comparable repository of our tradition.

To put an end to the spirit of inquiry that has characterized the West it is not necessary to burn the books. All we have to do is to leave them unread for a few generations. On the other hand, the revival of interest in these books from time to time throughout history has provided the West with new drive and creativeness. Great books have salvaged, preserved, and transmitted the tradition on many occasions similar to our own.

The books contain not merely the tradition, but also the great exponents of the tradition. Their writings are models of the fine and liberal arts. They hold before us what Whitehead called "the habitual vision of greatness." These books have endured because men in every era have been lifted beyond themselves by the inspiration of their example. Sir Richard Livingstone said: "We are tied down, all our days and for the greater part of our days, to the commonplace. That is where contact with great thinkers, great literature helps. In their company we are still in the ordinary world, but it is ordinary world transfigured and seen through the eyes of wisdom and genius. And some of their vision becomes our own."

Until very recently these books have been central in education in the West. They were the principal instrument of liberal education, the education that men acquire as an end in itself, for no other purpose than that it would help them to be men, to lead human lives, and better lives than they would otherwise be able to lead.

The aim of liberal education is human excellence, both private and public (for man is a political animal). Its object is the excellence of man as man and man as citizen. It regards man as an end, not as a means; and it regards the ends of life, and not the means to it. For this reason it is the education of free men. Other types of education or training treat men as means to some other end, or are at best concerned with the means of life, with earning a living, and not with its ends.

The substance of liberal education appears to consist in the recognition of basic problems, in knowledge of distinctions and interrelations in subject matter, and in the comprehension of ideas.

Liberal education seeks to clarify the basic problems and to understand the way in which one problem bears upon another. It strives for a grasp of the methods by which solutions can be reached and the formulation of standards for testing solutions proposed...

The liberal arts are not merely indispensable; they are unavoidable. Nobody can decide for himself whether he is going to be a human being. The only question open to him is whether he will be an ignorant, undeveloped one or one who has sought to reach the highest point he is capable of attaining. The question, in short, is whether he will be a poor liberal artist or a good one.

The tradition of the West in education is the tradition of the liberal arts. Until very recently nobody took seriously the suggestion that there could be any other ideal. The educational ideas of John

Locke, for example, which were directed to the preparation of the pupil to fit conveniently into the social and economic environment in which he found himself, made no impression on Locke's contemporaries. And so it will be found that other voices raised in criticism of liberal education fell upon deaf ears until about a half-century ago.

This **Western devotion to the liberal arts and liberal education must have been largely responsible for the emergence of democracy as an ideal. The democratic ideal is equal opportunity for full human development, and, since the liberal arts are the basic means of such development, devotion to democracy naturally results from devotion to them. On the other hand, if acquisition of the liberal arts is an intrinsic part of human dignity, then the democratic ideal demands that we should strive to see to it that all have the opportunity to attain to the fullest measure of the liberal arts that is possible to each.**

The present crisis in the world has been precipitated by the vision of the range of practical and productive art offered by the West. All over the world men are on the move, expressing their determination to share in the technology in which the West has excelled. This movement is one of the most spectacular in history, and everybody is agreed upon one thing about it: we do not know how to deal with it. It would be tragic if in our preoccupation with the crisis we failed to hold up as a thing of value for the world, even as that which might show us a way in which to deal with the crisis, our vision of the best that the West has to offer. That vision is the range of the liberal arts and liberal education. Our determination about the distribution of the fullest measure of these arts and this education will measure our loyalty to the best in our own past and our total service to the future of the world.

The great books were written by the greatest liberal artists. They exhibit the range of the liberal arts. The authors were also the greatest teachers. They taught one another. They taught all previous generations, up to a few years ago. The question is whether they can teach us. To this question we now turn...

Until recently great books were central in liberal education; but liberal education was limited to an elite. So great books were limited to an elite and to those few of the submerged classes who succeeded in breaking into them in spite of the barriers that society threw up around them. Where anybody bothered to defend this exclusion, it was done on the basis that only those with exceptional intelligence and leisure could understand these books, and that only those who had political power needed to understand them.

As the masses were admitted to political activity, it was assumed that, though they must be educated, they could not be educated in this way. They had to learn to read the newspaper and to write a business letter and to make change; but how could they be expected to study Plato or Dante or Newton? All that they needed to know about great writers could be translated for them in textbooks that did not suffer from the embarrassment of being either difficult or great.

The people now have political power and leisure. If they have not always used them wisely, it may be because they have not had the kind of education that would enable them to do so.

It is not argued that education through great books and the liberal arts was a poor education for the elite. It is argued that times have changed and that such an education would be a poor education for anybody today, since it is outmoded. It is remote from real life and today's problems. Many of the books were written when men held slaves. Many were written in a pre-scientific and pre-industrial age. What can they have to say to us, free, democratic citizens of a scientific, industrial era?

This is a kind of sociological determinism. As economic determinism holds that all activity is guided and regulated by the conditions of production, so sociological determinism claims that intellectual activity, at least, is always relative to a particular society, so that, if the society changes in an important way, the activity becomes irrelevant. Ideas originating in one state of society can have no bearing on another state of society. If they seem to have a bearing, this is only seeming. Ideas are the rationalizations of the social conditions that exist at any given time. If we seek to use in our own time the ideas of another, we shall deceive ourselves, because by definition these ideas have no application to any other time than that which produced them.

History and common sense explode sociological determinism, and economic determinism, too. There is something called man on this earth. He wrestles with his problems and tries to solve them. These problems change from epoch to epoch in certain respects; they remain the same in others. What is the good life? What is a good start? Is there a God? What is the nature and destiny of man? Such questions and a host of others persist because man persists, and they will persist as long as he does. Through the ages great men have written down their discussion of these persistent questions. Are we to disdain the light they offer us on the ground that they lived in primitive, far-off times? **As someone has remarked, "The Greeks could not broadcast the Aeschylean tragedy; but they could write it." ...**

The Disappearance of Liberal Education

The countries of the West are committed to universal, free, compulsory education. The United States first made this commitment and has extended it further than any other... It will not be suggested that they are receiving the education that the democratic ideal requires. The West has not accepted the proposition that the democratic ideal demands liberal education for all. In the United States, at least, the prevailing opinion seems to be that the demands of that ideal are met by universal schooling, rather than by universal liberal education. What goes on in school is regarded as of relatively minor importance. The object appears to be to keep the child off the labor market and to detain him in comparatively sanitary surroundings until we are ready to have him go to work...

The unique function of the educational system would appear to have something to do with the mind. No other agency in the community sets itself up, or is set up, to train the mind. To the extent to which the educational system is diverted to other objects, to that extent the mind of the community is neglected...

Education is supposed to have something to do with intelligence. It was because of this connection that it was always assumed that if the people were to have political power they would have to have education. They would have to have it if they were to use their power intelligently. **This was the basis of the Western commitment to universal, free, compulsory education. I have suggested that the kind of education that will develop the requisite intelligence for democratic citizenship is liberal education, education through great books and the liberal arts, a kind of education that has all but disappeared from the schools, colleges, and universities of the United States.**

Why did this education disappear? It was the education of the Founding Fathers. Now it is almost gone. I attribute this phenomenon to two factors, **internal decay** and **external confusion**...

We have repeated to ourselves so much of late the slogan, "America must be strong," that we have forgotten what strength is. We appear to believe that strength consists of masses of men and machines. I do not deny that they have their role. But surely the essential ingredients of strength are trained intelligence, love of country, the understanding of its ideals, and such devotion to those ideals that they become a part of the thought and life of every citizen.

We cannot hope to make ourselves intelligible to the rest of the world unless we understand ourselves. We now present a confusing picture to other people largely because we are ourselves confused. To take only one example, how can we say that we are a part of the great tradition of the West, the essence of which is that nothing is to be undiscussed, when some of our most representative citizens constantly demand the suppression of freedom of speech in the interest of national security? Now that military power is obsolescent, **the national security depends on our understanding of and devotion to such ancient Western liberties as free speech.** If we abandon our ideals under external pressure, we give away without a fight what we would be fighting for if we went to war. We abandon the sources of our strength.

How can we say that we are defending the tradition of the West if we do not know what it is?...

And this is the point: every man's mind ought to keep working all his life long; every man's imagination should be touched as often as possible by the great works of imagination; every man ought to push toward the horizons of his intellectual powers all the time. It is impossible to have "had" a liberal education, except in a formal, accidental, immaterial sense. Liberal education ought to end only with life itself... **That is why the Great Conversation never ends...**

The decay of education in the West, which is felt most profoundly in America, undoubtedly makes the task of understanding these books more difficult than it was for earlier generations. **In fact my observation leads me to the horrid suspicion that these books are easier for people who have had no formal education than they are for those who have acquired that combination of misinformation, unphilosophy, and slipshod habits that is the usual result of the most elaborate and expensive institutional education in America...**

In our colleges the curriculum is often so arranged that taking one course is made prerequisite to taking another. The pedagogical habit ingrained by such arrangements may prompt the question: What reading is prerequisite to reading great books? The answer is simply **None**. For the understanding of the great books it is not necessary to read background materials or secondary works about them...

Do you need a liberal education? We say that it is unpatriotic not to read these books. You may reply that you are patriotic enough without them. We say that you are gravely cramping your human possibilities if you do not read these books. You may answer that you have troubles enough already.

This answer is the one that Ortega attacks in *The Revolt of the Masses*. It assumes that we can leave all intellectual activity, and all political responsibility, to somebody else and live our lives as vegetable beneficiaries of the moral and intellectual virtue of other men. The trouble with this assumption is that, whereas it was once possible, and even compulsory, for the bulk of mankind, such indulgence now, on the part of anybody, endangers the whole community. It is now necessary for everybody to try to live, as Ortega says, "at the height of his times." **The democratic enterprise is imperiled if any one of us says, "I do not have to try to think for myself, or make the most of myself, or become a citizen of the world republic of learning." The death of democracy is not likely to be an assassination from ambush. It will be a slow extinction from apathy, indifference, and undernourishment... The aim of education is wisdom, and each must have the chance to become as wise as he or she can.**

This conversation continues with Nicholas Murray Butler:

The making of the American Constitution was a stupendous achievement of men who through reading, through reflection, through insight, and through practical experience, had fully grasped the significance of the huge task to which they had devoted themselves, and who accomplished that task in a way that has excited the admiration of the civilized world. Those men built a representative *republic*; they knew the history of other forms of government; they knew what had happened in Greece, in Rome, in Venice and in Florence; they knew what had happened in the making of the modern nations that occupied the continent of Europe. Knowing all this, they deliberately, after the most elaborate debate and discussion both of principles and details, produced the result with which we are so familiar... This government was founded by men whose minds were fixed upon the problems involved in the creation of political institutions. They were thinking of liberty, of representative government, of protection against tyranny and spoliation, and of ways and means by which public opinion might, in orderly fashion, express itself in statute laws, in judicial judgments and in executive acts. The task of the founders was a political task, and with what almost superhuman wisdom, foresight and skill they accomplished it, is recorded history... It is a noteworthy and singular characteristic of our American government that the Constitution provides a means for protecting individual liberty from invasion by the powers of government itself, as well as from invasion by others more powerful and less scrupulous than ourselves. The principles underlying our civil and political liberty are indelibly written into the Constitution of the United States, and the nation's courts are instituted for their protection...

The representative *republic* erected on the American continent under the Constitution of the United States is a more advanced, a more just and a wiser form of government than the socialistic and direct democracy which it is now proposed to substitute for it... To put the matter bluntly, there is underway in the United States at the present time a definite and determined movement to change our representative *republic* into a socialist democracy. That attempt, carried on by men of conviction, men of sincerity, men of honest purpose, men of patriotism, **as they conceive patriotism**, is the most impressive political factor in our public life of today... This attempt is making while we are speaking about it. It presents itself in many persuasive and seductive forms. It uses attractive formulas to which men like to give adhesion; but if it is successful, it will bring to an end the form of government that was founded when our Constitution was made and those we and our fathers and grandfathers have known and gloried in.

We began the destruction of the fundamental principles of representative government in this country when we reduced the representative to the position of a mere delegate; when we began, as is now quite commonly the case, to instruct a representative as to what he is to do when elected; when we began to pledge him, in advance of his election, that if chosen he will do certain things and oppose others – in other words, when we reduced the representative from the high, splendid and dignified status of a real representative chosen by his constituency to give it his experience, his brains, his conscience and his best service, and made him a mere registering machine for the opinion of the moment, whatever it might happen to be.[2]

That is a remarkably strong statement of what our heritage was and a solemn warning against the dangers toward which we have been drifting...

---

[2] Nicholas Murray Butler, *Why Should We Change Our Form of Government?*, New York, Columbia University, 1912

To close this preface, let's move to a thinker from the last quadrant of the twentieth century, from middle America; Dr. Russell Kirk, with whom I visited on more than one occasion:

> Though most men and women, in any age and any country, live almost unaware that they are governed by certain general ideas, nevertheless nearly everything we have is produced and sheltered by the moral and intellectual assumptions that people take for granted. One cannot see or feel or taste or hear ideas; yet without the existence of great ideas, human beings would be only animals, and could exist only as animals live. Only mankind possesses ideas. The success or failure of any human society depends upon how sound and true its ideas are. That a nation has prospered a great while – that it has been orderly and free and just and wealthy – is one very good proof that its ideas have been sound and true...
>
> At least three groups of ideas, or bodies of principle, invisibly control any people, whether those people are Australian bushmen or highly civilized modern nations. The first, and most important, of these bodies of principle is the set of moral convictions which a people hold: their ideas about the relationship between God and man, about virtue and vice, honesty and dishonesty, honor and dishonor. The second of these bodies of principle is the set of political convictions which a people hold: their ideas about justice and injustice, freedom and tyranny, personal rights and power, and the whole complex problem of living together peaceably. The third of these bodies of principle is the set of economic convictions which a people hold: their ideas about wealth and property, public and private responsibilities in the affair of making a living, and the distribution of goods and services...
>
> ...when these bodies of principle are weakened, and a people lose faith in the ideas by which they live, civilization decays. When these bodies of principle are increasing in strength and richness, we say a people are progressive; but when these bodies of principle are decaying in their influence upon men and women, we call such a people decadent. It is by the healthiness of our principles that we measure the success or failure of any society...
>
> ...they are the accumulated accomplishments of countless generations of human beings... Occasionally, in the procession of history, a man of genius contributes something new to these principles... some human beliefs are found to be sound and enduring, while others are found to be erroneous and obsolete...

Our religious and moral convictions had their origin in the experience and thought of the ancient Jews and Greeks and Romans. Our political ideas, for the greater part, are derived from Greek, Roman, medieval European, and especially English practice and philosophy… American civilization… it is a part of a great chain of culture which we sometimes call "Western Civilization"…

We cannot understand our American cause, therefore, unless we first understand the principles – moral, political, and economic – upon which the American people have formed their complex society. The American cause, the purpose and duty and mission of the United States in the contemporary world, has grown out of these bodies of principle and out of the practical American experience in the application of these principles. The American, as a type, is not a visionary, a dreamer: he acts upon long-established principles that have been confirmed as valid by the American historical experience. And the American cause is not some vague aspiration toward turning the world upside down, but a sober and prudent defense of beliefs and rights and institutions – the legacy of civilization – which today are threatened by violent and disastrous forces that would destroy not just our citizens but also our culture.

A man without principles is an unprincipled man. A nation without principles is an uncivilized nation. If a people forget their principles, they relapse into barbarism and savagery. If a people reject sound principles for false principles, they become a nation of fanatics. The thinking American nowadays has to defend sound principle on two fronts: one, the neglect of all principle, which leads to social and personal decadence; the other, the adopting of false principles, which plunges the world into anarchy…

No cause can be maintained long unless a considerable proportion of a people understand the meaning of that cause… the number of people who truly understand the complexity of the American cause has grown dangerously small…[3]

[3] Russell Kirk, *The American Cause*, Chicago, H. Regnery Co., 1957

MISSION

The purpose is to say something that must be said and say it with simplicity. The age calls for simple statements and restatements of simple truths. The prophets of doom are involved, **those who would bring light must be clear.** Our problem is the problem of moral decay and degeneration. From a handful of dust faith must come. There is more hope in a heather rose than in all the tons of Teutonic philosophy. I do not know how to say these things, but **God give me strength to say them.**

The shadow of another war already looms before us. **We have to think straight and think fast.**

Lin Yutang, *Between Tears and Laughter*

Thus again begin the ramblings…

INTRODUCTION

One afternoon in the summer of 1989 I spent hours on end in conversation with a friend. He was espousing a concept which seemed on the surface to be very sound. As the conversation drew to a close he told me: "My efforts will be directed to reach the great masses of the American public. I want to get the ear of the people. I'm prepared to devote a good portion of the rest of my life to spreading this doctrine to as wide a body as I can. **What do you think?**"

This proved to be a most embarrassing question, as this acquaintance of mine is a close friend and actually one of the few individuals whose judgment I truly value. Still, as I reflected, I was inclined to believe that over the last three decades I had had more contact with the masses than had my friend. I told him that it had taken me thirty-five years of **direct association** with **"the public"** to get this idea of "reaching the masses" **out of my head**, and that he would do well if he followed a similar course. He would find that the "common man" couldn't care less for his doctrine and probably less for himself. I went so far as to say that his expressed mission reflected that he had not done his homework well on the "mindset of the masses." I suggested that he study the story of the prophet Isaiah. He looked puzzled at my suggestion and asked what I meant by it.

Discussing the attitudes of too many in higher education and the media who would silence specific viewpoints in the promotion of their own, reminds me of a remark once forthcoming from Edmund Burke:

> **Because half a dozen grasshoppers under a fern make the field ring with their importunate chink, whilst thousands of great cattle, reposed beneath the shadow of the British oak, chew the cud are silent, pray do not imagine that those who make the noise are the only inhabitants of the field... or that, after all, they are other than the little, shriveled, meager, hopping, though loud and troublesome insects of the hour.**[1]

It occurs to me that the story of **The Remnant** is again worth recalling

---

[1] Edmund Burke, *Reflections on the Revolution in France*, New Rochelle, NY, Arlington House, 1966

now when so many wise individuals, pundits, and social engineers seem completely burdened by their obsession to "reach the people." It seems that everybody connected with television, talk radio, motion pictures, evangelism, advertisers, *et al.*, have as their "purpose of living" the ever motivating desire **to prove that truth is statistically derived** – i.e., "the greater the audience the more valuable and accurate the projected social agenda." I cannot recall a time when so many social critics have been so vigorously proclaiming their words and/or opinions to the public and telling us what we must do to be exempted from our social fate. Many do little more than preach to the choir or reinvent the wheel. To me, the story of Isaiah has something in it to steady and compose the human spirit until, in the words of Albert Jay Nock, **"this tyranny of windiness be overpast."** Let me, through the social critique of Nock, paraphrase the story:

> The career began at the end of King Uzziah's reign, say about 740 B.C. This reign was uncommonly long, almost half a century. It was one of those prosperous reigns, however, like the reign of Marcus Aurelius at Rome, where at the end the prosperity suddenly peters out, and things go by the board with a resounding crash.
>
> In the year of Uzziah's death, the Lord commissioned Isaiah to go out and warn the people of the wrath to come. Tell them what a worthless lot they are, "Tell them what is wrong, and why, and what is going to happen unless they have a change of heart and straighten up. Don't mince matters. Make it clear that they are positively down to their last chance. Give it to them good and strong, and keep on giving it to them. I suppose perhaps I ought to tell you," he added, "that it won't do any good. The official class and their intelligentsia will turn up their noses at you, and the masses will not even listen. They will all keep on in their own ways until they carry everything down to destruction, and you will probably be lucky if you get out with your life."
>
> Isaiah had been very willing to take on the job; in fact, he had asked for it; but this prospect put a new face on the situation. It raised the obvious question why, if all that were so, if the enterprise were to be a failure from the start, was there any sense in starting it?
>
> **"Ah," the Lord said, "you do not get the point. There is a Remnant out there that you know nothing about. They are obscure, unorganized, inarticulate, each one rubbing along as best he or she can. They need to be encouraged and braced up, because when everything has gone completely to the dogs, they are the ones who will come back and build up a new**

society, and meanwhile your preaching will reassure them and keep them hanging on. Your job is to take care of The Remnant, so be off now and set about it."

As the word masses is commonly used, it suggests combinations of poor and unprivileged people, laboring people, proletarians, and it means nothing like that, **it means simply the majority.** The mass-man is one who has neither the force of intellect to comprehend the principles ensuing in what we know as the humane life, nor the force of character to adhere to those principles steadily and strictly as laws of conduct. Because such people make up the great, the overwhelming majority of mankind, they are called collectively, the masses. The line of differentiation between "the masses" and "the Remnant" is set invariably by quality, not by quantity. **The Remnant are those who by force of intellect are able to comprehend the principles of freedom, and by force of character are able, at least measurably, to adhere to them; the masses are those who are unable to do either.**

Plato lived into the administration of Eubulus, when Athens was at the peak of its great era, and he speaks of the Athenian masses with all Isaiah's enthusiasm and fire, even comparing them to a herd of ravenous wild beasts. Curiously, too, he applies Isaiah's own word **"Remnant"** to the worthier portion of Athenian society; **"there is but a very small remnant,"** he says, of those who possess a saving force of intellect and force of character too small, precisely as in Judea, to be of any avail against the ignorant and vicious preponderance of the masses.

But Isaiah was a preacher and Plato a philosopher; and we tend to regard preachers and philosophers rather as passive observers of the drama of life than as active participants. Hence in a matter of this kind their judgment might be suspected of being a little uncompromising or a little naïve. We may therefore bring forward another witness who was preeminently a man of affairs, and whose judgment cannot lie under this suspicion. Marcus Aurelius was ruler of the greatest of empires, and in that capacity he not only had the Roman mass-man under observation, but he had him on his hands twenty-four hours a day for eighteen years. What he did not know about him was not worth knowing, and what he thought of him is abundantly attested to on almost every page of the little book of jottings[2] which

[2] Marcus Aurelius from A.D. 161 to 180 was emperor of Rome. *Meditations* was a series of spiritual expressions filled with wisdom and profound understanding of human behavior. It was one of the greatest works of ethical reflection ever written. The first English translation is available through The Remnant Trust.

he scribbled offhand from day to day, and which he meant for no eye but his own ever to see.

This view of the masses is the one that we find prevailing among the ancient authorities whose writings have come down to us. In the eighteenth century, however, certain European philosophers spread the notion that the mass-man, in his natural state, was not at all the kind of person that earlier authorities made him out to be, but on the contrary, that he was a worthy object of interest. His antisocial behavior was the effect of environment, an effect for which "society was somehow responsible." If only his environment permitted him to live according to his best abilities, he would undoubtedly show himself to be quite a fellow; and the best way to secure a more favorable environment for him would be to let him arrange it for himself. The French Revolution acted powerfully as a springboard for this idea, projecting its influence in all directions throughout Europe and the new world.[3]

That was Centuries Ago, What About Today?

At different times in our history, different cities have been the focal point of a radiating American spirit. In the late eighteenth century, for example, Boston was the center of a political radicalism that ignited a shot heard around the world – a shot that could not have been fired any other place but the suburbs of Boston. At its report, all Americans, including Virginians, became Bostonians at heart. In the mid-nineteenth century, New York became the symbol of the idea of a melting-pot America – or at least a non-English one – as the wretched refuse from all over the world disembarked at Ellis Island and spread over the land their strange languages and even stranger ways. In the early twentieth century, Chicago, the big city of big shoulders and heavy winds, came to symbolize the industrial energy and dynamism of America. If there is a statue of a hog butcher somewhere in Chicago, then it stands as a reminder of the time when America was railroads, cattle, steel mills and entrepreneurial adventures. If there is no such statue, there ought to be, just as there is a statue of a Minute Man to recall the Age of Boston, as the Statue of Liberty recalls the Age of New York.

Today, we must look to the city of Las Vegas, Nevada, as a metaphor of our national character and aspiration, its symbol a thirty-foot-high cardboard picture of a slot machine and a chorus girl. For Las

[3] Albert Jay Nock, *Isaiah's Job*, Irvington-on-Hudson, New York, Foundation for Economic Education, 1962

Vegas is a city entirely devoted to the idea of entertainment, and as such proclaims the spirit of a culture in which all public discourse increasingly takes the form of entertainment. Our politics, religion, news, athletics, education and commerce have been transformed into congenial adjuncts of show business, largely without protest or even much popular notice. The result is that we are a people on the verge of amusing ourselves to death.[4]

What is Past is Prologue?

I believe that most people are well intentioned. But I have great and ever increasing respect for the corrosive influence of bias, systematic distortions of thought, the power of rationalization, the guises of self-interest, and the inevitability of unintended consequences. I have more respect for people who change their views after acquiring new information than for those who cling to views merely because they held them thirty years ago. The world changes. Ideologues and zealots don't.

Educationally, I am a product of "The Age of Irrational Activism, the 1960s." It began with the philosophy of men, like Henri Bergson and Sigmund Freud, who emphasized the doctrines of struggle and survival from nonhuman nature to human society, and rejected rationalism as slow, superficial, and an inhibition on both action and survival. As Bergson said in his *Creative Evolution* (1907): "The Intellect is characterized by a natural inability to comprehend life. Instinct, on the contrary, is molded on the very form of life…"

This period felt that man, and nature, and human society were all basically irrational. Reason, regarded as a late and rather superficial addition in the process of human evolution, was/is considered inadequate (by many in the Academy) to plumb the real nature of man's problems, and was regarded as an inhibitor on the full intensity of his actions, an obstacle to the survival of himself as an individual and of his group (The State). Any effort to apply reason or science, based on rational analysis and evaluation, would be a slow and frustrating effort: slow because the process of human rationality is always slow, frustrating because it cannot delve into the real depths and nature of man's experience, and because it can always turn up as many and as good reasons for any course of action as it can for the opposite course of action. The effort to do this was dangerous, because the thinker became poised in indecision, the man of action

[4] Neil Postman, *Amusing Ourselves to Death: Public Discourse in the Age of Show Business*, New York, Penguin Group, 1986

> struck, eliminated the thinker from the scene, and survived to determine the future on the basis of continued action. To the theorist of these views, the thinker would always be divided, hesitant, and weak, while the man of action would be unified, decisive, and strong. Remember, goodness without wisdom often yields unintended evils. So history recorded some of the consequences of the 1960s.[5]

Let me again quote Dr. Carroll Quigley:

> Revelation is not oracular... Propositions do not descend on us from heaven ready made, but are [...] more a draft of work in progress than a final and completed document, for faith itself, though rooted in immutable truth is not crowning knowledge, and its elaboration in teaching, namely theology, is still more bound up with discourses progressively manifesting fresh truths or fresh aspects of the truth to the mind. So the individual community grows in understanding; indeed, they must if, like other living organisms, they are to survive by adaptation to a changing environment of history, ideas, and social pressure.[6]
>
> We must bring meaning back into human experience. This, like establishing an achieving outlook, can be done by going backward in our Western tradition to the period before we had any bourgeois outlook. Our society had both meaning and purpose long before it had any middle-class. Indeed, these are intrinsic elements in our society. In fact, the middle-class outlook obtained its meaning and purpose from the society where it grew up; it did not give meaning and purpose to the society. Capitalism, along with the middle-class outlook, became meaningless and purposeless when it so absorbed men's time and energies that men lost touch with the meaning and purpose of the society in which capitalism made a brief and partial experience. Enter, "stage right" **The Welfare State.**
>
> Unfortunately, very few people, even highly regarded experts on the subject, have any clear idea of what is the tradition of the West or how it is based on the fundamental need of Western civilization to reconcile its intellectual outlook with the basic facts of the various religious experiences. The reality of the world, time, and the flesh forced, bit by bit, abandonment of the Greek rationalistic dualism (as in Plato) that opposed spirit and matter and made knowledge exclusively a concern of the former, achieved by internal illumina-

[5] Carroll Quigley, *The World Since 1939: A History*, New York, Collier Books, 1968

[6] *Ibid.* Carroll Quigley quoting Leonard Boyle, *The Summa Theologiae of Saint Thomas Aquinas; Latin Text and English Translation,* Vol. I, New York, McGraw Hill, 1904, p.102

> tion. Aquinas, who is quoted above, also said, "Nothing exists in the intelligence which was not first present in the senses," and "we cannot shift from the ideal to the actual." On this epistemological basis was established the root foundations of both modern science and modern liberalism, with a very considerable boost to both from the nominalists of the century following Aquinas.
>
> Our socio-political world has constantly fallen into intellectual error because it never solved the epistemological problem of the relationship between the theories and concepts in men's minds and the individual.[7]

C.F. Kettering, the great American industrialist, wrote:

> I have no desire to meditate or philosophize upon the past. I have only one wish and that is to direct our eyes toward the infinite future... Nothing ever built arose to touch the skies unless some man dreamed that it should, some man believed that it could, and some man willed that it must.

This is the perfect formula for the restoration of *individual liberty* and *human dignity*.

The United States Supreme Court in *Wickard v. Filburn* stated: "It is hardly lack of due process for the government to regulate that which it subsidizes."

The enemy blocking our goal is *out-of-bounds government*: *And there's the problem!*

There is a truism, an old folk saying: "*He who pays the fiddler calls the tune.*" This certainly applies to the relationship between the government and we citizens. When government subsidizes – pays – it regulates; it calls the tune which determines the extent of our enslavement. For it is an observed fact that the road to the Command Society is paved with dictatorial regulations – i.e., enslavement edicts.

Is "enslavement" too harsh a term? The British thinker Herbert Spencer wrote in 1884 an unusual but thoughtful and realistic definition of slavery:

> What is essential to the idea of a slave? We primarily think of him as one who is owned by another... That which fundamentally distinguishes the slave is that he labors under coercion to satisfy another's desires... What [...] leads us to qualify our conception of slavery as more or less severe?

[7] *Ibid.*

> Evidently the greater or smaller extent to which effort is compulsorily expended for the benefit of another instead of for self-benefit.[8]

Reflect upon the countless subsidies today being sought, not merely by the socialist and welfare-staters, but by many who call themselves "free enterprisers." Each subsidy, when granted, gives birth to not one but to numerous regulations. The number of governments in the U.S.A. approximates 100,000. Consider the many regulations that limit creative action – most of them do – and explain our country's rapid decline into the Command Society: enslavement. Along with the enslavement occurs the deadening of private ownership, a fundamental feature of the free society.

Someone once wrote that the government type of enslavement is the satanic offspring of at least three hallucinations:

1. I AM WISE! With few exceptions, those wielding power over others are corrupted. Authority of this nature tends to intoxicate them; they see others as fallible but never themselves;
2. I AM IT! Government controls what it subsidizes. Elected and appointed holders of government office develop the mentality of *L'Etat c'est moi* – I am The State. They come to believe that the funds they use to subsidize are the government's own money, and they are the government, and thus, they are it;
3. I AM OMNIPOTENT! This is the little-god syndrome: "Be like me, do as I say, obey my edicts, and thou shalt be graced with the good life." The truth? Not one of them is any more competent to direct our mortal moments than to direct our spirits in the hereafter! This is to say that they can no more effectively direct creatively at the earthly level than they can direct Creation. *Managing the creative lives of others is beyond any man's competence*, but these characters don't even know this – a hallucination, indeed!

I repeat: *private ownership is a fundamental feature of the free society*. However, merely holding title to a piece of property does not mean ownership if control is absent. *One does not own that which one does not control.* In Mussolini's Italy, titles to enterprises were retained, but that fascist regime controlled wages, prices, hours worked, what goods and services could be produced, to whom sold, and so on. *Titles without control are utterly meaningless.*

---

[8] Herbert Spencer, *The Man Versus the State*, Caldwell, Id., The Caxton Printers Ltd, 1940

This is a point never to forget: The millions of regulations in our America today are controls! Thus, to the extent that regulations exist, to that extent has *government* ownership replaced *private* ownership.

Too many individuals demand that government bestow special privileges upon them? But their shameful demands would little perturb us were our government properly limited. Proper limitation means curbing all dictatorial, authoritarian action. This is a goal we approach only as more of us understand and insist that government mind its own business: invoking a common justice; keeping the peace; maintaining a fair field and no favoritism. Our goal of highest statesmanship has its origin in a highly moral citizenship, which is the personal responsibility of each of us.

Why is grass green? Leave free men and someone with eyes toward the infinite future will find the answer, just as in the past man discovered how to harness a mysterious energy: electricity. However, let us not say, "Give us freedom and the heavens will open unto us." *Freedom is not a gift but a blessing that is earned by learning and doing.* In such freedom, we serve one another – often unknowingly!

> That all men are... endowed by their Creator with certain unalienable rights, that among these are Life, Liberty, and the Pursuit of Happiness.[9]

Here we have the greatest wisdom ever written into a political document. It unseated government as the endower of men's rights and placed the Creator there! When citizens cannot turn to government for security, welfare, or prosperity, to whom or what do they turn? **To themselves?** Result? *Self-reliance and the greatest outburst of creative energy ever known* – miracles by the millions.

Why is the practice of freedom in America diminishing? On the surface, at least, it appears to be withering away. Why? Perhaps no one knows all the reasons, but an important one is that believers are lacking in understanding and defective in exposition. If we look to ourselves or our acquaintances, it is evident that none of us – when it comes to expertise in the philosophy of liberty – has enough candle power to cast much of a beam. This suggests a basic need to tie in with the source of light.

Common opinion, even among those who proclaim a liking for freedom, holds that our only task is to devise techniques for insinuating our present views into the minds of others – **as if our opinions were**

[9] The Declaration of Independence

wisdom unblemished, the latest and most enlightened word that could be imparted to others mechanically. Such reform efforts amount to no more than publicizing the scarcity of what we know, and the most likely reaction from others is to correlate the freedom philosophy with our emptiness and decide that they want none of it. We should realize that ideas can never be insinuated into the heads of others, for each person is in charge of his or her own doors of perception. We who believe in freedom should relinquish forever the habit of trying to make others carbon copies of ourselves.

The only methodology consistent with the philosophy of freedom puts the emphasis on inner reflection and self-probing; it avoids efforts to coercively project our views into the minds of others. Assuming studious preparation – that is, constantly drawing on all of the current and past wisdom within our capabilities – **individual reflection is the sole source of additional wisdom or enlightenment**, to the extent that as we brighten our own inner light, we dispel some of the darkness around us. Fortunately, there is nothing whatsoever one can do about the darkness that enshrouds others except to increase his or her own candle power and share it. **So let us look first and always to our own enlightenment. To expect a general enlightenment in society without any more enlightenment in particular individuals is an absurdity.**

> The free market, private ownership, limited government way of life – sometimes referred to as capitalism – is wasting away because so few understand its philosophical underpinnings and the prerequisites for its survival. Those interested in reversing this sorry trend are well advised to align themselves with the realities of the situation, so as not to waste energy in futile endeavors but, rather, to concentrate on the possible. Away with the fruitless that the fruitful may be pursued! ... Ask a hundred persons what capitalism is and get a hundred different answers, strikingly diverse, if not contradictory, ranging all the way from entrenched privilege and monopoly to an ideal concept of capitalism featured by freedom in transactions, free entry, competition, cooperation, voluntarism to each his own – in a word, a fair field and no favor. To proclaim oneself in favor of capitalism in today's babble of tongues is to evoke approval from a few and disfavor from the vast majority, so slight is the understanding of the issues involved.

An outstanding reason for this is the assumption that businessmen should be the key spokesmen for capitalism because presumably they are true exemplars and beneficiaries. The fact is that businessmen generally possess moral, ethical, intellectual, and ideological traits as varied as those to be found among students, teachers, politicians, football players, or any other occupational category. To fix upon businessmen as exemplars of freedom would be no more accurate than to classify them as socialists, or fiddlers, or gourmet cooks. **We are all a mix of every fault and virtue known to man.**

If a businessman is a capitalist in the sense that he upholds the ideal of a market economy, it is not because he is a businessman but, rather, that he is a student who sees through the fallacies of socialism and grasps the efficacy of freedom. Indeed, in the absence of a principled stand for capitalism, those of high energy with a strong desire to achieve and get ahead – entrepreneurs – are forever tempted to use their high positions in a political way to exploit the masses – that is, to become anti-capitalists. The exceptions, the entrepreneurs who maintain a principled capitalistic position, are men and women who have "worked against the grain" – an admirable moral and intellectual achievement. These are individuals who stand for freedom in spite of being in business. And bravo for them!

Professor Benjamin Rogge made this point decades ago and thereby gave a clue as to where our hope lies:

> ...Contrary to the popular impression, there is no reason to expect the businessman to be more committed to the system of economic freedom than anyone else. Not only is he not the greatest beneficiary of that system – he is not even the principal beneficiary. Again, contrary to popular impression, it is the "little man," the member of the masses who, far from being the exploited victim under capitalism, is precisely its principal beneficiary... The development and survival of man-made institutions depend upon someone's keen and unremitting desire to understand and sustain them. Without that incentive, actual or potential, we can forget about freedom. In whom, then, do we seek for this quality? We look first and foremost to the "little man" – little only in the sense that he is not a "big shot!" He is not one of those who, under authoritarian system, would have been a feudal lord, mercantilist, lord of the manor, maharajah. Nor in today's world, is he a commissar, or dictator, or political coercionist, or farm or labor business monopolist, or high-placed protectionist, or one who thinks he "has it made."[10]

We might describe the beneficiary as one to whom opportunity is still

[10] Benjamin Rogge, *Can Capitalism Survive?*, Indianapolis, The Liberty Fund, 1979

precious, who has not yet lived out his life, and is not ready for a closed system. He prefers to live his own life rather than beg from others or have others begging from him. The beneficiary is the growing man, one who wishes to become what he is not yet; an Abraham Lincoln or the bicycle repairmen; or a Larry Bird, Wilbur or Orville Wright; or a Thomas Alva Edison will suffice as examples.

The man who is still trying to improve himself is by all odds the principal beneficiary of capitalism or, if you prefer, the free market economy. This way of life in America accounts for the unrestrained release of creative human energy; accounts for untold millions able to reach over seventy years of age and to pursue whatever course our uniqueness, abilities, and aspirations suggest. These millions, had they entered the world of ten generations ago, would have been short-lived serfs! I repeat, we are the principal beneficiaries of capitalism – not of those practices so grossly misrepresented as capitalism, but of capitalism as it should be understood: the free and open market. So, the recovery of freedom must come from its principal beneficiaries, those who still aim to grow. And they, of course, are to be found at all economic and cultural levels, perhaps called **The Remnant.**

However, only when we, the principal beneficiaries of the free market economy, are aware of our blessings can we hope to become effective protagonists, for without such awareness, our improved circumstances and opportunities will be attributed to non-causes and we will lack the incentive to reverse the socialistic trend, to learn the principles and restore the practices of freedom and capitalism. **Until we see this to be a matter of self-interest, we will lack the initiative and there will be no chance for freedom – none whatsoever!**

Do we really want to become as Sven Birkerts projects in *The Gutenberg Elegies:* ***creatures of the hive*****?**

> **By moving from the order of print to the electronic, we risk the loss of the sense of obstacle as well as the feel of the particular that have characterized our experience over millennia. We are poised at the brink of what may prove to be a kind of *species mutation.* We had better consider carefully what this means.**
>
> 1. I believe that what distinguishes us as a species is not our technological prowess, but rather our extraordinary ability to confer meaning on our experience and to search for clues about our purpose from the world around us.
>
> 2. I believe, too, that meaning of this kind – call it "existential" meaning – has from the beginning been the product of our other

great distinguishing aptitude: the ability to communicate symbolically through language. Indeed language is the soil, the seedbed, of meaning. And the works of language, our literatures, have been the repository of our collective speculation.

I am not going to argue against the power and usefulness of electronic technologies. Nor am I going to suggest that we try to turn back or dismantle what we have wrought in the interests of an intensified relation to meaning. But I would urge that we not fall all over ourselves in our haste to filter all of our experience through circuitries. We are in some danger of believing that the speed and wizardry of our gadgets have freed us from the sometimes arduous work of turning pages in silence... it is inevitable that generation by generation all independence and idiosyncrasy and depth will be worn away; that we will move ever more surely in lockstep, turning ourselves into creatures of the hive, living some sort of diluted universal dream in a perpetual present...

A hundred million people form their ideas about what is going on in America and in the world from the same basic package of edited images – to the extent that the image itself has lost much of its once-fearsome power. Daily newspapers, with their long columns of print, struggle with declining sales, fewer and fewer people under the age of fifty read them; computers will soon make packaged information a custom product...

The outcry against the modification of the canon can be seen as a plea for old reflexes and routines. And the cry for multicultural representation may be a last-ditch bid for connection to the fading legacy of print. The logic is simple. When a resource is threatened – made scarce – people fight over it. In this case the struggle is over textual power in an increasingly nontextual age. The future of books and reading is what is at stake...

Whoever controls the reading list comes out ahead in the struggle for the hearts and minds of the young.

We can expect that curricula will be further streamlined, and difficult texts in the humanities will be pruned and glossed. One need only compare a college textbook from twenty years ago to its contemporary version. A poem by Milton, a play by Shakespeare – one can hardly find the text among the explanatory notes nowadays. Fewer and fewer people will be able to contend with the so-called masterworks of literature or ideas...

As the circuit supplants the printed page, our perception of history will inevitably alter...

We may even now be in the first stages of a process of social collectivization that will over time all but vanquish the ideal of the individual... There are no more wildernesses, no more lonely homesteads, and, outside of cinema, no more emblems of the exalted individual.

Literature and the humane values we associate with it have been depreciated, reincarnated in debased form. They have not been extinguished, for our culture will always need to pay lip service to them, but they have been rendered safely, nostalgically, irrelevant.

Think about it. Where in our society do we get so much as an inkling that writers matter? Or their books? Or their ideas? Visual is the order. The challenging writer is archaic. Anything archaic is shunned.

Difficult books have always depended on loyal coteries, but as these have dwindled we find publishers less and less willing to take a chance. Our culture is ruled by the pocketbook, by the psychology of the bottom line. The result is that our arts increasingly cater to the lowest common denominator... the very concept of the book as an object to be lingered over and palpated, something that seeps into the soul, has changed.

My core fear is that we are, as a culture, as a species, becoming shallower; that we have turned from [substance] – from the Judeo-Christians' premise of unfathomable mystery – and are adapting ourselves to the ersatz security of a vast lateral connectedness. That we are giving up on wisdom, the struggle for which has for millennia been central to the very idea of culture and that we are pledging instead to a faith in the web. What is our idea, our ideal, of wisdom these days? Who represents it? Who even invokes it? Our postmodern culture is a vast fabric of competing isms; we are leaderless and subject to the terrors, masked as the freedoms, of an absolute relativism. It would be wrong to lay all the blame at the feet of technology, but more wrong to ignore the great transformative impact of new technological systems – to act as if it's all just business as usual...

The devil no longer moves about on cloven hooves, reeking of brimstone. He is an affable, efficient fellow. He claims to want to help us all along to a brighter, easier future, and his sales pitch is very smooth. I was, as the old song goes, almost persuaded. I saw what it could be like, our toil and misery replaced by a vivid, pleasant dream. Fingers tap keys, oceans of fact and sensation get downloaded, are dissolved through the nervous system. Bottomless wells of data are accessed and manipulated, everything flowing at circuit speed. Gone

> the rock in the field, the broken hoe, the grueling distances. "History," said Stephen Dedalus, "is a nightmare from which I am trying to awaken." This may be the awakening, but it feels curiously like the fantasies that circulate through our sleep. From deep in the heart I hear the voice that says, "Refuse it."[11]

Yes – please refuse it!

Read the words from Ayn Rand, author of *Atlas Shrugged*:

> **Staleness is the dominant characteristic of today's (education) – and, at first glance, it may appear to be a puzzling phenomenon. Simply stated, most are bored!**
>
> There is an air of impoverished drabness, of tired routine, of stagnant monotony in all our (educational) activities – from stage and screen, to literature and the arts, to the allegedly intellectual publications and discussions (from TV to the classroom). There is little to see or to hear. Almost everything produces the effect of *déjà vu* or *déjà entendu*. **How long since you have read (or seen or heard) anything startling, different, fresh, unexpected: (A new idea, a new solution?)**
>
> Intellectually, people are wearing pasted jewelry copied from paste jewelry by artisans who have never seen the original gems. **Originality is an all but forgotten experience.** The latest fads [...] wither [...] at birth.
>
> **Evils are inherent in the vicious impropriety of the government subsidizing ideas.** Both chose to ignore the fact that any intrusion of government into the field of ideas, for or against anyone, withers intellectual freedom and creates an official orthodoxy, a privileged elite. **Today, it is called an ("education")...**
>
> Today, what we see in this country's intellectual field is one of the worst manifestations of power: **rule by favorites, by the unofficially privileged – by private groups with power, but without responsibility.** They are shifting, switching groups, often feuding among themselves, but united against outsiders; they are scrambling to catch momentary favors, their precise status unknown to their members, their rivals, or their particular patrons among the hundreds of Congressmen and the thousands of bureaucrats – who are now bewildered and intimidated by these Frankensteinian creations...
>
> The symptoms of today's (educational) disease are: conformity, with nothing to conform to – timidity expressed in a self-shrinking

[11] Sven Birkerts, *The Gutenberg Elegies*, Boston, Faber & Faber, 1994

> concern with trivia – a kind of obsequious anxiety to please the unknown standards of some nonexistent authority – and a pall of fear without object. Psychologically, this is the cultural atmosphere of a society living under censorship…
>
> America's abundance was not created by public sacrifices to "the common good," but by the productive genius of free men and women who pursued their own interests and the making of their own fortunes. They provided the people better jobs, higher wages, and less expensive goods with every new machine they invented, with every scientific discovery or technological advance – and thus the whole country was moving forward and profiting, every step of the way.
>
> The crisis our nation faces is a moral crisis… You and I must fight for capitalism, not as a "practical" issue, not as an economic issue, but, with the most righteous pride, **as a moral issue**. That is what future generations deserve, and nothing less should be our purpose…
>
> Government encouraged and financed education does not order men to believe that the false is true: **it merely makes them indifferent to the issue of truth or falsehood.**[12]

Editor's note: Remember Rand wrote this over half a century ago – doesn't it describe some citizens and our condition today?

> The attitude is so inclusive, so devout, that one is reminded of the troglodytic monster described by Plato, and the assiduous crowd at the entrance to its cave, trying obsequiously to placate it and win its favor, trying to interpret its inarticulate noises, trying to find out what it wants, and eagerly offering it all sorts of things that they think might strike its fancy.
>
> The main trouble with all this is its effect upon the mission itself. It necessitates an opportunist sophistication of one's doctrine which profoundly alters its character and reduces it to a single issue. If, say, you are a preacher, you wish to attract as large a congregation as you can, which means an appeal to the masses, and this in turn means adapting the terms of your message to the order of intellect and character that the masses exhibit. If you are an educator, say with a college on your hands, you wish to get as many students as possible, and you whittle down your requirements accordingly. If a writer, you aim at getting many readers; if a publisher, many purchasers; if a philosopher, many disciples; if a reformer, many converts; if a radio or TV talk show host or advertiser, the widest audience and

[12] Ayn Rand

subsequent highest ratings; and so on. But as we see on all sides, in the realization of these several desires the prophetic message is so heavily adulterated with trivialities in every instance that its effect on the masses is merely to harden them in their sins.[13]

Remember: truth is seldom statistically derived!

So long as the masses are taking up the tabernacle of *Sex in the City*, *Jerry Springer*, *Friends*, *Will & Grace*, *Survivor*, *Who Wants to be a Millionaire*, *South Park*, *MTV*, *Celebrity Poker*, *Fox News*, legalized distortion (advertising), and The National Football League, their images, and following the star of their words, we will have no lack of prophets to point the way that leadeth to the "more abundant life."

From Dhammapada:[14]

> All that we are is the result of what we have thought: it is founded on our thoughts, it is made up of our thoughts. If a man speaks or acts with an evil thought, pain follows him, as the wheel follows the foot of the one that draws the carriage.
>
> If a man speaks or acts with pure thought, happiness follows him, like a shadow that never leaves him...
>
> Buddha

May We Learn From History...

Reading history sometimes gives one a curious feeling in the pit of the stomach, for the similarities to the modern world are rather alarming. Unquestionably the Athenians were democrats; but unfortunately, democracies also commit suicide. Human art had never soared higher than in Athens; the light of sweet reason and a wide-awake curiosity had illuminated Her mind, and simplicity and harmony had beautified Her spirit. Athenian pride was justifiable. Modern presidents can boast of no greater achievements in their democracies, or in modern civilization in general, than Pericles did of the achievements of the Athenian way of life in his funeral speech in honor of the fallen heroes at the end of the first year of the Peloponnesian War. The tone is strikingly like an American presidential address:

> Before I praise the dead, I should like to point out by what principles of action we rose to power, and under what institutions and through

[13] Albert Jay Nock, *Isaiah's Job*

[14] The name of one of the early disciples of the Buddha, and therefore constantly chosen as their name in religion by Buddhist novices upon their entering the brotherhood.

> what manner of life our empire became great... Our form of government does not enter into rivalry with the institutions of others. We do not copy our neighbors, but we are an example to them. It is true that we are called a democracy, for the administration is in the hands of the many and not of the few. But while the law secures justice for all alike in private disputes, the claim of excellence is also recognized; and when a citizen is distinguished, he is preferred to the public service, not as a matter of privilege, but as a reward of merit. Neither is poverty a bar, but a man may benefit his country whatever be the obscurity of his condition... While we are thus unconstrained in our private intercourse, a spirit of reverence pervades our public acts; we are prevented from doing wrong by respect for authority and for the laws having especial regard to those unwritten laws which bring upon the transgressor of them the reprobation of the general sentiment.
>
> And we have not forgotten to provide for our weary spirits many relaxations from toil; we have regular games and sacrifices throughout the year; at home the style of life is refined; and the delight which we daily feel in all these things helps to banish melancholy. Because of the greatness of our city, the fruits of the whole earth flow in upon us; so that we enjoy the goods of other countries as freely as of our own... And in the matter of education, whereas they [the Spartans] from early youth are always undergoing laborious exercise which are to make youth brave, we live at ease, and yet are equally ready to face the perils which they face...[15]

Pericles could not have spoken better if he were giving a speech in honor of the heroes fallen at the World Trade Center. He could write the Thanksgiving Proclamation for 2010 in exactly the same words, for here is the essence of democracy as Pericles perceived it and as Thucydides reported it from memory (and his own imagination), and in the exact terms in which a *New York Times* or *Washington Post* editorial might have put it:

> For we are lovers of the beautiful, yet with economy, and we cultivate the mind without loss of manliness... An Athenian citizen does not neglect the State because he takes care of his own household; and even those of us who are engaged in business have a very fair idea of politics. We alone regard a man who takes no interest in public affairs, not as a harmless, but as a useless character; and if few of us

[15] Thucydides, *Peloponnesian War*, Bk. II, Ch. 36–39, Chicago, University of Chicago Press, 1989

> are originators, we are all sound judges of a policy. The great impediment to action is, in our opinion, not discussion preparatory to action. For we have a peculiar power of thinking before we act and of acting too, whereas other men are courageous from ignorance... To sum up: I say that Athens is the school of Hellas, and that the individual Athenian in his own person seems to have the power of adapting himself to the most varied forms of action with the utmost versatility and grace... I have dwelt upon the greatness of Athens because I want to show you that we are contending for a higher prize than those who enjoy none of these privileges...[16]

There was never a clearer defense of the strength of Athenian democracy and of the Athenian way of life. Unfortunately, it was an imperialist democracy, and the Greek Athenian way of life. Unfortunately, the Greek world remained half-slave and half-free. Athens had survived her "Great War I" – the Persian Wars and the defeat at Salamis; **it was rather the failure of moral leadership, the arrogance and stupidity (hubris) of the Athenians in failing to recognize the principle of freedom and equality for all Greek cities, that led to incessant wars and the final catastrophe, which was suicide**.

One could wish that Athenian and modern parallels were less exact. On the basis that human chicanery, the play of power politics, and the emotion of jealousy and fear are the same in all ages, Thucydides was quite right in his predictions. "But if he who desires a true picture of the events which have happened, and of **the like events which may be expected to happen hereafter in the course of human things**, shall pronounce what I have written to be useful, then I shall be satisfied."

The parallels are in fact uncomfortably and alarmingly exact.

> If we may believe Thucydides [says Will Durant], the democratic leaders of Athens, while making liberty the idol of their policy among Athenians, frankly recognized that the Confederacy of free cities had become an empire of force ... *the inherent contradiction between the worship of liberty and the despotism of empire co-operated with the individualism of the Greek states to end the Golden Age.*
>
> Thucydides, an Athenian, was ingenuous and impartial enough to tell us that the real cause of the Peloponnesian War was the domination of Athenian power. The Athenians were determined to enforce a *Pax Athenica*. They were for free trade, being themselves dependent upon imported grains from Egypt and Thrace, and were modern

[16] *Ibid.*, Bk. II, Ch. 40–42, Chicago, University of Chicago Press, 1989

> enough to enforce economic sanctions. Megarian products were excluded from Attica and the Empire. Megara and Corinth appealed to Sparta. Sparta intervened, and demanded the repeal of the embargo. Pericles agreed, but demanded in return the throwing open of Spartan cities to foreign trade. Sparta agreed, but countered with the demand that Athens acknowledge the full independence of all Greek cities. Pericles, however, refused to preside over the liquidation of the Athenian Empire. Thereupon Sparta declared war. Writes Thucydides, "The real though unavowed cause I believe to have been the growth of the Athenian power, which terrified the Lacedaemonians and forced them into war: but the reasons publicly alleged on either side were ... quite different.[17]

It's therefore correct to say that it was Pericles's Athens that ruined the Grecian world, and that the love of power and commercial imperialism were the causes of war. **Athenian arrogance and love of power resulted in a pattern of power politics very similar to that of the present day** – disaffection of allies, coercion in times of strength and cajolery in moments of weakness, shifting alliances and counter-alliances, internecine wars, and final exhaustion and ruin. Will Durant's judgment was as follows:

> Under him [Pericles] Athens had reached her zenith; but because her height had been attained in part through the wealth of an unwilling confederacy, and through power that invited almost universal hostility, the Golden Age was unsound in its foundations, and was doomed to disaster when Athenian statesmanship failed in the strategy of peace.
>
> That Thucydides could analyze the psychological motives of our modern statesmen so skillfully is merely evidence that **ancient and modern men are essentially alike**. Yielding and compromise would be construed as a sign of "weakness," even when Socrates chose to give himself thirty days to die. The seventy-year-old Socrates happened to believe in *satyagraha,* and in the integrity of spiritual principles. His accuser, Anytus, stood for law and order and even for public morality. Anytus went to the temple to worship. Anytus, too, was a good man, and a God-fearing man, by all public records. There was another man, Pontius Pilate, who once washed his hands of an important matter. Who ever said that Pontius Pilate was a bad man? He merely declined diplomatically to interfere in the

[17] Will Durant, *Life of Greece*, New York, Simon and Schuster, 1939

> private affairs of another nation, even though it involved the murder of an innocent man. There are in fact more historic analogies than one can stomach...
>
> There are too many similarities. The advantage of delving into Thucydides is that there the picture is focused into a smaller and simpler scale, its geography is foreshortened in time. Briefly, it was the conflict of Athenian sea power and Spartan land power, and the sad story of the failure of moral leadership. The dream of an all-Greek Federation petered out, owing to that moral failure and to the unwillingness or incapacity of Athens to solve the problem of empire versus freedom. We are wise after the fact and can put our finger on the arrogance and stupidity of the Athenians and the psychological cause of that failure. Let us only hope that **the dream of world federation** may have less the character of the Delian Confederacy, and that there be no Alexander from across the mountains to descend upon and desolate the Ionian plains and wipe out what was a world of glorious human achievements. **The tragic motivation of that historical drama was that the heroine, Athens, democratic and brilliant and arrogant, loved freedom for herself, but could not understand the equally passionate love of freedom of the other Greek cities.**[18]

We are not even beginning to scratch the surface of the moral malignant tumor that is called twenty-first-century culture. The region of the tumor being sensitive, politicians and publicists are too scared to touch its surface. That is why our governments have consistently followed the policy of "win the war first." For the time being, the win-the-war-first boys are having their way. The roots of all war – balance of power, domination by power, trade, and discrimination – are all there; not a single factor is lacking. **All the lessons we could have taken from the Greek world are being ignored**; all the sources of possible conflict, so plain now to the student of history, seem not to exist for the average planner of peace for our world. **The house built on sand by our learned architects will one day collapse...**

Since power, however, is by definition something dynamic and not static, there is no such thing as an actual "balance of power." Some powers grow and others weaken during a period; some alliances deteriorate, new ones are formed. Then the balance is upset once more and the nations of the world are plunged once more into bloodshed until a new "balance" is devised by a new generation of peace architects

[18] *Ibid.*

using the same old squares and compasses…

The adequacy of power politics as a principle must be called into question; the dependability of the cardinal principle of balance of power in building a stable peace must be debated, talked about, and challenged. **Only so can there be depth in our reasoning. The changes in our way of thinking must be basic if we are to succeed…**

> READING history may be a costly effort. Thucydides from Borders or Barnes & Noble may cost $25, but the failure to read it properly will be much more costly to our modern world. For today the issue of empire versus freedom is unsolved and ignored…

Let us take the idea of liberty, and see how its basis is failing. We shall see how the very content of freedom has changed, because the idea of man's "rights," on which liberty is based, has changed.

Let me share several quotes from decades ago by author and philosopher Walter Lippmann:[19]

> But first I must make clear that two of the Four Freedoms are not freedoms at all, and one of them has no meaning for me. A study of the Four Freedoms reveals that there are two "doubles" masquerading as Freedom that the Devil Economics has put there. **Freedom from fear is not freedom, but political security. Freedom from want is not freedom, but economic security.** Both may be achieved at the cost of human freedom, and probably will, if we think much about animal security. Nothing gives such a feeling of perfect freedom from want and fear to a dog as a collar around its neck. Its next meal is guaranteed. A bird in a cage has exchanged its freedom on the wing for freedom from the preying hawk and freedom from starvation in the snow. But a bird which deliberately flies into a cage cannot be said to be fighting for its freedom except by the most **caustic casuistry**. It is a mere trick of the English language, and "freedom from want" or "fear" is untranslatable into Chinese or French. What is *"liberté de misère"* or *"liberté de peur"*? We may, if we like, easily add a few more freedoms, like "Freedom from Disease," which is health, and "Freedom from Dirt," which is cleanliness, and "Freedom from the Telephone," which is peace and rest, *ad infinitum*.

[19] An address given at the annual meeting of The American Association for the Advancement of Science, December 29, 1940. It was printed in *The American Scholar* (publication of Phi Beta Kappa), Spring 1941 by Walter Lippmann. The author begins by discussing the four freedoms of Franklin Roosevelt.

And so when we speak of freedom, we must stick to the original meaning of the term, without "of" and without "from" – just plain good old freedom – **human freedom**. It is possible for man to have all Four Freedoms – the freedom to talk and think as he pleases and to be fed and sheltered in security – and yet be a slave.

That during the past forty or fifty years [**Editor's note: Now ten decades**] those who are responsible for education have progressively removed from the curriculum of studies the Western culture which produced [our] modern democratic state;

That the schools and colleges have, therefore, been sending out into the world [individuals] who no longer understand the creative principle of the society in which they must live;

That, deprived of their cultural tradition, **the newly educated … no longer possess in the form and substance of their own minds and spirits the ideas, the premises, the rationale, the logic, the method, the values of the deposited wisdom which are the genius of the development of Western civilization**;

That the prevailing education is destined, if it continues, to destroy Western civilization and is in fact destroying it.

> I believe there are more instances of the abridgement of freedom of the people by gradual and silent encroachments of those in power than by violent and sudden usurpations.
>
> James Madison, "On Dangers to Liberty"

That our civilization cannot effectively be maintained where it still flourishes, or be restored where it has been crushed, without the revival of the central, continuous, and perennial culture of the Western world;

And that, therefore, what is now required in the modern educational system is not the expansion of its facilities or the specific reform of its curriculum and administration but a thorough reconsideration of its underlying assumptions and of its purposes.

I realize quite well that this thesis constitutes a sweeping indictment of modern education. But I believe that the indictment is justified and that there is a prima facie case for entertaining this indictment.

Universal and compulsory modern education was established by the emancipated democracies during the nineteenth century. **"No other sure foundation can be devised,"** said Thomas Jefferson, **"for the preservation of freedom and happiness."** Yet as a matter of fact during the twentieth century the generations trained in these schools have either abandoned their liberties or they have not known, until the last desperate moment, how to defend them. The schools were to make men free. They have been in operation for some sixty or seventy years and what was expected of them they have not done. The plain fact is that the graduates of the modern schools are the actors in the catastrophe which has befallen our civilization. **Those who are responsible for modern education – for its controlling philosophy – are answerable for the results.**

They have determined the formation of the mind and education of modern [man]. As the tragic events unfold they cannot evade their responsibility by talking about the crimes and follies of politicians, businessmen, labor leaders, lawyers, editors, and generals. They have conducted the schools and colleges and they have educated the politicians, businessmen, labor leaders, lawyers, editors, and generals. **What is more they have educated the educators.**

They have had money, **lots of it**, fine buildings, big appropriations, great endowments, and the implicit faith of the people that the school was the foundation of democracy. If the results are "not as many wish," and indubitably they are not, on what ground can any of us who are in any way responsible for education disclaim our responsibility or decline to undertake a profound searching of our own consciences and a deep re-examination of our philosophy?

The institutions of the Western world were formed by men and women who learned to regard themselves as inviolable persons because they were rational and free. They meant by rational that they were capable of comprehending the moral order of the universe and their place in this moral order. They meant when they regarded themselves as free that within that order they had a personal moral responsibility to perform their duties and to exercise their corresponding rights. From this conception of the unity of mankind in a rational order the Western world has derived its conception of law – which is that all men and all communities of men and all authority among men are subject to law, and that the character of all particular laws is to be judged by whether they conform to or violate, approach or depart from the rational order of the universe and of man's nature. From this conception of law was derived the idea of constitutional government and of the consent of the governed and of civil liberty. Upon this conception of law our own institutions were founded.

This, in barest outline, is the specific outlook of Western men. This, we may say, is the structure of the Western spirit. This is the formation which distinguishes it. The studies and the disciplines which support and form this spiritual outlook and habit are the creative cultural tradition of Europe and the Americas. In this tradition our world was made. By this tradition it must live. **Without this tradition our world, like a tree cut off from its roots in the soil must die and be replaced by alien and barbarous things.**

It is necessary today in a discussion of this sort to define and identify what we mean when we speak of Western culture. This is in itself ominous evidence of what **an official historian of Harvard University once called "the greatest educational crime of the century against American youth – depriving him of his classical heritage."** For today there are many, the victims of this educational crime, who deny that there is such a thing as Western culture.

Yet the historic fact is that the institutions we cherish – and now we must defend against the most determined and efficient attack ever organized against them – are the products of a culture which, as [Gibbon] put it, "is essentially the culture of Greece, inherited from the Greeks by the Romans, transfused by the Fathers of the Church with the religious teachings of Christianity and progressively enlarged by countless numbers of artists, writers, scientists, and philosophers from the beginning of the Middle Ages up to the first third of the nineteenth century."

The men who wrote the American Constitution and the Bill of Rights were educated in schools and colleges in which the classic works of this culture were the substance of the curriculum. In these schools the transmission of this culture was held to be the end and aim of education.

> If all mankind minus one were of one opinion, and only one person were of the contrary opinion, mankind would be no more justified in silencing that one person than he, if he had the power, would be justified in silencing mankind.
>
> John Stuart Mill, "On Freedom of Speech"

Modern education, however, is based on a denial that it is necessary or useful or desirable for the schools and colleges to continue to transmit from generation to generation the religious and classical culture of the Western world. It is, therefore, much easier to say what modern education rejects than to find out what modern education teaches. Modern education rejects and excludes from the curriculum of necessary studies the [...] religious tradition of the West. It abandons and neglects as no longer necessary the study of the [...] classical heritage of the great works of great men and women.

Thus there is an enormous vacuum where until a few decades ago there was the substance of education. **And with what is that vacuum filled: it is filled with the elective, eclectic, the specialized, the accidental and incidental improvisations, and spontaneous curiosities of teachers and students. There is no common faith, no common body or principle, no common body of knowledge, no common moral and intellectual discipline.** Yet the graduates of these modern schools are expected to form a civilized community. They are expected to govern themselves. They are expected to have a social conscience. They are expected to arrive by discussion at common purposes. **When one realizes that they have no common culture is it astounding that they have no common purpose?** That they worship false gods? That only in war do they unite? **That in the fierce struggle for existence they are tearing Western society to pieces? They are the graduates of an educational system in which, though attendance is compulsory, the choice of the subject matter of education is left to the imagination of college presidents, trustees and professors, or even to the whims of the pupils themselves. We have established a system of education in which we insist that while everyone must be educated, yet there is nothing in particular that an educated [individual] must know.**

For it is said that since the invention of the steam engine we live in a new era so radically different from all preceding ages that the cultural tradition is no longer relevant, is in fact misleading. I submit to you that this is a rationalization, that this is a pretended reason for the educational void which we now call education. **The real reason, I venture to suggest, is that we reject the religious and classical heritage, first, because to master it requires more effort than we are willing to compel ourselves to make, and, too contentious to be faced with equanimity. We have abolished the old**

curriculum because we are afraid of it, afraid to face any longer in a modern democratic society the severe discipline and the deep, disconcerting issues of the nature of the universe, and of man's place in it and of his destiny.

I recognize the practical difficulties and the political danger of raising these questions and I shall not offer you a quick and easy remedy. For the present discussion all I am concerned with is that we should begin to recognize the situation as it really is and that we should begin to search our hearts and consciences...

In abandoning the classical culture of the West the schools have ceased to affirm the central principle of the Western philosophy of life – **that man's reason is the ruler of his appetites.** They have reduced reason to the role of servant to man's appetites. The working philosophy of the emancipated democracies is, as a celebrated modern psychologist has put it, that "the instinctive impulses determine the end of all activities... and the most highly developed mind is but the instrument by which those impulses seek their satisfaction."

The logic of this conception of the human reason must lead progressively to a system of education which sharpens the acquisitive and domineering and possessive instincts. And in so far as the instincts, rather than reason, determine the ends of our activity, the end of all activity must become the accumulation of power over men in the pursuit of the possession of things. So when parents and taxpayers in a democracy ask whether education is useful for life, they tend by and large to mean by useful that which equips the pupil for a career which will bring him money and place and power.

The reduction of reason to an instrument of each individual's personal career must mean also that education is emptied of its content. For what the careerist has to be taught are the data that he or she may need in order to succeed. Thus all subjects of study are in principle of equal value. There are no subjects which all belonging to the same civilization need to study. In the realms of knowledge the student elects those subjects which will presumably equip him for success in his (or her) career; for the student there is then no such thing as a general order of knowledge which he (or she) is to possess in order that it may regulate (one's) specialty...

It is this specialized and fundamentally disordered development of knowledge which has turned so much of man's science into the means of his own destruction. For as reason is regarded as no more than the instrument of men's desires, applied science inflates enormously the power of men's desires. Since reason is not the ruler of these desires, the power which science places in men's hands is ungoverned...

And, at last, education founded on the secular image of man must destroy knowledge itself. For its purpose is to train the intelligence of specialists in order that by trial and error they may find a satisfying solution of particular difficulties, then each situation and each problem has to be examined as a novelty. This is supposed to be "scientific." ... In fact it is a denial of that very principle which has made possible the growth of science.

For what enables men to know more than their ancestors is that they start with a knowledge of what their ancestors have already learned. They are able to do advanced experiments which increase knowledge because they do not have to repeat the elementary experiments. It is tradition which brings them to the point where advanced experimentation is possible. This is the meaning of tradition. This is why a society can be progressive only if it conserves its tradition.

The notion that every problem can be studied as such with an open and empty mind, without preconception, without knowing what has already been learned about it, must condemn men to a chronic childishness. For no man, and no generation of men, is capable of inventing for itself the arts and sciences of a high civilization. No one, and no one generation, is capable of rediscovering all the truths men need, of developing sufficient knowledge by applying a mere intelligence, no matter how acute, to mere observation, no matter how accurate.

> The men of any generation, **as Bernard of Chartres put it**, are like dwarfs seated on the shoulders of giants. If we are to "see more things than the ancients and things more distant" it is "due neither to the sharpness of our sight nor the greatness of our stature" but "simply because they have lent us their own."

For individuals do not have the time, the opportunity or the energy to make all the experiments and to discern all the significance that have gone into the making of the whole heritage of civilization. In developing knowledge men must collaborate with their ancestors. Otherwise they must begin not where their ancestors arrived but where their ancestors began. **If they exclude the tradition of the past from the curricula of the schools they make it necessary**

for each generation to repeat the errors rather than to benefit by the successes of its predecessors.

Having cut him off from the tradition of the past, modern secular education has isolated the individual. It has made him a careerist – without social connection – who must make his way – without benefit of man's wisdom – through a struggle in which there is no principle of order. This is the uprooted and incoherent modern "free man" that Mr. Bertrand Russell [...] described:

> [The man who sees] surrounding the narrow raft illumined by the flickering light of human comradeship, the dark ocean on whose rolling waves we toss for a brief hour; from the great night without, a chill blast breaks in upon our refuse; all the loneliness of humanity amid hostile forces is concentrated upon the individual soul, which must struggle along, with (want) of courage it can command, against the whole weight of the universe that cares nothing for its hopes and fears.
>
> ...The fundamental theory of liberty upon which all governments in this Union repose excludes any general power of **The State** to standardize its children by forcing them to accept instruction from public teachers only. The child is not the mere creature of **The State;** those who nurture him and direct his destiny have the right, coupled with the high duty, to recognize and prepare him for additional obligations.[20]

This is what the free man, in reality merely the freed and uprooted and dispossessed man, has become. But he is not the stoic that Mr. Russell would have him be. To "struggle alone" is more than the freed man can bear to do. And so he gives up his freedom and surrenders his priceless heritage, unable as he is constituted to overcome his insoluble personal difficulties and to endure his awful isolation.

The freedom of belief has a peculiarly American and seventeenth-century context, for the people of the Thirteen Colonies were pilgrims or religious refugees, who came to America that they might worship the God they chose and in the way they chose. But freedom of belief does not have such a ring in Chinese ears; it has absolutely no meaning to a Chinese, and it is not what the Chinese are fighting for. In the absence of religious wars and persecutions, freedom of belief is just accepted in Chinese national life; to fight for it is like taking an oath to fight for and maintain the blueness of the sky. Freedom of speech has been interfered with in certain periods of

[20] Lippmann quoting *Pierce v. Society of Sisters*, 268 U.S. 510, 69 L. Ed. 1070 at p.1078

Chinese history, as in Western democracies, and therefore it has still some meaning. But it is not broad enough, and is distinctly less comprehensive than just human freedom. I would not go to war with anybody just to protect freedom of speech; I could do with silence, or get around it to say all I want to say without landing in jail. I would consider as a worthy objective of this was only good old freedom, the freedom of all races and all people on this earth. On this issue we may not evade. Nor may we be less explicit about the freedom of the individual.

Nevertheless, the word "Freedom" has still a beautiful ring in America and the world. It means that the common people still believe in it – **in plain old, freedom...**

Similarly, when we want the right to a job or employment badly enough, we shall also be speaking of the "divine right to work," or to a salary or pension, or that men are "born employed," and at times it may even look more important to be "born employed" than to be "born free" or "born equal." **If we don't look out, someday we may discover that we are "born to a coupon," with the "inalienable right to a coupon" that no one shall metaphysically be able to take away from us**. Fundamentally, that is why we are forsaking the human rights and switching over to the economic rights.

So then the spiritual "values" are slipping and leave a vacuum. *Liberté, egalité, fraternité* have lost their prophetic Messianic ring. Democratic values, economic values, security values are being thrown into a witch's cauldron from which arises only a steam stinking with a strong totalitarian smell. Into this vacuum rush the confusing ideologies, and Communists, Socialists and Democrats exchange blows in the dark, not knowing who is fighting whom. Stalin is calling the U.S.S.R. a "democracy" and the Archbishop of Canterbury may be properly classified as a "red" by the N.Y. *Journal-American*. As for Pétain, he needs no ideology for his regime at all; it is neither Fascist, nor Socialist, nor Republican; he is neither Fuehrer, nor Duce, nor Dictator, nor President. For his ideology, he merely gasps "Work, Home, and Country!" No, it does not look as if there is going to be peace in Europe. The good old values have gone...

Editor's note: Remember this quote is decades old... and most is still relevant today.

But while we are arguing about the content of freedom and raising the question whether the concept of human freedom has not changed, we are threatened with another more serious and more

> fundamental matter, which has come about entirely unnoticed, and that is, *Freedom of the Will has disappeared.* Unless we recapture freedom of the will, we shall not have the strength to restore human freedom, and unless we restore human freedom, we shall accomplish nothing with the Four Freedoms, even if we attain them. Why has the Freedom of the Will disappeared? ...
>
> The dead hand of Science is upon the West. Science or the objective study of matter has colored man's thinking and brought us all three, Naturalism, Determinism, and Materialism. Science therefore has destroyed the human values. Naturalism has destroyed the belief in the power for good and cooperation. Materialism has destroyed subtlety and insight and faith in things unseen. Determinism has destroyed the capacity for hope...
>
> **The only whimper we can hear now is, "Give me security, or give me death!"**

Let me continue to quote Lippmann:

> When students cheat in examinations, it may be bad for them as individuals but for the community it means that the graduate is traveling with false papers and very shortly the papers – in this case the college degree – lose their value. **When military cadets cheat it is in effect a kind of treason, for it means they have not learned to do the things they will be assigned to do.** John Kennedy said his famous lines, "Ask not what your country can do for you – ask what you can do for your country." And the listening Nation nodded and smiled in agreement. But he said it not because the selfishness might become evident but because it is evident, and increasingly so. And it is historically true that a nation whose people take out more than they put in will collapse and disappear... The graduate of the modern school knows only by accident and by hearsay whatever wisdom mankind has come to in regard to the nature of man.
>
> **I recognize the practical difficulties and the political and social dangers of raising these questions and I shall not offer you a quick and easy remedy. For the present discussion all I am concerned with is that we should begin to recognize the situation as it really is and that we should begin to search our hearts and consciences... for solutions.**[21]

[21] Walter Lippmann, *The American Scholar*, publication of Phi Beta Kappa, Spring 1941

PART I

Condemn Those Who Think

Since the days of Socrates man has condemned those who think. Put to death by the voting of 501 of his peers – charged with "corrupting the youth" and "impiety" for having the audacity of suggesting that free men think – that round and bald, most Athenian of Athenians was reduced to the level of the masses. The functioning of pure democracy was shown in its true light of fraud. Even Plato was forced by the power of thought and reason to ***The Republic***. 2,500 years later little has changed. Men continue to condemn those who suggest others think. Early in the nineteenth century Ralph Waldo Emerson in his "American Scholar" address suggested:

> The great influence into the spirit of the scholar is the mind of the Past – in whatever form, whether of literature, of art, of institutions, that mind is inscribed. Books are the best type of the influence of the past, and perhaps we shall get at the truth – learn the amount of this influence more conveniently – by considering their value alone.
>
> The theory of books is noble. The scholar of the first age received into him the world around; brooded thereon; gave it the new arrangement of his own mind, and uttered it again. It came into him, life; it went out from him, truth. It came to him, short-lived actions; it went out from him, immortal thoughts. It came to him, business; it went from him, poetry. It was dead fact; now, it is quick thought. It can stand, and it can go. It now endures, it now flies, it now inspires. Precisely in proportion to the depth of mind from which it is issued, so high does it soar, so long does it sing... The state of society is one in which the members have suffered amputation from the trunk, and strut about so many walking monsters – a good finger, a neck, a stomach, an elbow, but never a man.
>
> Man is thus metamorphosed into a thing, into many things. The planter, who is man sent out into the field to gather food, is seldom cheered by any idea of the true dignity of his ministry. He sees his bushel and his cart, and nothing beyond, and sinks into the farmer, instead of Man on the farm. The tradesman scarcely ever gives an ideal worth to his work, but is ridden by the routine of his craft, and the soul is subject to dollars. The priest becomes a form; the attorney, a statute-book; the mechanic, a machine; the sailor, a rope of a ship.
>
> In this distribution of functions, the scholar is the delegated intellect. In the right state, he is Man Thinking. In the degenerate state, when the victim of society, he tends to become a mere thinker, or still worse, the parrot of other men's thinking...

> But the old oracle said, "All things have two handles: beware of the wrong one."[1]

Arriving now toward the middle of the twentieth century a former President of the University of Chicago, Robert Maynard Hutchins, wrote in *The Higher Learning In America*:

> The trouble with the popular notion of utility is that it confuses immediate and final ends. Material prosperity and adjustment to the environment are good more or less, but they are not good in themselves and there are other goods beyond them. The intellectual virtues, however, are good in themselves and good as means to happiness. By the intellectual virtues I mean good intellectual habits. The ancients distinguish five intellectual virtues: the three speculative virtues of intuitive knowledge, which is the habit of induction; of scientific knowledge, which is the habit of demonstration; and of philosophical wisdom, which is scientific knowledge, combined with intuitive reason, of things highest by nature, first principles and first causes. To these they add the two virtues of the practical intellect: art, the capacity to make according to a true course of reasoning, and prudence, which is right reason with respect to action.[2]
>
> In short, the intellectual virtues are habits resulting from the training of the intellectual powers. An intellect properly disciplined, an intellect properly habituated, is an intellect able to operate well in all fields. An education that consist of the cultivation of the intellectual virtues, therefore, is the most useful education, whether the student is destined for a life of contemplation or a life of action...
>
> I shall not be attentive when you tell me that the plan of general education I am about to present is remote from real life, that real life is in constant flux and change, and that education must be in constant flux and change as well. I do not deny that all things are in change. They have a beginning, and a middle, and an end. Nor will I deny that the history of the race reveals tremendous technological advances and great increases in our scientific knowledge. But we are so impressed with scientific and technological progress that we assume similar progress in every field. We renounce our intellectual heritage, read only the most recent books, discuss only current events, try to

[1] Ralph Waldo Emerson, "The American Scholar", *The Complete Works of Ralph Waldo Emerson,* Boston, New York, Houghton Mifflin Co., 1903–18

[2] Maynard Hutchins, *The Higher Learning In America*, New Haven, Yale University Press, 1936; quoting Cf. *Summa Theologica*, Part II, Q.57, Art. 2–4

keep the schools abreast or even ahead of the times, and write elaborate addresses on education and social change...[3]

The American Character

The American is a new man who acts on new principles; he must therefore entertain new ideas and form new opinions.

J. Hector St. John De Crèvecoeur

The problem of modern America is almost literally one of orientation. A century ago, Henry Thoreau described how, when he went out of doors uncertain where to go, his instinct always decided for him. "I turn round and round irresolute sometimes for a quarter of an hour, until I decide, for the thousandth time, that I will walk into the southwest or west. Eastward I go only by force; but westward I go free. Thither no business leads me. It is hard for me to believe that I shall find fair landscapes or sufficient wildness and freedom behind the eastern horizon. I am not excited by the prospect of a walk thither; but I believe that the forest which I see in the western horizon stretches uninterruptedly toward the setting sun, and there are no towns or cities in it of enough consequence to disturb me. Let me live where I will, on this side is the city, on that the wilderness, and ever I am leaving the city more and more and withdrawing into the wilderness. I should not lay so much stress on this fact if I did not believe that something like this is the prevailing tendency of my countrymen. I must walk toward Oregon and not toward Europe.[4]

All American experience, down to very recent times, was on the side of Thoreau. Oregon was no longer the wilderness; the Columbia River no longer rolled hearing "no sound save its own dashings," but was tamed by the greatest dams in the world and – towards the ocean, at least – rimmed with cities. But the westward drive was still potent; Americans rejoiced still in "the inward eye which is the bliss of solitude." It is only in this century that they have begun to learn, slowly, inadequately, humanly, that the world is really round, that to walk toward Oregon is to walk toward Europe. It has been a shock to their optimism, a shock to their view of their destiny. It is now necessary to turn from the lesson of Thoreau – or to apply it in a new world. Honolulu is west of Oregon;

---

[3] Maynard Hutchins, *The Higher Learning In America*

[4] D.W. Brogan, *The American Character*, New York, Alfred A Knopf, 1944, quoting Bernard De Voto, "Invocation", *The Year of Decision 1846*, New York, St. Martin's Press, 2000

China, "the Orient," is west of Honolulu; the Aleutians and Siberia are north and west. A contemporary of Thoreau knew that mere movement in one direction is not a solution.

> Were this world an endless plain, and by sailing eastward we could for ever reach new distances, and discover sights more sweet and strange than any Cyclades or Islands of King Solomon, then there were promise in the voyage. But in pursuit of those far mysteries we dream of, or in tormented chase of that demon phantom that, some time or other, swims before all human hearts; while chasing such over this round globe, they either lead us on in barren mazes or midway leave us whelmed.[5]

The world is round, and so you come to Europe (or Europe comes to you) by the back if not by the front door. The world runs north and south as well as east and west. Brazil is a neighbor of Africa as well as of the United States; Canada is a neighbor of Siberia as well as of Greenland.

And it is not only a world that has closed in on the United States (or on whose once remote borders the United States now presses with unconscious weight and power). It is a world in which all nations have to make deep adjustments in their mental habits, have to take stock of what is living and what is dead in their traditions. But that adjustment must, all the same, be made in the terms of the living tradition, according to the spirit. "These are the times that try men's souls," wrote Thomas Paine in 1776. These are the times that try men's powers of sympathetic imagination, of mutual understanding, for without these there will be no enduring structure of peace and order built...

The Framers of the American Constitution put as their first aim the provision of the political means to "a more perfect union." They did not aim at perfect union, at the ironing-out of all regional differences, at the destruction of all regional independence. One of the organizers of the movement that led to framing the Constitution did, indeed, want complete union, did want to abolish local autonomy. But the ideas of Alexander Hamilton were so remote from any possibilities in the America of 1787 that they were more or less politely ignored by his colleagues, and Hamilton left the Convention in disgust. When the Constitution was put before the people, Hamilton was an effective fighter for it and as the first Secretary of the Treasury he helped to get

---

[5] *Ibid.*, quoting Herman Melville, *Moby Dick*, New York, The Modern Library, 1930, Chapter LII

the machine running. But he was not a maker of the Constitution because he thought it was not good enough, that what the United States needed was complete union, the fusion of the thirteen states into a unitary body politic...

To have created a free government, over a continental area, without making a sacrifice of adequate efficiency or of liberty is the American achievement. It is a unique achievement in world history.

And because that achievement is tied up in fact and in legend with the Constitution, with the political system which makes the Constitution work, with a long historical experience (long, as modern political history goes), the American people are entitled to more than tolerance: they are entitled to sympathetic understanding in their worship of their own system of political and social institutions. And sympathetic understanding must begin with understanding of the obstacles to unity that faced and still face the People of the United States...

In the nineteenth century, thirty million immigrants entered the United States and increasingly they came from parts of Europe that had contributed little to the population of the thirteen colonies. It is doubtful if the beneficiaries of the Constitution today, the present "People of the United States," are in a majority of cases the posterity of the American people of 1789 for whose descendants' liberty as such thought was taken.

The three most important racial groups of recent immigrant origin are, at the moment, Germans, Italians, and Poles in that order. And although there were in America a few Italians like Jefferson's friend, Philip Mazzei, and although the Polish leaders Kosciusko and Pulaski played an important role in the American Revolution, there were, for all practical purposes, no Poles and no Italians in the United States of 1789...

Religion became a matter of conduct, of good deeds, of works with only a vague background of faith. It became highly functional, highly pragmatic; it became a guarantee of success, moral and material. The world of which Henry Ward Beecher on one side and Colonel Ingersoll on the other were such representative specimens was not quite the world of Harnack and Renan, Newman, Libbon, and Gore, Loisy, Denifle, and Denny. Theological schools turned from the theology to a form of anthropology – a moralistic and optimistic form, but anthropology all the same. The "proper study of mankind is man" was the evasion by which many American divines escaped the necessity for thought about God.

In the twentieth century, this policy suddenly ceased to be adequate. The fight over "fundamentalism," whether it took the form of the so-called "monkey trial" at Dayton, Tennessee, or the listing of "evolution" as one of the serious causes of stress between daughters and parents in Muncie, Indiana, or the fight in the Princeton Theological Seminary over the place of orthodox Calvinism in the last home town of Jonathan Edwards, was a fight over a very real problem. In the making of America, views about the relationship of God and Man had played a great part. If the God of the first settlers, and the God of the frontier who had converted so many tens of thousands in the straw pens of so many camp meetings, was no longer the God of the new universities, of the new technology, what was to replace Him? Could anything replace Him but "Democracy" made into an object of worship, or business, or success? Nobody knew; nobody knows, yet... [**Note: Elections in 2000 and 2004 for U.S. President.**]

America is promises but America is words, too. It is built like a church on a rock of dogmatic affirmations. "We hold these truths to be self-evident, that all men are created equal, that they are endowed by their Creator with certain unalienable Rights, that among these are Life, Liberty and the pursuit of Happiness." "We the People of the United States, in order to form a more perfect Union, establish justice, insure domestic tranquility, provide for the common defense, promote the general welfare, and secure the blessings of liberty to ourselves and our posterity, do ordain and establish this Constitution." These are only two of the most famous assertions of faith in things unseen, of dogmatic articles denied in good faith by many non-Americans but asserted in good faith by millions of Jefferson's countrymen from July 4th, 1776 to this day. How absurd an ambition for a people to attempt, by a written constitution, to "establish justice"! It is an ambition to make lawyers laugh and philosophers weep. "To promote the general welfare"; what is this entity so confidently labeled? What would a Marxian or a Machiavellian make of it? What an overleaping ambition of the Supreme Court to apply not known statute or case law but "the rule of reason"! What complacent courage in the founders of the Massachusetts Bay Company to identify the decision of John Winthrop, Richard Saltonstall, and the rest to transplant themselves to New England with "the greatness of the work in regard of the consequence, God's glory and the churches good"! Nevertheless, Massachusetts was founded, and a Saltonstall is governor in this year of grace, 1944, more than three hundred years later. There have been other consequences, too. What (possibly non-spontaneous) wisdom was shown by Lord Baltimore and the other Catholics of Maryland who in 1649 noted the evils arising from "the enforcing of the conscience in matters of Religion" and so came out for the toleration of all Christians – this in an age when the Inquisition was still going strong, a year after the Peace of Westphalia, the year of the massacre at Drogheda by Cromwell, a generation before the revocation of the Edict of Nantes? With what Hebraic confidence in their mission did the people of Massachusetts in 1780 acknowledge "with grateful hearts the goodness of the great Legislator of the universe, in affording us, in the course of His Providence, an opportunity, deliberately and peaceably, without fraud, violence or surprise, of entering into an original, explicit, and solemn compact with each other; and of forming a new constitution of civil government, for ourselves and posterity; and devoutly imploring His direction in so interesting a design, do agree upon, ordain and establish, the following Declaration of Rights and Frame of Government, as the Constitution of the Commonwealth of Massachusetts." Only a lively conviction of divine interest and direction could have justified so extravagant a hope as that by the mere separation of the legislative, executive, and judicial powers the people of Massachusetts or any people could establish a "government of laws and not of men."...

If we would first know where we are and whither we are tending, we could better judge what to do and how to do it... "A house divided against itself cannot stand." I believe this government cannot endure permanently half slave and half free. I do not expect the Union to be dissolved; I do not expect the house to fall; but I do expect it will cease to be divided. It will become all one thing, or all the other.

Lincoln was speaking against a kind of internal isolationism, against a belief that a great internal cleavage, tolerable, practically if not morally, in an earlier and far less integrated stage in American history, could continue to be tolerable when railways had brought two different societies into close, competitive neighborhood and had accelerated the growth of two very different societies. The consequence of failure to face the problem of the house divided was the Civil War – a crude and expensive way of settling a problem that could *perhaps* have been settled otherwise. Historical analogies, though always dangerous, are often valuable, too, and from Lincoln we can at least learn the need for patience and the need for candor, the need for doing what can be done and for not letting all possible good things be the enemy of realizing one good.

The house must cease to be divided if we are to prevent one of the ice ages of history from coming upon us. But it will have to be a house of many mansions, not an enormous room where bored and frightful prisoners regret the varied life they have known...

The American people can contribute to the world community only as Americans. As Americans they have much to give, materially and spiritually: a well-founded optimism about their own possibilities; a well-founded belief that some of the problems of unity in the absolute essentials, combined with diversity in all departments of life where diversity is possible, have been solved in the American historical experience. The problem set us and all peoples by the technological unification of the world is extremely difficult. It will be hard to solve, at best, and it may easily be made insoluble by pretense that its basic difficulty either does not exist or can easily be got round – the difficulty of creating an effective sense of common duty and common interest among the separate and quite different peoples of the world. That separateness, that difference, need not be insuperable obstacles if they are first allowed for and their origins understood. It is, I have been told, one of the most formidable of Chinese imprecations to wish that your enemy lived "in interesting times." We live in very interesting times; times not to be made better by any simple formula. Understanding each other is not enough, but it is an indispensable beginning.[6]

Paul Shorey [a former professor at the University of Chicago] said:

> If literature and history are a Heraclitean flux of facts, if one unit is as significant as another, one book, one idea, the equivalent of another ... we may for a time bravely tread the mill of scholastic routine, but in the end the soul will succumb to an immense lassitude and bafflement. But if ... the flux is not all, if the good, the true, and the beautiful are something real and ascertainable, if these eternal ideals re-embody themselves from age to age essentially the same in the imaginative visions of supreme genius and in the persistent rationality and sanity of the world's best books, then our reading and study are redeemed, both from the obsessions of the hour, and the tyranny of quantitative measures and mechanical methods.[7]

Our erroneous notion of progress has thrown the classics and the liberal arts out of the curriculum, overemphasized the empirical sciences, and made education the servant of any

[6] *Ibid.*

[7] Maynard Hutchins, *The Higher Learning in America*, quotes Paul Shorey

contemporary movements in society, no matter how superficial. In recent years this attitude has been accentuated by the world-wide depression and the highly advertised political, social, and economic changes resulting from it. We have been very much upset by all these things. We have felt that it was our duty to educate the young so that they would be prepared for further political, social, and economic changes. Some of us have thought we should try to figure out what the impending changes would be and frame a curriculum that embodied them. Others have even thought that we should decide what changes are desirable and then educate our students not merely to anticipate them, but also to take part in bringing them about.

One purpose of education is to draw out the elements of our common human nature. These elements are the same in any time or place. The notion of educating a man to live in any particular time or place, to adjust him to any particular environment, is therefore foreign to a true conception of education. Education implies teaching. Teaching implies knowledge. Knowledge is truth. The truth is everywhere the same. Hence education should be everywhere the same.[8] I do not overlook the possibilities of differences in organization, in administration, in local habits and customs. These are details. I suggest that the heart of any course of study designed for the whole people will be, if education is rightly understood, the same at any time, in any place, under any political, social, or economic conditions. Even the administrative details are likely to be similar because all societies have generic similarity. If education is rightly understood, it will be understood as the cultivation of the intellect…

Material prosperity, peace and civil order, justice and the moral virtues are means to the cultivation of the intellect. So Aristotle says in the *Politics:* "Now, in men reason and mind are the end towards which nature strives, so that the generation and moral discipline of the citizens ought to be ordered with a view to them." An education which served the means rather than their end would be misguided.

I agree, of course, that any plan of general education must be such as to educate the student for intelligent action. It must, therefore, start him on the road toward practical wisdom. But the question is what is the best way for education

[8] *Ibid.* quotes: "It is therefore evident that, as regards the general principles whether of speculative or practical reason, truth or rectitude is the same for all, and is equally known by all," *Summa Theologica,* Part II, Q. 94, Art. 4.

to start him and how far can it carry him? Prudence or practical wisdom selects the means toward the ends that we desire. It is acquired partly from intellectual operations and partly from experience. But the chief requirement for it is correctness in thinking. Since education cannot duplicate the experiences which the student will have when he graduates, it should devote itself to developing correctness in thinking as a means to practical wisdom, that is, to intelligent action.

As Aristotle put it in the *Ethics,* "...while young men become geometricians and mathematicians and wise in matters like these, it is thought that a young man of practical wisdom cannot be found. The cause is that such wisdom is concerned not only with universals, but with particulars, but a young man has no experience, for it is length of time that gives experience." Since practical wisdom is "a true and reasoned capacity to act with regard to the things that are good or bad for man," it would seem that education can make its best contribution to the development of practical wisdom by concentrating on the reasoning essential to it.

A modern heresy is that all education is formal education and that formal education must assume the total responsibility for the full development of the individual. The Greek notion that the city educates the man has been forgotten. Everything that educated the man in the city has to be imported into our schools, colleges, and universities. We are beginning to behave as though the home, the church, the state, the newspaper, the radio, the movies, the neighborhood club, and the boy next door did not exist. All the experience that is daily and hourly acquired from these sources is overlooked, and we set out to supply imitations of it in educational institutions. The experience once provided by some of these agencies may be attenuated now; but it would be a bold man who would assert that the young person today lived a life less full of experience than the youth of yesterday. Today as yesterday we may leave experience to other institutions and influences and emphasize in education the contribution that it is supremely fitted to make, the intellectual training of the young. The life they lead when they are out of our hands will give them experience enough. We cannot try to give it to them and at the same time perform the task that is ours and ours alone...

If there are permanent studies which every person who wishes to call himself educated should master; if those studies constitute our intellectual inheritance, then those studies should be the center of a general education. They cannot be ignored because they are difficult, or unpleasant, or because they are almost totally missing from our curriculum today... But educators cannot permit the students to dictate the course of study unless they are prepared to confess that they are nothing but chaperons, supervising an aimless, trial-and-error process which is chiefly valuable because it keeps young people from doing something worse...

Since there was no content to education, we might as well let students follow their own bent. They would at least be interested and pleased and would be as well educated as if they had pursued a prescribed course of study. This overlooks the fact that the aim of education is to connect man with man, to connect the present with the past, and to advance the thinking of the race. If this is the aim of education, it cannot be left to the sporadic, spontaneous interests of children or even of undergraduates...[9]

It cannot be assumed that students at any age will always select the subjects that constitute education. If we permit them to avoid them, we cannot confer upon them insignia which certify to the public that they are in our opinion educated. In any field the permanent studies on which the whole development of the subject rests must be mastered if the student is to be educated...

A classic is a book that is contemporary in every age. That is why it is a classic. The conversations of Socrates raise questions that are as urgent today as they were when Plato wrote. In fact they are more so, because the society in which Plato lived did not need to have them raised as much as we do. We have forgotten how important they are...

Since the proposed curriculum is coherent and comprehensible, and since it is free from the triviality that now afflicts our program, students will respond to it if the teachers will give them a chance to do it.

---

[9] *Ibid.* quoting Plato, *Republic*, Book IX: "'And it is plain,' I said, 'that this is the purpose of the law, which is the ally of all classes in the state, and this is the aim of our control of children, our not leaving them free before we have established, so to speak, a constitutional government within them and, by fostering the best element in them with the aid of the like in ourselves, have set up in its place a similar guardian and ruler in the child, and then, and then only we leave it free.'"

It may be said that the course of study is too difficult. It is not too difficult for students who can read or who can be taught to do so. For ease of reading, as well as other qualities, *The Federalist,* an American classic, is superior to some recent treatises on government and public administration; Herodotus is more sprightly than most modern historians of the ancient world; and Plato and Aristotle are as intelligible as contemporary philosophers.

No, students can do the work if the faculties will let them. Will the faculties let them? I doubt it. The professors of today have been brought up differently. Not all of them have read all the books they would have to teach. Not all of them are ready to change the habits of their lives. Meanwhile they are bringing up their successors in the way they were brought up, so that the next crop will have the habits they have had themselves. And the love of money, a misconception of democracy, a false notion of progress, a distorted idea of utility, and the anti-intellectualism to which all these lead conspire to confirm their conviction that no disturbing change is needed.

The times call for the establishment of a new college or for an evangelistic movement in some old ones which shall have for its object the conversion of individuals and finally of the teaching profession to a true conception of general education. Unless some such demonstration or some such evangelistic movement can take place, we shall remain in our confusion; we shall have neither general education nor universities; and we shall continue to disappoint the hopes of our people.

Upon education our country must pin its hopes of true progress, which involves scientific and technological advance, but under the direction of reason; of true prosperity, which includes external goods but does not overlook those of the soul; and of true liberty, which can exist only in society, and in a society rationally ordered.[10]

---

[10] *Ibid.*

The Harvard Red Book, Mansfield Review

Enter stage right, Mansfield and his review of the Harvard Red Book:

> General education was presented in a book, the once-famous Red Book – *General Education in a Free Society* – that should still impress readers in our time. The Red Book has an introduction by President James Bryant Conant, who appointed the committee of stalwarts – administrators and professors – who put together the curriculum and wrote the report initiating and explaining "general education." With the strong leadership of the president, the report was designed for cohesion and achieved it. It was designed ambitiously not only for Harvard but also for "a free society" in which, of course, Harvard would be a leader not only of private higher education but of all education, public and private, from primary schools (discussed in the report) to graduate education. Throughout, the authors made reference to the requirements and hopes of American democracy.
>
> The Red Book did not assume that general education was easy to achieve. It identified problems in education as such, some of them intensified in a democracy: how to combine the citizen and the whole man; how to serve both the gifted (traced to Thomas Jefferson's insistence on promoting the talented) and the average (championed by Andrew Jackson); how to reconcile the practice of free inquiry with the need for "firm belief" by both the gifted and the average; and the related difficulty of seeking new insights while preserving tradition. It also squarely faced the difference between science, or natural science, on the one hand, and the social sciences and the humanities, on the other – a general problem that [...] was the greatest concern of President Conant and his committee...
>
> "Goethe does not render Sophocles obsolete, nor does Descartes supersede Plato." No doubt many lesser figures of the past are lost in oblivion; and there could easily be agreement that these four are great thinkers worth studying. But they are worth studying because these four differ among themselves and offer views still necessary to consider...
>
> Hence the core curriculum. I have dwelt on general education because the core program is best understood as a privative defined by what it lacks more than by any positive idea of its own. Its only positive idea was the requirement for moral reasoning...
>
> The core curriculum never defined a core. Generated from the faculty rather than promoted, still less imposed, from above, it

produced a vague consensus of the most powerful departments. Core areas were carefully not named for departments but they were close enough to departments to gain their consent. The core has been a professors' curriculum based on the premise that what professors want to teach is the same as what students need to know, and which society needs them to know. In fact, the core has been better than that, better than its lack of theory might have portended. The prestige of teaching in the core – rather than languishing in the periphery! – has been an attraction for the more ambitious professors, and the need for getting the consent of a core committee has kept them from simply teaching their pet ideas, as tended to happen in the later stages of general education. But in too many cases the idea of *not teaching something necessary to know* has imposed itself. Some angle must be found that will look interesting to students not mainly interested in the subject matter of the course. Thus the professors' curriculum tended to become a curriculum designed to appeal to students. After a while that appeal began to fade, and the students who flocked to core courses in huge numbers began to hold them in disdain...

Education is a choice divided into two aspects: what students want and what students should have. These are two different things, but neither can exclude the other. What students want should not be accepted without revision, nor on the other hand should it be denied them merely because they want it. What they should have needs to be connected to what they want even though the two will never coincide. What students want for their education comes spontaneously from them; what students should have has to be imposed or at least offered insistently against the flow of their desires. What students want spontaneously at this time is going to be influenced by two forces that need to be resisted by the faculty...

Partisanship is one. Most of our students arrive with, or soon acquire, liberal political inclinations, and these need to be countered by experience with arguments from the other side and also by courses that teach students detachment, from their own or even from any political inclination...

The second is risk-avoidance for the sake of a future career or to enhance the prospect of getting admitted to the top graduate and professional schools. There is a pressing need to make our curriculum more demanding, and this should be a major goal of our curriculum review. Students should be asked to give more time to their courses and less time to extra-curricular activities. Just as students seem to be looking for more substance in the curriculum, so too they sense that Harvard has become too easy...

Now I have some more particular recommendations inspired by these reflections on recent history...

We can be sure that America's responsible role in the world or America's imperialist temptation – take your choice – will be of spontaneous interest to our students and to us. This material is familiar to us in the clusters of questions associated with multiculturalism and globalization. But now we face Islamic radicalism, which casts doubt on the ready reception or absorption of foreign nations and cultures into our country, *a fortiori* into our understanding of the world. In theory we say the world is diverse, in practice we act as if we believe it to be homogeneous. Is there such a thing as an enemy, a real Other that we cannot and ought not tolerate...?

The proposed emphasis on international relations falls into the category of things students spontaneously want. We also need to make sure that they understand their own country. Far too little is taught about America at Harvard. The Government department has too few courses on America; little on the Supreme Court, for example, and less on American foreign policy. The History department has no course on the American Revolution or on the American Founding. Courses in American history and politics should be part of the recommended or required part of the curriculum...

Western Civilization needs to be taught, if only for the power it has shown in dominating the world. But to avoid the objection that it is too self-centered a topic, it could be treated from the angle of modernity as above or of greatness as below. A course that begins with Homer and ends somewhere in the vicinity of Nietzsche, with selected stops between, still makes lots of sense. Such a course can find room for our concerns for minorities and women without being dominated by those concerns (I believe Homer has something to say about both of them).

Moral reasoning. Despite my irreverence above, moral reasoning is the best part of the Core and we should retain it as a requirement. It should be kept as a way to ensure that great books are read, for most of the Moral Reasoning courses have had to include Aristotle and Kant and a few others of their class. Our students still suffer from superficial, unreasoning moralism, and President Bok was right to think a course in Moral Reasoning would be beneficial all around...

We must not be afraid to make judgments of greatness in our teaching, explicit or not, and we should show students how to recognize it in its diversity. Relativism is not a crazy position to hold if it means that we lack proof of the major conflicting principles guiding our lives, but it is debilitating if it induces us to level all principles, equating petty and great, and thus dismiss greatness from our view. I believe in the great books because I think that all human thoughts derive from these few masters, *i maestri di color che sanno*. But the derivations are interesting too, more relevant and urgent...[11]

General Education in a Free Society

The heart of the problem of a general education is the continuance of the liberal and humane tradition. Neither the mere acquisition of information nor the development of special skills and talents can give the broad basis of understanding which is essential if our civilization is to be preserved. No one wishes to disparage the importance of being "well informed". But even a good grounding in mathematics and the physical and biological sciences, combined with an ability to read and write several foreign languages, does not provide a sufficient educational background for citizens of a free nation. For such a program lacks contact with both man's emotional experience as an individual and his practical experience as a gregarious animal. It includes little of what was once known as "the wisdom of the ages," and might nowadays be described as "our cultural pattern." It includes no history, no art, no literature, no philosophy. Unless the educational process includes *at each level of maturity* some continuing contact with those fields in which value judgments are of prime importance, it must fall short of the ideal. The student in high school, in college and in graduate school must be concerned, in part at least, with the words "right" and "wrong" in both the ethical and the mathematical sense. Unless he feels the import of those general ideas and aspirations which have been a deep moving force in the lives of men, he runs the risk of partial blindness.

There is nothing new in such educational goals; what is new in this century in the United States is their application to a system of universal education. Formal education based on "book learning" was once only the possession of a professional class; in recent times it became more widely valued because of social implications. The restricted nature of the circle possessing certain linguistic and historical knowledge greatly enhanced the prestige of this knowledge. "Good taste" could be standardized in each generation by those who

[11] Harvey C. Mansfield, "A More Demanding Curriculum", *Claremont Review of Books*, Winter 2004

knew. But, today, we are concerned with a general education – a liberal education – not for the relatively few, but for a multitude...[12]

Finally, we should like to remind you of the words you used to the Board of Overseers in your *Annual Report* of January 11, 1943, in describing your purpose in appointing the committee. You then wrote: "The primary concern of American education today is not the development of the appreciation of the 'good life' in young gentlemen born to the purple. It is the infusion of the liberal and humane tradition into our entire educational system. Our purpose is to cultivate in the largest possible number of our future citizens an appreciation of both the responsibilities and the benefits which come to them because they are Americans and are free..."[13]

Education in the United States: The Problem

> We need no Homer to praise us. Rather, we have opened the whole earth and sea to our enterprise and raised everywhere living memorials to our fortune.
>
> Pericles, as reported by Thucydides

> Youth is the time when the character is being molded and easily takes any impress one may wish to stamp on it. Shall we then simply allow our children to listen to any stories that anyone happens to make up and so receive into their minds ideas often the very opposite to those we shall think they ought to have when they are grown up?
>
> Plato, *Republic*

These two statements from another democracy pose broadly the problem of this report. They are in essence contradictory. The first breathes the pride of a free society which, through the released energy of its citizens, had achieved a power, wealth, and height of material progress unknown until that time. The second concerns the effects of this creative freedom. It reflects a time when many shades of opine, many forms of special knowledge, many standards of life and conduct, beat confusedly upon the young, and it asks how under those circumstances they might be expected to reach a settled outlook. The achievements proclaimed in the first statement thus set

[12] James Bryant Conant, "Introduction", *General Education in Free Society: A Report of the Harvard Committee*, Cambridge, Mass., Harvard University Press, 1945

[13] Letter of Transmittal to President James Bryant Conant from The Harvard Committee, *General Education in Free Society: A Report of the Harvard Committee*, Cambridge, Mass., Harvard University Press, 1945

the question of the second. Taken together they reflect two characteristic facets of democracy: the one, its creativity, sprung from the self-trust of its members; the other, its exposure to discord and even to fundamental divergence of standards precisely because of this creativity, the source of its strength.

General education, as education for an informed responsible life in our society, has chiefly to do with the second of these questions, the question of common standards and common purposes. Taken as a whole, education seeks to do two things: help young persons fulfill the unique, particular functions in life which it is in them to fulfill, and fit them so far as it can for those common spheres which, as citizens and heirs of a joint culture, they will share with others. Obviously these two ends are not wholly separable even in idea – much less can preparation for them be wholly separate. Who does not recall from school or college some small, seemingly quite minor subject which through a teacher or on reflection took on inclusive meaning? Yet to analyze is inevitably to separate what in fact clings together, and this report on general education will perforce deal mainly with preparation for life in the broad sense of completeness as a human being, rather than in the narrower sense of competence in a particular lot...

One of the great tragedies of our time has been the change of teaching from a calling to something like an industry. The fault, as has been argued, is at once with the colleges, which have turned their backs; with the schools of education, which have taught everything except the indispensable thing, the love of knowledge; and with American society itself, which has tolerated the conditions under which many students and their teachers still labor. The remedy is a joint concern both of the public and of people who so believe in the importance of high school teaching as the floor and foundation of democracy that they will go into it as a calling...

You cannot, it is clear, gather together masses of young people and expect them all to behave like young Aristotles. Young people have always brought with them to school the unsettlements and vapors of adolescence, and now when nearly all go to high school the scope of these unsettlements is multiplied geometrically. It is one thing to have a relatively few students of superior gifts and stable backgrounds; it is another to have the present Babel of gifts and backgrounds. Granting, then, that it is at best not easy for the young to see their way through the mists of feeling, it follows that the school cannot hope to accomplish its proper tasks without allowing for and somehow harnessing these feelings. Hence the only way of escaping the excesses of athletics, cliques, and general anti-intellectualism – these groupings, pathetic or harmful, for outlets which neither the community nor the school otherwise provides – is to recognize what the school legitimately should provide. This recognition in turn brings one face to face with teaching in all its varied phases.

It was argued earlier that the low pay of teaching could not be considered as something apart from the caliber and devotion of those who go into it, and that the one would rise only with the other. If the sufferings of our time have shown anything, they have shown that human beings are not led by economic motives alone but equally by visions, however distorted, of causes to be served. The failures of teaching are not therefore ascribable only to the pay, however cryingly it demands improvement, but to the failure of colleges, teachers' colleges, and the country as a whole to make of teaching the high calling that it must be. But, it was further argued, improvement will also depend on a sound and thoroughgoing democracy in the schools. We understand by democracy the interworking of two complementary forces, the Jeffersonian and the Jacksonian, the one valuing opportunity as the nurse of excellence, the other as the guard of equity. If, therefore, equal opportunity no longer lies in the curriculum alone but also in the wider functions which have been cast on the school by the conditions of modern life, the commands of democracy extend to these as well. All are teachers, and all equally necessary, who give to young people through the curriculum or beyond it the opportunity which makes for completeness of life, and improvement in teaching will depend of this wider vision of who the teacher is.

Are Jeffersonionism and Jacksonianism in fact complementary or do they struggle against each other? Much of our future will be written in answer to this question. The terms are of course vague and relative. Thus we have criticized the school system as too Jeffersonian, because it gives quite different honor to academic and technical subjects from which students go on to relatively assured futures, from any that it gives to subjects pursued by humbler students. The standard of our education is a strongly middle-class standard, which must disappoint and may embitter those (perhaps half of all the students in the high school) who find themselves cast for another role. Their good is still almost wholly to be discovered. On the other hand, it can equally be said that the high school is Jacksonian, in that it largely fails to find and force the able young person. And the same, as has been noted, applies to outer influences, radio and moving picture, which aim, often calculatingly, at the mass. It has been gloomily said that no man and no society can do two things well at the same time. Certainly the human tendency is to see one goal as to forget the other, and writers on education have not uncommonly erred with this fault, setting either a standard of culture which coolly neglects the great mass of indulging in a flat and colorless egalitarianism. But the belief that one good is purchasable always and only at the expense of another ultimately goes back to a belief in the natural right of the stronger; it runs counter both to religious faith and to the best experience of civilization. The hope of the American school system, indeed of our society, is precisely that it can pursue two goals simultaneously: give scope to ability and raise the average. Nor are these two goals so far apart, if human beings are capable of common sympathies...

We have tried so far to sketch in broad outline the growth of American education and to indicate the factors which have determined growth. The very momentum of its development, like that which has marked American life generally, left a legacy of disturbance and maladjustment undreamed of in simpler times. A passage from Machiavelli's *Discourses* comes to mind in which, after asking why the Roman Republic showed signs of confusion in the period of its fastest growth, he observes that such confusion was inevitable in so vicious a state. "Had the Roman Commonwealth," he concludes, "grown to be more tranquil, this inconvenience would have resulted that it must at the same time have grown weaker, since the road would have been closed to that greatness to which it came. For in removing the causes of her tumults, Rome must have interfered with the causes of her growth." Just so in the United States, the most ideally planned educational system would have found itself in conflict with the unforeseen forces set loose by the growth and development of the country. But this very growth, the source of the gravest problems to education, is at the same time the index of its strength and promise...

It was remarked at the end of the previous chapter that a supreme need of American education is for a unifying purpose and idea. As recently as a century ago, no doubt existed about such a purpose; it was to train the Christian citizen. Nor was there doubt how this training was to be accomplished. The student's logical powers were to be formed by mathematics, his test by the Greek and Latin classics, his speech by rhetoric, and his ideals by Christian ethics. College catalogues commonly began with a specific statement about the influence of such a training on the mind and character. The reasons why this enviable certainly both of goal and of means has largely disappeared already been set forth. For some decades the mere excitement of enlarging the curriculum and making place for new subjects, new methods, and masses of new students seems quite pardonably to have absorbed the energies of schools and colleges. It is fashionable now to criticize the leading figures of that expansive time for failing to replace, or even to see the need of replacing, the unity which they destroyed. But such criticisms, if just in themselves, are hardly just historically. A great and necessary task of modernizing and broadening education waited to be done, and there is credit enough in its accomplishment. In recent times, however, the question of unity has become insistent. We are faced with a diversity of education which, if it has many virtues, nevertheless works against the good of society by helping to destroy the common ground of training and outlook on which any society depends.

It seems that a common ground between some, though not all, of the ideas underlying our educational practice is the sense of heritage. The word heritage is not here taken to mean mere retrospection. The purpose of all education is to help students live their own lives...

In this concern for heritage lies a close similarity between religious education in the great classic books. Exponents of the latter have, to be sure, described it as primarily a process of intellectual discipline in the joint arts of word and number, the so-called *trivium* (grammar, logic, rhetoric) and *quadrivium* (arithmetic, geometry, astronomy, music). But, since the very idea of this discipline goes back to antiquity and since the actual books by which it is carried out are in fact the great books of the Western tradition, it seems fairer, without denying the disciplinary value of such a curriculum, to think of it as primarily a process of opining before students the intellectual forces that have shaped the Western mind. There is a sense in which education in the great books can be looked at as a secular continuation of the spirit of Protestantism. As early Protestantism, rejecting the authority and philosophy of the medieval church, placed reliance on each man's personal reading of the Scriptures, so this present movement, rejecting the unique authority of the Scriptures, places reliance on the reading of those books which are taken to represent the fullest revelation of the Western mind. But be this as it may, it is certain that, like religious education, education in the great books is essentially an introduction of students to their heritage.

Nor is the sense of heritage less important, though it may be less obvious, a part of education for modern democratic life. To the degree that the implications of democracy are drawn forth and expounded, to that degree for the long-standing impulse of education toward shaping students to a relieved ideal is still pursued. Consider the teaching of American history and of modern democratic life. However ostensibly factual such teaching may be, it commonly carries with it a presupposition which is not subject to scientific proof: namely, the presupposition that democracy is meaningful and right. Moreover, since contemporary life is itself a product of history, to study it is to tread unconsciously, in the words of the hymn, where the saints have trod. To know modern democracy is to know something at least of Jefferson, though you have not read him; to learn to respect freedom of speech or the rights of the private conscience is not to be wholly ignorant of the *Aeropagitica* or the *Antigone,* though you know nothing about them. Whether, as philosophers of history argue, being conditioned by the present we inevitably judge the past by what we know in the present (since otherwise the past would be unintelligible) or whether human motives and choices do not in reality greatly change with time, the fact remains that the past and the present are parts of the same unrolling scene and, whether you enter early or late, you see for the most part the still-unfinished progress of the same issues...

There is doubtless a sense in which religious education, education in the great books, and education in the modern democracy may be mutually exclusive. But there is a far more important sense in which they work together to the same end, which is belief in the idea of man and society that we inherit, adapt, and pass on.

This idea is described in many ways, perhaps most commonly in recent times, as that of the dignity of man. To the belief in man's dignity must be added the recognition of his duty to his fellow men. Dignity does not rest on any man as a being separate from all other beings, which he in any case cannot be, but springs from his common humanity and exist positively as he makes common good his own. This concept is essentially that of the Western tradition: the view of man as free and not as slave, an end in himself and not a means...

It is impossible to escape the realization that our society, like any society, rests on common beliefs and that a major task of education is to perpetuate them...

The Greek idea of an orderly universe, of political freedom under rationally constructed laws, and of the inner life itself as subject to the ways of reason, was certainly not achieved without skepticism, observation, or the test of experience. The ancient atomists and medical writers and, to a large extent, Socrates himself relied precisely on induction from observed facts. Socrates, the teacher and the gadfly of the Athenian city, impressed on his pupils and the public at large the duty of man to reflect on his beliefs and to criticize his presuppositions. Socrates was an individual proclaiming that man should form his opinions by his own reasoning and not receive them by social indoctrination. And yet, it was this same Socrates who died in obedience to the judgment of the state, even though he believed the judgment to be wrong. Again, historical Christianity has been expressed and consistently concerned with the importance of this life here on earth. The doctrine of the Incarnation, that God took the form of man and inhabited the earth, declares this concern. While perhaps for Greek thought, only the timeless realm had importance, in Christian thought the process of history is vested with absolute significance. If the ideal of democracy was rightly described above in the interwoven ideas of the dignity of man (that is, his existence as an independent moral agent) and his duty to his fellow men (that is, his testing by outward performance), the debt of these two ideas to the similarly interwoven commandments of the love of God and the love of neighbor is obvious...

Science has done more than provide the material basis of the good life; it has directly fostered the spiritual values of humanism. To explain, science is both the outcome and the source of the habit of forming objective, disinterested adjustments based upon exact evidence. Such a habit is of particular value in the formation of citizens for a free society. It opposes to the arbitrariness of authority and "first principles" the direct and continuing appeal to things as they are. Thus it develops the qualities of the free man. It is no accident that John Locke, who set forth the political doctrine of the natural rights of man against established authority, should have been also the man who rejected the authority of innate ideas.

Students of antiquity and of the Middle Ages can therefore rightly affirm that decisive truths about the human mind and its relation to the world were laid hold of then, and yet agree that, when new application of these truths was made through a more scrupulous attention to fact, their whole implication and meaning were immensely enlarged. Modern civilization has seen this enlargement of meaning and possibility; yet it is not a new civilization but the organic development of an earlier civilization. The true task of education is therefore so to reconcile the sense of pattern and direction deriving from heritage with the sense of experiment and innovation deriving from science that they may exist fruitfully together, as in varying degree they have never ceased to do throughout Western history.

Belief in the dignity and mutual obligation of man is the common ground between these contrasting but mutually necessary forces in our culture. As was pointed out earlier, this belief is the fruit at once of religion, of the Western tradition, and of the American tradition. It equally inspires the faith in human reason which is the basis for trust in the future of democracy. And if it is not, strictly speaking, implied in all statements of the scientific method, there is no doubt that science has become its powerful instrument. In this tension between the opposite forces of heritage and change poised only in the faith in man, lies something like the old philosophic problem of the knowledge of the good. If you know the good, why do you seek it? If you are ignorant of the good, how do you recognize it when you find it? You must evidently at one and the same time both know it and be ignorant of it. Just so, the tradition which has come down to us regained the nature of man and the good society must inevitably provide our standard of good. Yet an axiom of that tradition itself is the belief that no current form of the received ideal is final but that every generation, indeed every individual, must discover it in a fresh form. Education can therefore be wholly devoted neither to tradition nor to experiment, neither to the belief that the ideal in itself is enough nor to the view that means are valuable apart from the ideal. It must uphold at the same time tradition and experiment, the ideal and the means, subserving, like our culture itself, change within commitment...

The concept of liberal education first appeared in a slave-owning society, like that of Athens, in which the community was divided into freemen and slaves, rulers and subjects. While the slaves carried on the specialized occupations of menial work, the freemen were primarily concerned with the rights and duties of citizenship. The training of the former was purely vocational; but as the freemen were not only a ruling but also a leisure class, their education was exclusively in the liberal arts, without any utilitarian tinge. The freemen were trained in the reflective pursuit of the good life; their education was unspecialized as well as unvocational; its aim was to produce a rounded person with a full understanding of himself and of his place in society and in the cosmos.

Modern democratic society clearly does not regard labor as odious or disgraceful; on the contrary, in this country at least, it regards leisure with suspicion and expects its "gentlemen" to engage in work. Thus we attach no odium to vocational instruction. Moreover, in so far as we surely reject the idea of freemen who are free in so far as they have slaves or subjects, we are apt strongly to deprecate the liberal education which went with the structure of the aristocratic ideal. Herein our society runs the risk of committing a serious fallacy. Democracy is the view that not only the few but that all are free, in that everyone governs his own life and shares in the responsibility of the management of the community. This being the case, it follows that all humans stand in need of an ampler and rounded education. The task of modern democracy is to preserve the ancient ideal of liberal education and to extend it as far as possible to all the members of the community. In short, we have been apt to confuse accidental with fundamental factors, in our suspicion of the classical ideal. To believe in the equality of human beings is to believe that the good life, and the education which trains the citizen for the good life, are equally the privilege of all. And these are the touchstones of the liberated man: first, is he free; that is to say, is he able to judge and plan for himself, so that he can truly govern himself? In order to do this, his must be a mind capable of self-criticism; he must lead that self-examined life which according to Socrates is alone worthy of a free man. Thus he will possess inner freedom, as well as social freedom. Second, is he universal in his motives and sympathies? For the civilized man is a citizen of the entire universe; he has overcome provincialism, he is objective, and is a "spectator of all time and all existence." Surely these two are the very aims of democracy itself...

We must distinguish between liberalism in education and education in liberalism. The former, based as it is on the doctrine of individualism, expresses the view that the student should be free in his choice of courses. But education in liberalism is an altogether different matter; it is education which has a pattern of its own, namely, the pattern associated with the liberal outlook. In this view, there are truths which none can be free to ignore, if one is to have that wisdom through which life can become useful. These truths are the truths concerning the structure of the good life and concerning the factual conditions by which it may be achieved, truths comprising the goals of the free society...

Education must look to the whole man. It has been wisely said that education aims at the good man, the good citizen, and the useful man. By a good man is meant one who possesses an inner integration, poise, and firmness, which in the long run come from an adequate philosophy of life. Personal integration is not a fifth characteristic in addition to the other four and coordinate with them; it is their proper fruition. The aim of liberal education is the development of the whole man; and human nature involves instincts and sentiments as well as the intellect. Two dangers must be mentioned. First, there is the danger of identifying intelligence with the qualities of the so-called intellectual type – with bookishness and skill in the manipulation of concepts. We have tried to guard against this mistake by stressing the traits of relevant judgment and discrimination of values in effective thinking. Second, we must remember that intelligence, even when taken in its widest sense, does not exhaust the total potentialities of human nature. Man is not a contemplative being alone. Why is it, then, that education is conceived as primarily an intellectual enterprise when, in fact, human nature is so complex? For instance, man has his emotions and his drives and his will; why should education center on the training of the intellect? The answer is found in the truth that intelligence is not a special function (or not that only) but a way in which all human powers may function. Intelligence is that leaven of awareness and reflection which, operating upon the native powers of men, raises them from the animal level and makes them truly human. By reason we mean, not an activity apart, but rational guidance of all human activity. Thus the fruit of education is intelligence in action. The aim is mastery of life; and since living is an art, wisdom is the indispensable means to this end...

The first proposition is at once a confession and a question – a confession of ignorance and a question calling for an answer. The line of reasoning in this report so far has been briefly this. First, our national life and, more broadly, our culture do in fact predicate certain traits of mind and ways of looking at man in the world. Second, these traits and outlooks embrace both heritage and change, which in turn correspond, though not exactly and certainly in no wooden, perfunctory way, to general and special education, the one concerned with the more slowly changing relationships within knowledge as a whole, the other with its more quickly changing parts. Third, a successful democracy (successful, that is, not merely as a system of government but, as democracy must be, in part as a spiritual ideal) demands that these traits and outlooks be shared so far as possible among all the people, not merely the privileged few. But, fourth, there exist in fact great differences among people, not only of opportunity, which have been and can be improved, but of gifts and interests, which either cannot be improved so quickly or, in the case of interests, are and should ideally be varied. Our ignorance, which seems to us a widespread ignorance, and our question, which is the question of the nation and age, follow these four steps as a fifth. It is, *how can general education be so adapted to different ages and, above all, differing abilities and outlooks, that it can appeal deeply to each, yet remain in goal and essential teaching the same for all?* The answer to this question, it seems not too much to say, is the key to anything like complete democracy...

No society can be organized simply for the advancement of the fittest or, in the more polite modern term, for mobility. If it were, it would cease to be a society in the sense of Aristotle's famous definition: "The state originates in the need for subsistence; it continues through the wish for the good life." In so far as society looks to the good life, then it has common aims, the inculcation of which is at least as important a task of education as the furtherance of this or that individual. Ideally, indeed, the success of an individual is meaningless or harmful except as it is the mark of his superior service to the common good...

Traits of Mind

At the time of his examination the average student hardly remembers more than 75 per cent of what he was taught. If he were a sophomore when he took the course, how much does he recall by the time of his graduation, how much five years later, how much, or how little, when he returns on his twenty-fifth reunion? Pondering on all this, the pessimist might well conclude that education is a wholly wasteful process. He would of course be wrong, for the simple reason that education is not a process of stuffing the mind with facts. Yet he would be partly right because the student soon forgets not only many facts but even some general ideas and principles. No doubt we are exaggerating. Those students practically who have been able to unite what they learned in school or college with later studies or with their jobs do retain a surprising amount of information. Nevertheless, the real answer to the pessimist is that education is not merely the imparting of knowledge but the cultivation of certain aptitudes and attitudes in the mind of the young. As we have said earlier, education looks both to the nature of knowledge and to the good of man in society. It is to the latter aspect that we shall now turn our attention – more particularly to the traits and characteristics of mind fostered by education.

By characteristics we mean aims so important as to prescribe how general education should be carried out and which abilities should be sought above all others in every part of it. These abilities, in our opinion, are: *to think effectively, to communicate thought, to make relevant judgments, to discrimination among values.* They are not in practice separable and are not to be developed in isolation. Nor can they be even analyzed in separation. Each is an indispensable coexistent function of a sanely growing mind. Nonetheless, since exposition requires that one thing be discussed at one time, our description of these abilities must take them up in turn.

By *effective thinking* we mean, in the first place, logical thinking: the ability to draw sound conclusions from premises. Yet by logical thinking we do not mean the equipment of the specialist or what a student would learn by taking a course in formal logic. We are concerned with the student who is going to be a worker, or a businessman, or a professional man, and who does not necessarily look forward to a career in scholarship or in pure science. As a plain citizen he will practice his logical skills in practical situations – in choosing a career, in deciding whom to vote for, or what house to buy, or even in choosing a wife. But perhaps the last case is just the point where logical skills fail, although European parties might disagree.

Logical thinking is the capacity to extract universal truths from particular cases and, in turn, to infer particulars from general laws. More strictly, it is the ability to discern a pattern of relationships – on the one hand to analyze a problem into its component elements, and on the other to recombine these, often by the use of imaginative insight, so as to reach a solution. Its prototype is mathematics which, starting with a few selected postulates, makes exact deductions with certainty. Logical thinking is involved to a degree in the analysis of the structure of a painting as well as in that of a geometric system. In moving toward a solution, the trained mind will have a sharp eye for the relevant factors while zealously excluding all that is irrelevant; and it will arrange the relevant factors according to weight. For instance, in voting during a presidential election our citizen should consider whether the candidate has sound policies, whether he has the ability to get on with Congress, whether he has a good grasp of international relations, and, in these troubled times, whether he has an understanding of military strategy. These are some of the factors which are relevant to the problem in hand. But the looks of the candidate most probably, and his religious denomination surely, are irrelevant. Prejudice brings in irrelevancies and logic should keep them out.

Effective thinking, while starting with logic, goes further so as to include certain broad mental skills. Thus an effective thinker is a man who can handle terms and concepts with skill and yet does not confuse words with things; he is empirical in the widest sense of the word, looking outward to nature. He is not satisfied merely with noting the facts, but his mind ever soars to implications. He knows when he knows and when he does not; he does not mistake opinion for knowledge. Furthermore, effective thinking includes the understanding of complex and fluid situations, in dealing with which logical methods are inadequate as mental tools. Of course thinking must never violate the laws of logic, but it may use techniques beyond those of exact mathematical reasoning. In the fields of the social studies and history, and in the problems of daily life, there are large areas where evidence is incomplete and may never be completed. Sometimes the evidence is incomplete and may never be completed. Sometimes the evidence may be also untrustworthy; but, if the situation is practical, a decision must be made. The scientist has been habituated to deal with properties which can be abstracted from their total background and with variables which are few and well defined. Consequently, where the facts are unique and unpredictable, where the variables are numerous and their interactions too complicated for precise calculation, the scientist is apt to throw up his hands in despair and perhaps turn the situation over to the sentimentalist or the mystic. But surely he would be wrong in so doing; for the methods of logical thinking do not exhaust the resources of reason. In coping with complex and fluid situations we need thinking which is relational and which searches for cross bearings between areas; this is thinking in a context. By its use it is possible to reach an understanding of historical and social materials and of human relations, although not with the same degree of precision as in the case of simpler materials and of recurring events. As Aristotle says, "It is the mark of an educated man to expect no more exactness than the subject permits."

A further element in effective thinking is the imagination, by which we mean whatever is distinctive in the thinking of the poet. Logical thinking is straight, as opposed to crooked, thinking; and that of the poet may be described as curved thinking. Where the scientist operates with abstract conceptions the poet employs sensuous images; imagination is the faculty of thinking in terms of concrete ideas and symbols. Instead of reading a prosaic analysis of exuberant vitality, we may get a direct vision of it in Manet's portrait of the boy with the flute. We may study human nature in the psychologist's abstract accounts of it, or we may see it in the vivid presentations of imagined individuals like Othello, Becky Sharp, Ulysses, and Anna Karenina. The reader might demur that imagination has little to do with effective thinking. Yet the imagination is most valuable in the filed of human relations. Statistics are useful, but statistics alone will not carry us very far in the understanding of human beings. We need an imagination delicately sensitive to the hopes and the fears, the qualities and the flaws of our fellow man, and which can evoke a total personality in its concrete fullness. In practical matters, imagination supplies the ability to break with habit and routine, to see beyond the obvious and to envisage new alternatives; it is the spur of the inventor and the revolutionary, no less than of the artist.

It may be noted that the three phases of effective thinking, logical, relational, and imaginative, correspond roughly to the three divisions of learning, the natural sciences, the social studies, and the humanities, respectively.

Communication – the ability to express oneself so as to be understood by others – is obviously inseparable from effective thinking. In most thinking, one is talking to oneself; and good speech and writing are the visible test and sign of good thinking. Conversely, to speak clearly one must have clear ideas. You cannot say something unless you have something to say; but in order to express your ideas properly you also need some skill in communication. There is something else too: the honest intent to make your ideas known, as against the desire to deceive or merely to conceal. Communication is not speaking only but listening as well; you cannot succeed in communicating your ideas unless the other person wishes to hear and knows how to listen. As there are two kinds of language, oral and written, communication breaks up into the four related skills of speaking and listening, writing and reading.

Communication is that unrestricted exchange of ideas within the body politic by which a prosperous intellectual economy is secured. In its character as the sharing of meanings it is the instrument by which human beings are welded into a society, both the living with the living and the living with the dead. In a free and democratic society the art of communication has a special importance. A totalitarian state can obtain consent by force; but a democracy must persuade, and persuasion is through speech, oral or other. In a democracy issues are aired, talked out of existence or talked into solution. Failure of communication between citizens, or between the government and the public, means a breakdown in the democratic process. Nevertheless, whereas people have been brought together nearer than ever before, in a physical sense, by the improving of mechanisms of transportation, it cannot be said that mutual understanding among individuals and among peoples has made a corresponding advance. Skills, crafts, professions, and scholarly disciplines are apt to surround themselves by high walls of esoteric jargon. Other barriers are erected through the tendency to convert communication into propaganda, whether it be political propaganda, or economic propaganda, as for instance in some types of advertising. Thus, effective communication depends on the possession not only of skills such as clear thinking and cogent expression but of moral qualities as well, such as candor.

In older days, a course on rhetoric was a normal part of the curriculum. Rhetoric to us suggests oratory, and today we are suspicious of or at least indifferent to oratory. Yet the art of rhetoric meant the simple skill of making one's ideas clear and cogent; it did not necessarily mean high-flown speeches. The simplest example of communication is conversation. It is a truism to say that conversation is a lost art. The question is, where was it lost? If we carry on less, or less good, conversation than our ancestors did, is it because we have lost the art, or because, having become technicians, we have little to say that is suitable for general conversation, or because we are much more interested in doing things – driving, for example, or playing bridge? Learned persons are apt to disparage conversation as trivial or frivolous, but unjustly so. If you are looking for the uncovering of important truths during a dinner party, of course you may be disappointed; but that is because you will be looking for the wrong thing. The contribution of general conversation is the revelation and impact of personality. While nothings are being bandied about and trivial words, like the lightest balloons, are launched into the air, contact with personalities is being achieved through characteristic inflections and emphases, through readiness or shyness of response. In conversation the idea is inseparable from the man; conversation is useful because it is the most unforced and natural means of bringing persons together into a society. Beyond its social function, conversation is a delight in itself. It is an art, yet it loses its value if it becomes artificial. Its essence is spontaneity, impetus, movement; the words of a conversation are evanescent, things of the moment, while written words are formalized, rigid, and fixed. Starting with simple things like the weather and minor personal happenings, it proceeds to weave a pattern of sentiments and ideas, and through these of persons, which is fugitive just because it is alive.

Perhaps we have wandered too far from the serious – or should we say the ponderous – aspects of our problem. Yet we had a point to make: that language needs to be neither high learning nor high literature in order to be communication. What we have in mind is the language of a businessman writing a plain and crisp letter, of a scientist making a report, of a citizen asking straight questions, of human beings arguing together on some matter of common interest.

The *making of relevant judgments* involves the ability of the student to bring to bear the whole range of ideas upon the area of experience. It is not now a question of apprehending more relationships within ideas but of applying these to actual facts. The most competent instructor of military science is not necessarily the best officer in the field. An adequate theory of ball playing is conceivable, but an abstract knowledge of it would not make a good ballplayer any more than a course on poetics, however good, would make a good poet. It is not the power to distinguish or state the universal formula, for separated contemplation, which heightens our skill. It is the power to use the formula in the new concrete situations as they fleet past us which education aims to advance. In Plato's myth the philosopher who has obtained the vision of the good must return to the cave and use his vision in order to guide himself among the shadows. Initially and inevitably he is confused; only after long habituation is he able to find his way around and properly to apply his concepts to his concrete experience. There is no rule to be learned which could tell the student how to apply rules to cases; the translation from theory to practice involves an art all its own and requires the skill which we call sagacity or judgment.

To some degree every school or college is separated from life by high walls, visible or invisible; it holds reality at arm's length. And up to a point this is necessary and proper. While it is true that the present is our only fact, nevertheless we cannot see the present so long as we are immersed in it; we need the perspective afforded by distance in time and in space. One of the aims of education is to break the stranglehold of the present upon the mind. On the other side is the fact that youth is instinctive and ardent; to subject youth to a steady diet of abstractions alone would be cruel and unnatural. Moreover, abstractions in themselves are meaningless unless connected with experience; and for this reason all education is in some sense premature. The adult who rereads his great authors realizes how much he had missed of their meaning when he read them in school or college. Now his reading is more rewarding because his range of experience is greater. One might conceive fancifully of another scheme of life in which work comes first and education begins later, say at forty-five. The advantages of this scheme are obvious. Not only would the mature student be amply equipped with the depth of experience necessary for the understanding of the great authors, but the financial problem would be solved. The student would have saved enough money from his work, or perhaps his children would support him.

But such utopias are not for us; we have to deal with harsh realities. Education must be so contrived that the young, during the very process of their schooling, will realize the difference between abstractions and facts and will learn to make the transition from thought to action. A young man who has been nourished with ideas exclusively will be tempted by the sin of intellectual pride, thinking himself capable of dealing with any problem, independently of experience. When he later comes into contact with things, he will stumble or perhaps in self-defense withdraw into sterile cleverness. As we have seen, the aptitude of making relevant judgments cannot be developed by theoretical teaching; being an art, it comes from example, practice, and habituation. The teacher can do a great deal nonetheless; he can relate theoretical content to the student's life at every feasible point, and he can deliberately simulate in the classroom situations from life. Finally, he can bring concrete reports of actual cases for discussion with the students. The essential thing is that the teacher should be constantly aware of the ultimate objectives, never letting means obscure ends, and be persistent in directing the attention of the student from the symbols to the things they symbolize.

Discrimination among values involves choice. The ability to discriminate in choosing covers not only awareness of different kinds of value but of their relations, including a sense of relative importance and of the mutual dependence of means and ends. It covers also much that is analogous to method in thinking; for example, the power to distinguish values truly known from values received only from opinion and therefore not in the same way part of the fabric of experience. Values are of many kinds. There are the obvious values of character, like fair play, courage, self-control, the impulse of beneficence and humanity; there are the intellectual values, like the love of truth and the respect for the intellectual enterprise in all its forms; there are the aesthetic values, like good taste and the appreciation of beauty. As for the last, people are apt to locate beauty in picture galleries and in museums and to leave it there; it is equally, if not more, important to seek beauty in ordinary things, so that it may surround one's life like an atmosphere.

Add to all this that the objective of education is not just knowledge of values but commitment to them, the embodiment of the ideal in one's actions, feelings, and thoughts, no less than an intellectual grasp of the ideal. The reader may object that we are proposing a confusion, that we are suggesting the turning of school or college into a moral reformatory or a church. For is not the purpose of educational institutions to train the mind and the mind only? Yet it is not easy, indeed it is impossible, to separate effective thinking from character. An essential factor in the advancement of knowledge is intellectual integrity, the suppression of all wishful thinking and the strictest regard for the claims of evidence. The universal community of educated men is a fellowship of ideals as well as of beliefs. To isolate the activity of thinking from the morals of thinking is to make sophists of the young and to encourage them to argue for the sake of personal victory rather than of the truth. We are not so naïve as to suggest that theoretical instruction in the virtues will automatically make a student virtuous. Rather, we assert that the best way to infect the student with the zest for intellectual integrity is to put him near a teacher who is himself selflessly devoted to the truth; so that a spark from the teacher will, so to speak, leap across the desk into the classroom, kindling within the student the flame of intellectual integrity, which will thereafter sustain itself.

The problem of moral values and character is more complex. Here the college does not play quite the same role as the school. Clearly we have a right to expect the school to be engaged directly in moral education. But although the college shares in this responsibility, it cannot be expected to use the same direct approach. The college will have to confine itself to providing a proper discrimination of values and will trust to the Socratic dictum that the knowledge of the good will lead to a commitment to the good. Nevertheless, we must recognize a difference between the responsibility of both school and college to train the intellect and their responsibility to form character. In some sense, the former responsibility is a unique one for the educational institution. But in the sphere of moral instruction the school shares its responsibilities with numerous other institutions, of which the family is the most important. Moreover, the school's responsibility is less than that of the family in this field. To use an earlier figure there is danger in regarding the school as a modern Atlas to whom is entrusted the bearing of the whole task of the formation of man. To change the metaphor, a wise society does not put all its eggs in one basket. By the same token, the school cannot remain uninterested in the task of moral education. Just as liberal education, while strictly liberal, must somehow be oriented toward vocationalism, so in this general way will school and college be oriented toward moral character.

Discrimination in values is developed by the study of all the three areas of learning. We have seen that the humanities point both to moral and aesthetic values. It may be true, as we have said earlier, that ethical neutrality is a guiding rule for the historian as scholar. Nevertheless, the historian or social scientist, as *teacher*, should probably go further and present to the student the human past and human institutions not merely as facts but as attempted embodiments of the good life in its various phases. In the natural sciences facts are studied in abstraction from values. But this separation, while pragmatically valid, leads to disaster if treated as final. Values are rooted in facts; and human ideals are somehow a part of nature.

The Humanities

One need not make the altogether excessive claim that the humanities are the whole of either liberal or general education in order to recognize their central importance. If we recommend that the study of literature continue the four years of secondary school (though possibly not as a major or full-time subject in each year), we do not mean that literature is the only one of the humanistic studies which is legitimately part of the secondary curriculum. We do suggest that it is, for those years, the central humanistic study – that it offers peculiar opportunities for achieving the goals previously set forth. The first of these opportunities is direct access to the potentialities and norms of living as they are presented to the mental eye by the best authors. All the other aims in the teaching of literature are subordinate to this. All work in literature should be concerned chiefly with making these visions accessible. When they are seen, when the words open to the reader, the teacher's task is performed. Unless this direct view is to some considerable degree achieved, we have failed. **Above all we must be aware of getting in the light, between the work and the reader.** Summaries or restatements of what the masters were trying to say are often worse than useless. They can be mere dust in the learner's eye.

A natural doubt thus rises at the start. If by "the best authors" we mean the best, rather than good contemporary writing, or writing aimed expressly at different mental stages, or otherwise tempered to assumed limitations of experience in the readers, are not those "best authors" too hard – too hard, that is, for school study under present conditions, large classes, lack of relevant background, teaching power, and the rest? The doubt is reasonable as well as natural. The greatest work stretches any mind. For young minds the stretching may never begin or it may be of the wrong sort. Questions of differentiation obviously enter. We should not sacrifice the interests of the many to those of the few. Nonetheless, it is legitimate to consider first what would be best for those most able to profit, making then what modifications are required to suit the needs of others.

The root argument for using, wherever possible, great works in literature courses is briefly this: ours is at present a centrifugal culture in extreme need of unifying forces. We are in real danger [...] of losing touch with the human past and therefore with one another. The remedy is not in more knowledge about the past. That has been piled up as such knowledge never was for any former generation. Its sudden, all but overwhelming, increase is one of our chief difficulties. The humanities as recently as the sixteenth century were a compact and compassable literature. They cover now not only all literature, philosophy, music, but also "anything that has anything to do with anything in the Metropolitan Museum," and have thereby ceased to be the bond and covenant between men that they once were. Not even the great scholar can any longer see the human story staidly or whole, and the epitome confronts the rest of us. As Shelley said, "Epitomes are the moths of just history; they eat the poetry out of it," and the poetry is our need. It is through the poetry, the imaginative understanding of things in common, that minds most deeply and essentially meet. Therefore the books – whether in verse or prose, whether epic, drama, narrative, or philosophy – which have been the great meeting points and have most influenced the men who in turn have influenced others are those we can least afford to neglect, if ways can be found of opening better access to them. It is a safe assumption that a work which has delighted and instructed many generations of ordinary readers and has been to them a common possession, enriching and enriched, is to be preferred to a product which is on its way to limbo and will not link together even two school generations. On the question of difficulty, it is relevant to refer to Mr. Whitehead's dictum in *Aims of Education,* "If it were easy the book ought to be burned, for it cannot be educational..."

There is a need for versions of the great works cleared of unnecessary and unrewarding obstacles and made by abridgment and reflective editing more accessible to general readers. We believe that in the interests of teaching and public reading alike it is time for scholarship to turn some part of its best energies to the service of the present. Great books are being read increasingly in abridgments. If these are not made by scholars they will be made by relatively incompetent hands. Only the scholar knows enough to distinguish the parts of Homer, Plato, the Old Testament, Bacon, Dante, Shakespeare, or Tolstoy which are essential to their value for contemporary general readers from the parts which concern only the special student. But the scholar, by his training, his competitive position, above all his professional idea, is as a rule unconcerned with this problem. The seeking out of inessentials needed if these authors are to be read with profit by non-specialist, or read widely at all, is a highly delicate process. A separation within the sentence is often needed, an extremely careful weighing of profit and loss, a balancing of one sort of clarity, scope, or fidelity against another. Only the mature scholar saturated with his author can judge of these things; only he can bring together the phrases which supplement and explain one another or cut out with a minimum of disturbance the obstructive detail, the unimportant qualification, or the irrelevant reference. How far this process of clarification or simplification should be carried is, of course, in every instance the prime question. Nothing but a fine awareness both of the material and of the reader's resources will answer it...

When Aristotle said that "man is by nature a political animal" he did not mean that man invariably seeks public office or habitually engages in what we may think of as the activities of the politician. He meant, rather, that civilized man lives in a politically organized society, that only in such a society can he live a satisfactory life. He was reflecting the doctrine of his teacher, Plato, and of his teacher's teacher, Socrates, as also when he said that "virtue and goodness in the state are not a matter of chance but the result of knowledge and purpose." Not all people were, in his estimation, adapted to the highest form of civic life. But even among those whose capacities fitted them for life in society, their natural endowments were but the beginning. "All else is the work of education, we learn some things by habit and some by instruction." Like Plato and Socrates before him, he believed with unquestioning faith that education for life in organized society is essential to the well-being of the state. It is, in other words, a condition of the good life for all citizens.

The education which seeks to promote active, responsible, and intelligent citizenship is ordinarily general rather than special education. It is not, to be sure, reserved for formal education since the shaping of the future citizen takes place mainly at home, at church, on the street or playground, before and outside of school and college. But neither the school nor the college can defensibly fail to attempt the promotion of the kind of citizenship upon which the well-being of our entire way of life depends.

Nor do the social studies include all those which have a very real bearing upon life in society. In some measure every subject in the curriculum helps achieve this great goal of general education. But the social studies have a more immediate relationship to civic education than do the other studies of the secondary-school years, and even though they are concerned with other aspects of general education than training for a life of civic responsibility, this is their distinctive justification...

Political wisdom has always been founded in some part upon knowledge of the past, and upon comprehension of those values which are either implicit in institutions or which have been nobly expressed by statesmen and philosophers. To say this is not to question the value of an understanding of immediate political and economic affairs. It is only to say that a study of immediate problems is ordinarily inadequate since the immediate problem is itself, in some measure, the product of tradition and of inherited ideas. We urge not the necessity of antiquarianism, but rather that kind of education which, specifically directed at wise and responsible citizenship, includes the formal study of history and the social sciences. Interest in, and good will toward, civic affairs are invaluable but inadequate.

The need for differentiation, discussed in the previous chapter, will probably result in certain variations of subject matter in the social studies with different groups of students. It is of course clear that the goals remain the same. But differences in background and in intellectual competence will call for variety in materials and teaching methods. As between those students who are preparing for college and those who do not expect to continue their formal education beyond high school, we see but slight grounds for differentiation in subject matter. Those whose formal education ends with high school, as well as those who intend to go on to technical institutions or to liberal colleges, need that cultural literacy which springs only from the study of history...

While we think that general history, and especially European history, has been unhappily neglected in many schools, both public and private, during the past few decades, we do not, to repeat, propose that every school should provide precisely the same course. Certainly colleges should not attempt to require for entrance this or any other single pattern of courses even though they may, and we think should, expect of students some substantial work in European or in general history as well as in American history. But there are obvious dangers in prescribing the particular methods by which these aims should be obtained. There may, for example, be in a given school a teacher who is devoted to ancient history, and a course in Greek or Roman history can be made a vital part of the education of future citizens, even though, no matter how well taught, it would not afford that familiarity with the background of the modern world which is necessary to an understanding of the great society in which we live. Such a course might, that is to say, be an extremely valuable basis upon which to build later work in modern European and American history, even though it would not be a substitute for either. The need for experimentation in teaching the societal sciences will continue. It would be most unwise to cast them in rigid mold. The enthusiasm of a teacher for his subject is always of first importance. But even when all of these factors are taken into account, it may be doubted whether any of them can justify the exclusion of European and American history from the list of courses which best subserves the purpose of general education...

The old and much criticized maxim, "Politics without history has no roots," expresses a sound view if only it be wisely interpreted and applied. It does not necessarily mean that politics (which, as once understood, embraced economics and sociology) should be taught only in historical terms. But the political, economic, and social problems of today do have historical roots, just as they will supply the roots of other problems in the future. Connections with the past and some knowledge of these problems are essential to an understanding of the complexity of the political organism.

The movement toward a "realistic" study of government and economics has unquestionably produced a clearer picture of contemporary problems and processes. But the understanding that has resulted has often been shallow, partly because of neglect of historical forces, partly through lack of attention to the role played by relatively abstract principles of politics and economics. Nearly fifty years ago Justice Holmes said, "Theory is the most important part of the dogma of the law, as the architect is the most important man who takes part in the building of a house." The generalization is as valid for the social sciences as for law and architecture, yet the teaching of these subjects is rarely based upon the principle which Holmes expressed. One result is that the slogans and catchwords of the movement are accepted as statements of profound truth; another is a skeptical relativism which recognizes no standard of value except success. There is no better safeguard against these unhappy conditions than the study of some of the speculative doctrines, as well as some of the statements of political and social faith, which served the men of the past – the men from whom we inherit the institutions for whose perpetuation and improvement we are responsible. A wise student of American history and government recently remarked that we today have no substitute for the old books of maxims and precepts of free government which formerly constituted a basic part of instruction in the schools. The lack to which he referred is a serious one, even though the old collections of maxims seem dogmatic and not entirely relevant today. But some of the classic statements of political and social theory can profitably be used either in courses in European or American history or in those dealing with civics or American life. Obviously there will be a need for careful selection of such materials in relation to the capacities of students, and we do not suggest *The Politics* or *The Wealth of Nations* in high-school courses. But there exists statements of the essential principles of democracy which should be made available to all students; other statements, as with algebra or advanced work in foreign languages, would be suitable only for a somewhat limited group. Thus Mill's *On Liberty* or his *Representative Government* probably could be studied profitably by only a minority of high-school students. Some parts of Jefferson's *Notes on Virginia* and some numbers of *The Federalist* might be read by a somewhat larger proportion, provided the teacher has the training and the capacity to explain their place in the growth of American polity and is able to discuss their relevance to contemporary affairs. Nearly all students should have an opportunity to read some of the major constitutional documents and certain of the great speeches of Pitt, Burke, Lincoln, Wilson, and Roosevelt. Passages from many of them have become the common possession of literate men. Primarily they are eloquent testimonies of faith in a free society. They are also illustrations in the history of constitutional democracy and statements of the principles which have shaped and continue to shape the asocial order in which we live. As such they warrant analysis as well as repetition...

No discussion of the problems of teaching the social studies would be complete without a recognition of the restraints sometimes imposed on teachers by outside persons or groups in the community. These limitations or compulsions come ordinarily from those who believe, or profess to believe, that they are expressing the true principles of Americanism. They too often forget that the basic doctrine of faith is freedom of thought and speech, as they fail to recall the disastrous effects in many countries of abandoning that freedom. It may readily be agreed that teachers must be aware of their grave responsibility in discussing debated and debatable political and social ideas and movements. Their role is analysis, discussion, teaching – not stump oratory. But recognition of the nature of that role must not be allowed to become an excuse for strangling the freedom to investigate and to discuss controversial issues. That freedom is essential to the continuation of the American way of life. Teachers are citizens and their students will soon be expected to take up the obligations of citizenship. Unless teachers are free to enjoy the privileges of citizenship outside the classroom, and to carry on in the classroom the spirit and practice of inquiry and discussion, the rights of teachers and of students will have been sacrificed to a principle of enforced conformity which has been far more productive of the spirit of revolt than of intelligent participation in the democratic process. Change is inevitable in politics, as in science and in the art of war. Our constitutional system is based on that assumption, and orderly changes, as the founders knew, can proceed only out of free discussion. To those who are entirely content with the existing condition of affairs, any consideration of proposals for amendment may appear to be both unpatriotic and unconstitutional. To them we would recall the statement of Jefferson, made at the age of seventy-three, after he had spent nearly a decade in reflecting on his forty years of public life:

> Laws and institutions must go hand in hand with the progress of the human mind. As that becomes more developed, more enlightened, as new discoveries are made, new truths disclosed, and manners and opinions change with the change of circumstances, instructions must advance also, and keep pace with the times. We might as well require a man to wear still the coat which fitted him when a boy, as civilized society to remain ever under the regimen of their ancestors... (*Writings*, Paul L. Ford, ed., X, pp.42–43)

The fact that an educational institution grants a diploma on the basis of the completion of courses and the passing of examinations does not imply that its aim is wholly to impart learning. As we suggested in the second chapter, learning is also for the sake of cultivating basic mental abilities; in short, to foster the powers of reason in man. The ability to think in accordance with the facts and with the laws of inference, to choose wisely, to feel with discrimination is what distinguishes man from the animals and endows him with intrinsic worth. Yet reason, while an end, is a means as well – a means to the mastery of life. The union of knowledge and reason in the integrated personality – this is the final test of education. We are not now denying the central position of reason or of knowledge as ministering to reason; we are only urging that reason is or must strive to become master of a highly complex inner kingdom consisting of many and diverse members, all of which go into the making of a complete man. To put the matter bluntly, the educational process has somewhat failed of its purpose if it has produced the merely bookish youth who lacks spirit and is all light without warmth. But to leave the matter in these terms is to make for dangerous confusion; we must safeguard our statement from the misunderstandings to which it has exposed...

While traditionally man has been viewed as primarily as rational desires and sentiments which becloud and sometimes sway his reason. To be sure, classical philosophers recognized the existence of the passions, but they tended to regard the latter as alien intrusions and an unwanted complication. Yet passions, although dangerous because primitive and even savage, are a source of strength if properly guided; they supply the driving forces for achievement. Lord Bryce once said that if government were in the hands of the young many mistakes would be made, but if government were run by old men nothing would be done. According to the ancient myth, reason is the charioteer that directs but is not the horse that pulls the chariot. In the complete man we look for imitative, zest and interest, strength and resolution, driving power. In a free society much of improvement, in or outside of government, comes from the initiative and the dogged perseverance of private citizens; and the clash of ambitions in the struggle for the rewards of life, when regulated by the rules of fair play and a concern for the common good, is a source of social progress.

The danger in the preceding account is that the various components of the human person might be wrongly viewed as isolated elements or faculties, each leading an autonomous existence. For instance, reason is not a faculty operating separately from interest and zest. Without a zeal for knowledge, without the impulse of curiosity, the thinker will remain lazy and unproductive. And yet, while ordinarily the perfection of one human power depends on the parallel development of the other powers, there are important and unpredictable exceptions. It is not true, for example, that a healthy body is always necessary for the existence of a vigorous mind. There are cases of great men in the arts and sciences who, all their lives, fought against sickness; there have been persons eminent in a special field who were not rounded individuals. Human personality is enough of a mystery to prelude our making sweeping and rigid prescriptions.

Furthermore, the concept of the whole man is not adequate as an aim of education. The innate drives, the sentiments and force of will, are neutral, capable of developing in either direction, and may become antisocial unless they are "moralized," unless they are made to serve as tools in the hand of duty. The complete man must be a good man. Moral character arises from the molding of the native power to ideal aims. The final secular good is the dedication of the self to an ideal higher than the self – the devotion to truth and to one's neighbor...

Virtually all college teachers will agree that students should have a sound training in the essential techniques of English composition in high school, and that they should there have developed some facility of expression; that, in other words, they should come to college prepared to go ahead without the necessity of learning, or even of reviewing, the essentials of spelling, grammar, and syntax. We realize that composition is a never-ending discipline which can be only begun in schools and must be continued in college. But most college teachers, and this seems to be true in virtually every country, complain that the high schools do not equip their students with the capacity to write their own language clearly and grammatically, and that, therefore, the colleges must do a kind of work in composition which the schools should have done and which the schools should be able to do better than the colleges. The result has been that in most colleges there is some remedial requirement in English composition...

Proposed Courses in General Education: The Humanities

It is proposed that the course in the area of the humanities which will be required of all students be one which might be called "Great Texts of Literature." The aim of such a course would be the fullest understanding of the work read rather than of men or periods represented, craftsmanship evinced, historic or literary development shown, or anything else. These other matters would be admitted only in so far as they are necessary to allow the work to speak for itself. Otherwise they should be left for special, not general, education.

Literature is surrounded by a numerous company of attendant studies which profess to guide the student in the right approach, the proper understanding, the full enjoyment. These attendant studies occasionally assume the main place. Thus at various times philology, history of language, history of literature, biography of authors, discussion of literary form, criticism, prosody, and grammar may be found occupying the student's time and energy even to the utter neglect of that for which alone these worthy subjects were born.

As scholarship, which once had only a shelf of Greek and Latin authors to tend, becomes ever more extensive, more coordinated, and more official, this danger of forgetting its prime purpose inevitably increases. The ancillary studies can and do at innumerable points assist the specialist in his professional effort to throw light upon literature. They belong unquestionably to his own full professional equipment. It is his business to father them and to train successors in their use. Moreover, progress in these studies is tangible, **almost measurable**. Progress in ability to take from literature what man most needs is, in comparison, intangible. Relatively it is unexaminable. What can be examined is largely knowledge about literature. But the knowledge it has to give as a part of general, as opposed to special, education is of another sort. It is knowledge though. It comes only through immersion in the literature. Knowledge about, though its origin and aim may be simply to aid the immersion, can in fact prevent and hinder its own purpose.

The scholar is of course aware of this. He has learned this lesson in his own progress through many a hard struggle to recover perspective. But if his chief occupation has been research and the training of others in research, a special effort of imagination is needed to distinguish what is, or might be, helpful to himself in reading a master from what will help a beginner who neither possesses nor will ever possess anything resembling his own background or equipment. Here is the difficulty in designing a course in great literature for all students: that the modes of treatment proper to the specialist are a distraction to those who are not to become experts. A mere listing of books to be read would convey little without some specification of the mode of treatment. But a specification would amount to the course itself. And here we meet another difficulty. There is not one best way of introducing people to Homer or Plato or Dante. Or, if there is, which it is not known. **Freedom for the instructor is essential. He only teaches, in this field, by letting his students watch the play of a mind with a mind, that their minds may play in turn.** The play he shows them must be representative of "the all in each of all minds," to use Coleridge's phrase, but it cannot be tied down to another man's notions of what is educative. And yet if a course in literature is to deserve to be compulsory there must be wide agreement both as to what is attempting and how it will attempt that.

A third difficulty is that there are no known ways of describing ends or means in these matters which will not be construed by different readers to very different effects. Nonetheless, with the prime aims as defined above in mind, it may be said that the more specific aim is familiarity with as much of the greatest writing as can be read and pondered in the limited time available. The proportion of reading to pondering is of course the turning point. There must be time for reflection or the familiarity will remain too verbal. This cuts down the amount that can be read. But since the best commentary on an author is frequently some more of his writing, and since great books are great in part through the power of their design, the amount for single authors cannot be cut beyond a point. **The outcome is that fewer books can be chosen.** Each must be read completely enough for its parts to help one another to the full. Probably, therefore, a course which chose eight great books would be trying to do too much. A list from which a selection would be made might include Homer, one or two of the Greek tragedies, Plato, the Bible, Virgil, Dante, Shakespeare, Milton, Tolstoy.

Both lectures and group discussion are desirable as aids to this reading. The main purpose of the lectures would be to launch certain themes for the discussions. Each of these books can be thought about and talked over through course after course. Careful husbandry of time will be needed. It will not be possible to consider more than some selection of those things in each book for which it has been most regarded; and this selection will need all the instructor's wisdom. It will include the greatest, most universal, most essential human preoccupations first. Whatever is left unnoticed is sacrificed in the interests of these. The treatment which is attempted of these great themes can only do its best to be worthy of them. They themselves are its inspiration. Beyond all techniques of pedagogy and scholarship these books have been masters of method. The instructor can only seek to be a means by which the authors teach the course.

Some doubt may be felt whether the heights of these books may not be beyond the reach of large masses of the students. But they have always been admittedly beyond the reach of the vast majority of even their best readers. That has not made them less educative. And indeed the chief reason for the course, and the best argument for experimenting with it, is that too many students today have too little contact with thoughts which are beyond them (apart from the specialties) and that many are in fact passionately if inarticulately hungry for greatness in the common cares of man...

We considered the possibility of suggesting as a title for such a course "The Evolution of Free Society," but that title carries with it implications of indoctrination which would be unacceptable to many, and which might, indeed, convey an entirely false idea of its intentions. For while we agree that Harvard College should assume "a full and a conscientious responsibility for training men in the nature of the heritage which they possess, and in the responsibilities which they must assume as free men for its enlargement and perpetuation," we do not believe that the course should be one which would attempt to convince students of the eternal perfection of existing ideas and institutions. The central objective of the course would be an examination of the institutional and theoretical aspects of the Western heritage.

It would be inappropriate for us to outline in detail a scheme of this course, or even to indicate all the topics with which it would be concerned. Its content and procedure should be worked out by the staff charged with its execution and later modified on the basis of experience in actually giving the course. In order to indicate somewhat more clearly the character of the course we have in mind we shall, however, suggest a number of topics and writing with which it could deal appropriately.

Any course which attempts to consider the nature of the Western heritage must raise more questions than it professes to answer. It should open up questions of ends as well as means, of values and objectives as well as of institutional organization. But it should also include an analysis of some of the great attempts which have been made to find answers to these questions. The course would, in other words, include an historical analysis of certain significant movements and changes in Western society together with the reading of substantial portions of certain of the classics of political, economic, and social thought which those changes have helped to produce.

In a single course it would be folly to attempt a comprehensive survey of the entire range of European institutional development and social thinking form the time of the Greeks to the present day, and no such project is proposed. We believe that the course should be selective, not inclusive. It will, for example, probably be thought desirable to spend some time at the beginning in reading portions of two or three of the great foundation treatises of political and social thought which came out of the civilization of classic antiquity. It may be doubted whether any other books succeed so well in raising certain of the persistent problems of organized life in society as do those of Plato and Aristotle. The study could not at this point be a thorough one in the sense in which advanced work in a field of concentration would be thorough, but it might prove to be intensely valuable in indicating the nature of some of the more enduring problems. Along with the reading of portions of such books might well go lectures on the character of the Greek city-state, and possibly some consideration of the impact of the Roman Empire upon the culture, law, and political life of the ancient world...

The modern college dates from the Renaissance, when it was created, more or less in opposition to the then long-established European universities, as a place where students might live together and with their teachers for the purpose of receiving a rounded preparation – spiritual, intellectual, physical – for active life. It took its inspiration from the classical ideal of the complete man and was originally aristocratic in tone, a training place for the kind of universal gentleman described in Castiglion's *Courtier* or sketched in Shakespeare's picture of Hamlet as "the courtier's, scholar's, soldier's eye, tongue, sword." But in England, where this concept of the college alone took firm root, it was also shaped by the Puritan, anti-aristocratic forces of the Reformation, which stressed not so much the rounded gentleman as the pastor and the religiously formed man of affairs. A passage from S.E. Morrison's *The Founding of Harvard College* (pp.56–57) catches amusingly the fusion of ideas which was carried from the old to the new Cambridge.

One can hardly exaggerate the importance of this intrusion of "young gentlemen" into the English universities, for there they remained, and to Harvard they have come. Owing to the fact that England simultaneously received the reformation, the renaissance, and this notion of a gentleman's education, there was brought about an unwilling compromise between gentility and learning, a rubbing of shoulders between the poor scholar and the squire's son, that has made the English and American college what it is today: the despair of educational reformers and logical pedagogues, the astonishment of Continental scholars, a place which is neither a house of learning nor a house of play, but a little of both; and withal a microcosm of the world in which we live. To this sixteenth-century compromise, become a tradition, we owe that common figure of the English-speaking world, "a gentleman and a scholar."

Such were several among the leading founders of New England and of Harvard: both Winthrops and both Saltonstalls, Downing and Bradstreet, Bellingham, and Peter Bulkeley, of whom Cotton Mather wrote, "His education... was Learned, it was Genteel and... Pious." To Harvard they brought a new zeal for scriptural religion and the humanist tradition. From her opening day, Harvard has included a large proportion of young men who had no professional intentions. They have been complained of by their more serious preceptors, these three hundred years. They have committed every sort of folly and extravagance. New colleges such as Williams and Amherst have been founded in order to provide a place where poor but pious youth could be educated for the ministry, uncontaminated by the "rakehells," "bloods," and "sports" of Harvard – and the same class of students have flocked to the new colleges. Even after countless examples of gentlemen who have become scholars and scholars who have become gentlemen by this illogical commingling, there are some people who would admit none to our colleges but serious students, and others who would set a standard of luxury and expense impossible for poor students. As long as Harvard remains true to her early tradition, rich men's sons and poor, serious scholars and frivolous wasters, saints and sinners, puritans and papists, Jews and Gentiles will meet in her Houses, her Yard, and her athletic fields, rubbing off each other's angularities, and learning from friendly contact what cannot be learned from books.

But one further point should be noticed. It was remarked that democracy, by broadening the basis of government to include all the people, ideally demands of all the education formerly reserved for a privileged class. The distinction has ceased between inferiors trained only for practical tasks and superiors broadly trained for government. The Renaissance collegiate education was, in effect, precisely an education of governors – men rounded and supple enough to make decisions and sufficiently well educated to do so with perspective and a sense of standards. It is the mantle of this tradition which has descended on the modern college – even to some degree on the modern high school. Since the governor is now the citizen and no longer merely the gentleman and the aristocrat, then this "gentleman's education" has become the citizen's education...

Finally, a similarly loose but perhaps useful contrast can be applied to teaching. It has been said that teaching has naturally two phases: the Olympian and the earthly. In the Olympian phase, the teacher, actually or figuratively at some distance from the student, expounds the objective majesty of the subject – a majesty which exists, so to speak, whether the student heeds or not, which is greater than he and greater than the teacher, something austere and almost impersonal, a facet of the world. In the human phase, the teacher sits on the same level, as the student discussing the truth as it appears to each. The individual adjustment which each makes to the truth is then uppermost, and as the teacher examines, he can also be examined. We would not say that the Olympian phase of teaching is proper to the university and the human phase to the college.

Graduate instruction obviously involves discussion and personal oversight. Yet it is true that, in so far as the college aims to develop the total person, then it must attach special importance to this human phase of teaching. The justification of all teaching to some extent, and of this kind especially, is the premises of the democratic way of life: teaching is important because the human being has value in himself – not as a potential scholar but as he actually is with his actual capacities and limitations. From this premise follows what was said earlier about the place of tutoring, advising, and small discussion groups in the college as a whole and in connection with the Houses. The university college must use both methods, the human as well as the Olympian, to fulfill its proper purpose...

In Mencius's famous parable:

> The trees of Niu hill were once beautiful. Being in the suburbs of a great city, however, they were hewn down with axes and bills. Could they retain their beauty? Still, through the growth from the vegetative life day and night, and the nourishing influence of the rain and the dew, they were not without buds and sprouts springing out. But then came the cattle and the goats, and browsed upon them. Thence came the bare and stripped appearance of the hill. People seeking this think it was never finely wooded. But is this the nature of the hill?
>
> Even so of what properly belongs to man. Is what is left of any man's mind ever without love and justice, without courtesy and knowledge of right and wrong? The way in which man loses his proper goodness of mind is like the way in which the trees were denuded by hatchets. Hewn down day after day, can it retain its excellence? But there is some growth of its life night and day, and in the calm air of the morning, just between night and day, the mind feels in a degree these desires and aversions which are proper to humanity; but then it is fettered and destroyed by what a man does during the day. This happens again and again, the night breath is not enough to preserve the proper goodness, and he becomes not far different from the birds and beasts. When people see this, they think his mind never had these endowments. But is this man's propensity?
>
> If it gets its nourishment, there is nothing which will not grow. If it loses its nourishment, there is nothing that will not perish.

A few years before this Plato was writing:

> As it is, we have given a true account of the soul in its present appearance. But we have looked at it in a state like that of the sea-god Glaucus: whose original nature can no longer be readily discerned by the eye, because the members of his body have been broken off or

> crushed and in every way marred by the waves, and incrustations have grown over him of seaweed and shells and stones, so that he is more like any wild beast than his natural self. The soul which we behold has been brought to a similar state by a thousand evils.

Modern philosophy puts the same point this way:

> Now, let us go quite a way from physics and consider an oak tree. There is evidence, we saw, for the norm of an oak tree. A botanist or horticulturist could tell us in great detail what is the *normal* growth and appearance of any particular variety of oak. Give the oak suitable soil, water, sun, fertilizer, and freedom from other vegetation, from insects, and the like, and the normal oak will be exemplified. The law of the oak will exhibit itself in concrete existence just as the law of gravitating mass exhibited itself in the dropped ball. But plant the oak in poor soil or on a windswept hill, or in a thick forest, and it will be distorted from its normal growth just as the planet was from the normal gravitational path. This distortion will be a resultant of the forces of other laws in which the characters of the oak participate in conjunction with the normal law of growth of the oak.
>
> The same distortions occur for the same reasons in the norms of animals, of men, and of human societies. (Stephen C. Pepper, *World Hypotheses*, p.179)

Man, these agree, has his norm, and the account of education we are giving here agrees too, without, however, professing to give an adequate statement of the norm. The apprehension of the norm – by approximation to it – is education itself, which is thus its own aim. Books about education are not competitors.

But we can discuss the means to be used and the dangers to be met, and in so doing we must ignore neither the influences of the schools upon the community nor its influences upon their products. Mencius's hatchetman and his goats hew and browse alike within and without the schools. It is what happens after the schooling period and what should and should not happen which concerns us now. If we are tempted to blame the schools for the bare and stripped appearance of too many ex-students in later life, we should not forget what the world is endlessly doing to them. And here what happens in the immediate post-school years has especial importance...

Leisure, the name the future will have to give to unemployment, is opening out before mankind as widely as the Pacific Ocean spread before Cortez. It is no wild surmise that a chief adjustment we will have to make soon is the replacement of needful toil by other occupations. We are making it already or failing to make it with every reduction in hours of labor. And the dangers of idleness, we know today, are very far from being merely proverbial. We have seen how a Hitler can turn people from unemployment to war. We have not yet seen as clearly how education can be made not merely a preventative but, in William James's phrase, the moral equivalent of war. To use a previous figure of speech this means a Jacksonian raising of the many by education.

The unparalleled growth – we almost said eruption – in our school system was the point with which this report began. A parallel growth or eruption to be expected in post-school invitations and aids to further learning seems to be what its conclusions indicate. In the measure in which the schools succeed this development becomes the more likely. General education perpetuates itself, if only by seeking endlessly to discover what it itself is. In Chapter I we compared the present diversity of offerings in the high school to a clouded mirror reflecting dimly the diversity of our society itself. One great function of adult education is to provide a still more comprehensive reflection, but cleared and refocused by our utmost endeavor to the vision of those who have passed out of tutelage, to become in the measure of their awareness guardians of the republic...

Yet education is primarily self-teaching. The classroom is to show the student how to instruct himself and to save him time in this attempt. Its aim is to aid him toward enterprising independence, toward free curiosity, and toward persistence in self-learning...

Hector's words in *Troilus and Cressida*:

The wound of peace is surety
Surety secure.

Or, as Poor Richard had it, "He that is secure is not safe."

Such dangers, however, are a spur to a widened and livelier sense of responsibility, individual and collective. Enlargement of the common concern is indeed the distinctive character of our age. Not very long ago the mass of mankind could and did leave peacemaking, for example, to statesmen. Today most people feel some of its weight on their shoulders. Even one generation back, how other people lived was not their business; but all men are neighbors now. Among and beyond all the local and personal motives which drive men to pursue education, this budding collective responsibility year by year grows in power. And as it grows it profoundly influences some immediate motives. The desire to get on in the world or to advance the status of the workers, the two chief drives which have animated out-of-school education hitherto, are being transformed by it into wider interests far more favorable both to growth in democracy and to the final causes for which society itself is only a means. "War is the great educator," as enemy propagandists have said, though hardly with this in mind. It has shown us that in technical instruction we have been sadly unambitious and unenterprising. It has shown us equally that in general education the strongest incentive comes from the whole man's awareness of his share in the common fate, of his part in the joint undertaking.[14]

The Closing of the American Mind

Decades later, as the twentieth century drew to a close, Allan Bloom, also from the University of Chicago, in his classic work *The Closing of the American Mind* continued the controversy. Hear first Saul Bellow in the foreword:

Bloom tells of a student who, after a reading of the *Symposium*, said that it was hard today to imagine the magic Athenian atmosphere, "in which friendly men, educated, lively, on a footing of equality, civilized but natural, came together and told wonderful stories about the meaning of their longing. But [adds Bloom] such experiences are always accessible. Actually, this playful discussion took place in the midst of a terrible war that Athens was destined to lose, and Aristophanes and Socrates at least could foresee that this meant the decline of Greek civilization. But they were not given to culture despair, and in these terrible political circumstances, their abandon to the joy of nature proved the viability of what is best in man, independent of accidents, of circumstance. We feel ourselves too dependent on history and culture... What is essential about [...] any of the Platonic dialogues is reproducible in almost all times and places... This thinking might be what it is all for. That's where we are beginning to fail. But it is right under our noses, improbable but always present..."

The heart of Professor Bloom's argument is that the university, in a society ruled by public opinion, was to have been an island of intellectual freedom where all views were investigated without restriction. Liberal democracy in its generosity made this possible, but by consenting to play an

[14] *General Education in Free Society: A Report of the Harvard Committee*, Cambridge, Mass., Harvard University Press, 1945

active or "positive," a participatory role in society, the university has become inundated and saturated with the backflow of society's "problems." Preoccupied with questions of Health, Sex, Race, War, academics make their reputations and their fortunes and the university has become society's conceptual warehouse of often harmful influences. Any proposed reforms of liberal education which might bring the university into conflict with the whole of the U.S.A. are unthinkable. Increasingly, the people "inside" are identical in their appetites and motives with the people "outside" the university. This is what I take Bloom to be saying, and if he were making a polemical statement merely it would be easy enough to set aside. What makes it formidably serious is the accurate historical background accompanying the argument. He explains with an admirable command of political theory how all this came to be, how modern democracy originated, what Machiavelli, Hobbes, Locke, Rousseau and the other philosophers of enlightenment intended, and how their intentions succeeded or failed.

The heat of the dispute between Left and Right has grown so fierce that the habits of civilized discourse have suffered a scorching. Antagonists seem no longer to listen to one another. It would be a pity if intelligent adversaries were not to read Professor Bloom's book with disinterested attention. It makes an important statement and deserves careful study. What it provides, whether or not one agrees with its conclusions, is an indispensable guide for discussion, not a mere skimming of the tradition, but a completely articulated, historically accurate summary, a trustworthy résumé of the development of the higher mental life in the democratic U.S.A.

Saul Bellow

Closing of the American Mind begins:

> This essay – a meditation on the state of our souls, particularly those of the young, and their education – is written from the perspective of a teacher. Such a perspective, although it has grave limitations and is accompanied by dangerous temptations is a privileged one. The teacher, particularly the teacher dedicated to liberal education, must constantly try to look toward the goal of human completeness and back at the natures of his student here and now, ever seeking to

understand the former and to assess the capacities of the latter to approach it. Attention to the young, knowing what their hungers are and what they can digest, is the essence of the craft...

There is one thing a professor can be absolutely certain of: almost every student entering the university believes, or says he believes, that truth is relative. If this belief is put to the test, one can count on the students' reaction: they will be uncomprehending. That anyone should regard the proposition as not self-evident astonishes them, as though he were calling into question 2 + 2 = 4. These are things you don't think about. The students' backgrounds are as various as America can provide. Some are religious, some atheists; some are to the Left, some to the Right; some intend to be scientists, some humanists or professionals or businessmen; some are poor, some rich. They are unified only in their relativism and in their allegiance to equality. And the two are related in a moral intention. The relativity of truth is not a theoretical insight but a moral postulate, the condition of a free society, or so they see it. They have all been equipped with this framework early on, and it is the modern replacement for the inalienable natural rights that used to be the traditional American grounds for a free society. That it is a moral issue for students is revealed by the character of their response when challenged – a combination of disbelief and indignation: "Are you an absolutist?" the only alternative they know, uttered in the same tone as "Are you a monarchist?" or "Do you really believe in witches?" This latter leads into the indignation, for someone who believes in witches might well be a witch-hunter or a Salem judge. The danger they have been taught to fear from absolution is not error but intolerance. Relativism is necessary to openness; and this is the virtue, the only virtue, which all primary education for more than fifty years has dedicated itself to inculcating. Openness – and the relativism that makes it the only plausible stance in the face of various claims to truth and various ways of life and kinds of human beings – is the great insight of our times. The true believer is the real danger. The study of history and of culture teaches that all the world was mad in the past; men always thought they were right, and that led to wars, persecutions, slavery, xenophobia, racism, and chauvinism. The point is not to correct the mistakes and really be right; rather it is not to think you are right at all.

The students, of course, cannot defend their opinion. It is something with which they have been indoctrinated. The best they can do is point out all the opinions and cultures there are and have been. What right, they ask, do I or anyone else have to say one is better than the others? If I pose the routine questions designed to confuse them and make them think, such as, "If you had been a British administrator in India, would you have let the natives under your governance burn the widow at the funeral of a man who had died?" they either remain silent or reply that the British should never have been there in the first place. It is not that they know very much about other nations, or about their own. The purpose of their education is not to make them scholars but to provide them with a moral virtue – openness.

Every educational system has a moral goal that it tries to attain and that informs its curriculum. It wants to produce a certain kind of human being. This intention is more or less explicit, more or less a result of reflection; but even the neutral subjects, like reading and writing and arithmetic, take their place in a vision of the educated person. In some nations the goal was the pious person, in others the warlike, in others the industrious. Always important is the political regime, which needs citizens who are in accord with its fundamental principle. Aristocracies want gentlemen, oligarchies men who respect and pursue money, and democracies lovers of equality. Democratic education, whether it admits it or not, wants and needs to produce men and women who have the tastes, knowledge, and character supportive of a democratic regime. Over the history of our republic, there have obviously been changes of opinion as to what kind of man is best for our regime...

Lack of education simply results in students seeking for enlightenment wherever it is readily available, without being able to distinguish between the sublime and trash, insight and propaganda. For the most part students turn to the movies, ready prey to interested moralisms such as the depictions of Gandhi or Thomas More – largely designed to further passing political movements and to appeal to simplistic needs for greatness – or to insinuating flattery of their secret aspirations and vices, giving them a sense of significance...

Thus, the failure to read good books both enfeebles the vision and strengthens our most fatal tendency – the belief that the here and now is all there is.

The only way to counteract this tendency is to intervene most vigorously in the education of those few who come to the university with a strong urge for *un je ne sais quoi*, who fear that they may fail to discover it, and that the cultivation of their minds is required for the success of their quest…

They pointed toward a road of learning that leads to the meeting place of the greats! …

This nation's impulse is toward the future, and tradition seems more of a shackle to it than an inspiration. Reminiscences and warnings from the past are our only monitor as we careen along our path…

In short, philosophy was only a word, and literature a form of entertainment. Our high schools and the atmosphere around them put us in this frame of mind. But a great university presented another kind of atmosphere, announcing that there are questions that ought to be addressed by everyone but are not asked in ordinary life or expected to be answered there. It provided an atmosphere of free inquiry, and therefore excluded what is not conducive to or is inimical to such inquiry. It made a distinction between what is important and not important. It protected the tradition, not because tradition is tradition but because tradition provides models of discussion on a uniquely high level. It contained marvels and made possible friendships consisting in shared experiences of those marvels. Most of all there was the presence of some authentically great thinkers who gave living proof of the existence of the theoretical life and whose motives could not easily be reduced to any of the baser ones people delight in thinking universal. They had authority, not based on power, money or family, but on natural gifts that properly compel respect. The relations among them and between them and students were the revelation of a community in which there is a true common good. In a nation founded on reason, the university was the temple of the regime, dedicated to the purest use of reason and evoking the kind of reverence appropriate to an association of free and equal human beings…

The great democratic danger, according to Tocqueville, **is enslavement to public opinion. The claim of democracy is that every man decides for himself. The use of one's natural faculties to determine for oneself what is true and false and good and bad is the American philosophic method.** Democracy liberates from tradition, which in other kinds of regimes determines the judgment. Prejudices of religion, class and family are leveled, not only in principle but also in fact, because none of their representatives has an intellectual authority. Equal political right makes it impossible for church or aristocracy to establish the bastions from which they can affect men's opinions. Churchmen, for whom divine revelation is the standard, aristocrats in whom the reverences for antiquity are powerful, fathers who always tend to prefer the rights of the ancestral to those of reason, are all displaced in favor of the equal individual. Even if men seek authority, they cannot find it where they used to find it in other regimes. Thus the external impediments to the free exercise of reason have been removed in democracy...

However, since very few people school themselves in the use of reason beyond the calculation of self-interest encouraged by the regime, they need help on a vast number of issues – in fact, all issues, inasmuch as everything is opened up to fresh and independent judgment – for the consideration of which they have neither time nor capacity...

Every man in democracy thinks himself individually the equal of every other man, this makes it difficult to resist the collectivity of equal men. If all opinions are equal, then the majority of opinions, on the psychological analogy of politics, should hold sway. It is very well to say that each should follow his own opinion, but since consensus is required for social and political life, accommodation is necessary. So, unless there is some strong ground for opposition to majority opinion, it inevitably prevails. This is the really dangerous form of the tyranny of the majority, not the kind that actively persecutes minorities but the kind that breaks the inner will to resist because there is no qualified source of nonconforming principles and no sense of superior right. **The majority is all there is. What the majority decides is the only tribunal. It is not so much its power that intimidates but its semblance of justice. Tocqueville found that Americans talked very much about individual right but that there was a real monotony of thought and that vigorous independence of mind was rare. Even those who appear to be free-thinkers really look to a constituency and expect one day to be part of a majority. They are creatures of public opinion as much as are conformists – actors of nonconformist in the theatre of the conformists who admire and applaud nonconformity of certain kinds, the kinds that radicalize the already dominant opinions...**

The university must come to the aid of unprotected and timid reason. The university is the place where inquiry and philosophic openness come into their own. It is intended to encourage the non-instrumental use of reason for its own sake, to provide the atmosphere where the moral and physical superiority of the dominant will not intimidate philosophic doubt. And it preserves the treasury of great deeds, great men and great thoughts required to nourish that doubt.

Freedom of the mind requires not only, or not even especially, the absence of legal constraints but the presence of alternative thoughts. The most successful tyranny is not the one that uses force to assure uniformity but the one that removes the awareness of other possibilities that makes it seem inconceivable that other ways are viable, that removes the sense that there is an outside. It is not feelings or commitments that will render a man free, but thoughts, reasoned thoughts. Feelings are largely formed and informed by convention. Real differences come from difference in thought and fundamental principle. Much in democracy conduces to the assault on awareness of difference...

Reason and competence are to be underlined here. "Intellectual honesty," "commitment" and that kind of thing have nothing to do with the university, belong in the arenas of religious and political struggle, only get in the way of the university's activity, and open it to suspicion and criticism of which it has no need. Freedom of thought and freedom of speech were proposed in theory, and in the practice of serious political reformers, in order to encourage the still voice of reason in a world that had always been dominated by fanaticisms and interests. How freedom of thought and speech came to mean the special encouragement and protection of fanaticism and interests is another of those miracles connected with the decay of the ideal of the rational men in the United States. They were not particularly concerned with protecting eccentric or mad opinions or lifestyles. Such protection, which we now often regard as the Founders' central intention, is only an incidental result of the protection of reason, and it loses plausibility if reason is rejected. These authors did not respect the many religious sects or desire diversity for its own sake. The existence of many sects was permitted only to prevent the emergence of a single dominant one...

The humanities are the specialty that now exclusively possesses the books that are not specialized, that insist upon asking the questions about the whole that are excluded from the rest of the university, which is dominated by real specialties, as resistant to self-examination as they were in Socrates's day and now rid of the gadfly.

The humanities have not had the vigor to fight it out with triumphant natural science, and want to act as though it were just a specialty. But, as I have said over and over again, however much the humane disciplines would like to forget about their essential conflict with natural science as now practiced and understood, they are gradually undermined by it. Whether it is old philosophic texts that raise now inadmissible questions, or old works of literature that presuppose the beginning of the noble and the beautiful, materialism, determinism, reductionism, homogenization – however one describes modern natural science – deny their importance and their very possibility. Natural science asserts that it is metaphysically neutral, and hence has no need for philosophy, and that imagination is not a faculty that in any way intuits the real – hence art has nothing to do with truth. The kinds of questions children ask: Is there a God? Is there freedom? Is there punishment for evil deeds? Is there certain knowledge? What is a good society? were once also the questions addressed by science and philosophy. But now the grown-ups are too busy at work, and the children are left in a day-care center called the humanities, in which the discussions have no echo in the adult world. Moreover, students whose nature draws them to such questions and to the books that appear to investigate them are very quickly rebuffed by the fact that their humanities teachers do not want or are unable to use the books to respond to their needs.

This problem of the old books is not new. In Swift's *Battle of the Books* one finds Bently, the premier Greek scholar of the eighteenth century, on the side of the moderns. He accepted the superiority of modern thought to Greek thought. So why study Greek books? This question remains unanswered in classics departments. There are all sorts of dodges, ranging from pure philological analysis to using these books to show the relation between thought and economic conditions. But practically no one even tries to read them as they were once read – for the sake of finding out whether they are true. Aristotle's *Ethics* teaches us not what a good man is but what the Greeks thought about morality. But who really cares very much about that? Not any normal person who wants to lead a serious life.

All the things I have said about books in our time help to characterize the situation of the humanities, which are the really exposed part of the university. They have been buffeted more severely by historicism and relativism than the other parts. They suffer most from democratic society's lack of respect for tradition and its emphasis on utility. To the extent that the humanities are supposed to treat of creativity, professors' lack of creativity becomes a handicap.

The humanities are embarrassed by the political content of many of the literary works belonging to them. They have had to alter their contents for the sake of openness to other cultures. And when the old university habits were changed, they found themselves least able to answer the question "Why?", least able to force students to meet standards, or to attract them with any clear account of what they would learn. One need only glance at the situation of the natural sciences in all these respects to see the gravity of the problem faced by the humanities. Natural science is sovereignly indifferent to the fact that there were and are other kinds of explanations of natural phenomena in other ages or cultures. The relation between Einstein and Buddha is purely for educational TV, in programs put together by humanists. Whatever its practitioners may say, they are sure its explanations are true, or truth. They do not have to give reasons "why," because the answer seems all too evident.

The natural sciences are able to assert that they are pursuing the important truth, and the humanities are not able to make any such assertion. That is always the critical point. Without this, no study can remain alive. Vague insistence that without the humanities we will no longer be civilized rings very hollow when no one can say what "civilized" means, when there are said to be many civilizations that are all equal. The claim of "the classic" loses all legitimacy when the classic cannot be believed to tell the truth. The truth question is most pressing and acutely embarrassing for those who deal with the philosophic texts, but also creates problems for those treating purely literary works. There is an enormous difference between saying, as teachers once did, "You must learn to see the world as Homer or Shakespeare did," and saying, as teachers now do, "Homer and Shakespeare had some of the same concerns you do and can enrich your vision of the world." In the former approach students are challenged to discover new experiences and reassess old; in the latter, they are free to use the books in any way they please…

[Editor's note: Or not use them at all as is the growing norm!]

These are the shadows cast by the peaks of the university over the entering undergraduate. Together they represent what the university has to say about man and his education, and they do not project a coherent image. The differences and the indifferences are too great. It is difficult to imagine that there is either the wherewithal or the energy within the university to constitute or reconstitute the idea of an educated human being and establish a liberal education again.

However, the contemplation of this scene is in itself a proper philosophic activity. The university's evident lack of wholeness in an enterprise that clearly demands it cannot help troubling some of its members. The questions are all there. They only need to be addressed continuously and seriously for liberal learning to exist; for it does not consist so much in answers as in the permanent dialogue. It is in such perplexed professors that at least the idea might persevere and help to guide some of the needy young persons at our doorstep. **The matter is still present in the university; it is the form that has vanished. One cannot and should not hope for a general reform. The hope is that the embers do not die out.**

Men may live more truly and fully in reading Plato and Shakespeare than at any other time, because then they are participating in essential being and are forgetting their accidental lives. The fact that this kind of humanity exists or existed, and that we can somehow still touch it with the tips of our outstretched fingers, makes our imperfect humanity, which we can no longer bear, tolerable. The books in their objective beauty are still there, and we must help protect and cultivate the delicate tendrils reaching out toward them through the unfriendly soil of students' souls. Human nature, it seems, remains the same in our very altered circumstances because we still face the same problems, if in different guises, and have the distinctively human need to solve them, even though our awareness and forces have become enfeebled...

Throughout this book I have referred to Plato's *Republic*, which is for me *the* book on education, because it really explains to me what I experience as a man and a teacher, and I have almost always used it to point out what we should not hope for, as a teaching of moderation and resignation. But all its impossibilities act as a filter to leave the residue of the highest and non-illusory possibility. The real community of man, in the midst of all the self-contradictory simulacra of community, is the community of those who seek the truth, of the potential knowers, that is, in principle, of all men to the extent they desire to know. But in fact this includes only a few, the true friends, as Plato was to Aristotle at the very moment they were disagreeing about the nature of the good. Their common concern for the good linked them; their disagreement about it proved they needed one another to understand it. They were absolutely one soul as they looked at the problem. This, according to Plato, is the only real friendship, the only real common good. It is here that the contact people so desperately seek is to be found. The other kinds of relatedness are only imperfect reflections of this one trying to be self-subsisting, gaining their only justification from their ultimate relation to this one. This is the meaning of the riddle of the improbable philosopher-kings. They have a true community that is exemplary for all other communities.

This is a radical teaching but perhaps one appropriate to our own radical time, in which proximate attachments have become so questionable and we know of no others. This age is not utterly insalubrious for philosophy. Our problems are so great and their sources so deep that to understand them we need philosophy more than ever, if we do not despair of it, and it faces the challenges on which it flourishes. I still believe that universities, rightly understood, are where community and friendship can exist in our times. Our thought and our politics have become inextricably bound up with the universities, and they have served us well, human things being what they are. But for all that, and even though they deserve our strenuous efforts, one should never forget that Socrates was not a professor, that he was put to death, and that the love of wisdom survived, partly because of his *individual* example. This is what really counts, and we must remember it in order to know how to defend the university.

This is the American moment in world history, the one for which we shall forever be judged. Just as in politics the responsibility for the fate of freedom in the world has developed upon our universities, and the two are related as they have never been before. The gravity of our given task is great, and it is very much in doubt how the future will judge our stewardship.[15]

Today as the twenty-first century begins, I recall several motivating theaters of discourse:

I

One must view with profound respect the infinite capacity of the human mind to resist the inroad of useful knowledge.

Bertrand Russell

II

To think is easy. To act is hard. But the hardest thing in the world is to act in accordance with your thinking.

Goethe

[15] Allan Bloom, *The Closing of the American Mind*, New York, Simon and Schuster, 1987

III

> The rules fall away in chunks and in the vacant places we have a generality: "It's all right because everybody does it." ... It does remind me of something. Have you ever seen a kennel of beautiful, highly bred and trained and specialized bird dogs? And have you seen those same dogs when they are no longer used? In a short time their skills and certainties and usefulness are gone. They become quarrelsome, fat, lazy, cowardly, dirty, and utterly disreputable and worthless, and all because their purpose is gone and with it the rules and disciplines that made them beautiful and good.
>
> Is that what we are becoming, a national kennel of animals with no purpose and no direction? For a million years we had a purpose – simple survival – the finding, planting, gathering, or killing of food to keep us alive, of shelter to prevent our freezing. This was a strong incentive. Add to it a defense against all kinds of enemies and you have our species' history. But now we have food and shelter and transportation and the more terrible hazard of leisure. I strongly suspect that our moral and spiritual disintegration grows out of lack of experience with plenty. Once, in a novel, I wrote about a woman who said she didn't want a lot of money. She wanted just enough. To which her husband replied that just enough doesn't exist. There is no money or not enough money. A billionaire still hasn't enough money.
>
> **John Steinbeck**[16]

...And so The Remnant, first mentioned in Isaiah, proceeds!

Ideas do rule the world!

[16] John Steinbeck, *America and Americans*, New York, Viking Penguin, 2002

PART II

Fat Plus Fantasy Equals Fluff

From the past **A Remnant** speaks: Our political process has become contradictory. Liberal as well as conservative ideologies have become more irrelevant and trivial. America, a nation of people once known for its dogged optimism, is often in despair. Quackery and dishonesty flourish and are reported daily. Honest, hard-working people seem to be limited in choice between apathy, resignation or blind revolt. Has the American dream become a lost cause? **Our tri-centennial celebration could be a wake!**

Remember something: **Edison didn't complain about darkness. Seeing the need for change, Ford didn't demand laws to hassle horses. Bell didn't lobby against late letters. Carver didn't demonstrate against spoiled soil. And the Wright brothers didn't file a class action suit against gravity. These men could have... Lobbied, Politicked, Pressured, Organized, Demonstrated, Demanded, Threatened, Coerced or otherwise applied pressure to win GOVERNMENT intervention in the form of privileges and exemptions. Can you imagine what the world would be like if they had?**

Think about this: Manipulative management (government or otherwise) is producing a society that provides real satisfaction in work only to a tiny minority. Manipulations produce tensions of two sorts: the discomfort that comes when people feel forced every day to be less than they could be; and the frustration we feel when we see the growing gap between what we could achieve and what we do achieve... Originality simply cannot be managed and originality is what keeps societies alive.

Great achievements by individuals are seldom planned... **The ballpoint pen was conceived by a sculptor. Two musicians discovered the Kodachrome process. Alexander Fleming discovered penicillin accidentally when one of his cultures was contaminated. The idea for the safety razor occurred to a young traveling salesman one morning while he was shaving. Then it took many anxious months to figure out how razors could be produced in quantity.** "If I had been technically trained," **said King Gillette,** "I would have quit." **The zipper was invented by a mechanical engineer in 1891. Clothing manufacturers steadfastly refused to use it until 1923, when B.F. Goodrich finally put zippers on goulashes.** The most noble of tasks, at first, always seems impossible.

The job for America must be to replace the idea of material

success with the idea of the soul. I believe there is building in America a new silent plurality – a growing group who believe that our complaints are organic and beyond the reach of politics as we now practice it. More and more of us are sensing that our country is in a kind of trouble that cannot be cured by conventional political action, but by its unfamiliar opposite – by de-politicizing, or de-managing (*decentralizing*) a society that has outgrown its present structures and is not working. The silent plurality may be longing to fix America without politics and wondering where to begin. There is little debate that the Bill of Rights has lost most of its meaning. There is no effective limit on government's power to tax and command, to destroy the value of our money, to invade our privacy, to wage war, and to strap us into our automobiles. But we the people can, when we want to, redefine our rights and force the front office to accept whatever definitions we devise.

Who was it who wrote:

> You are what you make of yourself. When you compromise your code of ethics, your integrity, you steal from others. Each theft results in less worth stealing, as well as a belief that what is left isn't worth saving.

The battle today in the United States is joined between the "so-called" liberal and conservative persuasions.

Leadership revolves around the ideas of Adam Smith of the eighteenth century and Karl Marx of the nineteenth century, between advocates of capitalism and advocates of socialism. The one believes in individual freedom, personal ownership of property, and individual responsibility; the other disbelieves in each of these qualities, centering power in the State.

The third idea competing for leadership is compassion, "caring for others" as it is stated in the popular language. There is no place for "caring" under totalitarianism or authoritarianism, of course, because ideology rules under that political philosophy. In democratic countries, where "caring" has reached large proportions, it has done so because there is no philosophy to which people commit themselves. While no one doubts that we should be concerned for our brothers, sisters and even our enemies, it is impossible to care for anyone without having some ideas to which we can direct those for whom we say we care.

To "care" and have no beliefs is to be naïve. **Even the notion of justice, which has been based on the nature of property for hundreds of years, has been used by believers in "compassion first of all" to mean socialism and can only result in confusion.** The definition of justice as the redistribution of property is a legitimization of theft, and no free society can exist on that basis.

We assume that if a country is democratic it has reached the pinnacle of possibility. We assume, further, that the leaders of that country are politicians. Both assumptions are wrong.

Democracy is only a form of government, and a democratic government has to have sound principles of governance. There is no reason that a totalitarian government cannot have sound principles and govern a country better than a democracy. The failure of non-democratic governments is not that they are totalitarian but that they are resistant to change, **and that the lust for power in dictatorial politicians prevents peaceful change for the better. The advantage of democracy, conversely, is that change is possible; but, of course,** we have to have wisdom in understanding what needs to be changed, and change without wisdom is hardly virtue.

Voltaire preferred monarchy to democracy, on the ground that in a monarchy it was only necessary to educate one man; in a democracy you must educate millions, and the grave-digger gets them all before you can educate ten percent of them.

Sir Henry Maine:

> Everywhere intelligence has fled from the hustings of democracy as from an engulfing torrent. Fools are in the saddle and ride mankind... Originally liberty meant freedom from feudal tyranny and tolls; originally equality meant the admission of the middle classes, along with the aristocracy and the clergy, to the honors and spoils of government... When the masters fell out the people fell in. When the men fell out women fell in. Now we are all in the morass together; and it becomes a problem... how we can find someone to drag us out, when every one is in? ... Democracy results from the wholesale denudation of individuality which we achieve through standardized education and the press.[1]

Will Durant commented on the problems of democracy:

> Aristocracy is rule by the best, not necessarily rule by birth. We want

---

[1] Sir Henry Maine

> aristocracy, we fester and rot for lack of it; but this does not mean that we hunger to be ruled by counts and earls and dukes; it means that we wish to be governed by our ablest men. In every walk of life we meet with men and women trained and equipped for achievement; but in politics they find the road barred beyond passing. America must open the road.[2]

We have been misled by a confusion between humanism and humanitarianism, not knowing the difference in meaning between the two words. We think of ourselves as humanitarians, but this means we are interested in improving the lot of mankind, and particularly, in this materialistic age, of improving the economic well-being of "the whole world." We want to improve the condition of the poor in the Third World countries, or wherever they may be. We pass stacks of legislation in our country in our war on poverty, to assist the fatherless, the crippled, or whoever else is in need of assistance. Our effort is to save mankind by classes.

Said Thomas Carlyle of the humanitarians:

> A gospel of Brotherhood not according to any of the four old Evangelists and calling on men to repent, and each amend his own wicked existence, that they might be saved; but a Gospel rather, as we often hint, according to the new fifth Evangelist Jean-Jacques, calling on men each to amend the whole world's wicked existence and be saved by making the Constitution.[3]

In the meantime, the security, serenity, peace, strength, and comfort that flow from genuine religion have given way to an obsession for material comfort. In our panic for material comfort, we lose the dignity of man.

We have false ideas about the equality of classes, wishing all men to be equal. We have wished all men to have an equal chance to happiness, which is hard to understand, and we have wished all men to be equal in opportunity, which is impossible to accomplish though it would be wonderful if it were possible. As inheritors of the passion for equality that issued from the tradition of the Reformation and democracy, we have attempted to abolish the distinction of classes, saying that hierarchically

---

[2] Will Durant

[3] Thomas Carlyle, *The French Revolution: A History*, Everyman's Library, 1931

organized society is wrong. Society does have and must have hierarchical levels, and one only has to open one's eyes to observe this truth. One man is not above another man before God and the law, but, apart from these basic fundamentals, one man is subject to another all of the time. I am subject to you in this relation as you are subject to me in that relation, and so for each man, in my subject relation, you must be obedient. In my dominant role, I must assert authority and you must obey. In your dominant role, you must assert your authority and the refusal to be obedient at the proper time has developed rebellious spirits, which undermine society. Society can be healthy only by the correct appreciation of proper subjection and authority.

The chief lesson to be learned is that we are led by ideas, with men as channels of ideas, and that our present materialistic and technological education is insufficient for the resolution of the problems before us.

Centuries past, it was written:

> In our day the tyrant came to us in open defiance of our rights, with hostility and violence, with sword and cannon. Through tears, prayers, and blood we threw him off and drove him out. Now he is among you again, but not in open war upon your houses and lands, but in subtle disguise, bearing gifts of free money, free food, free houses, and free security; trading them to you in the name of equality, rights, and liberty: offering the goods he took from you by heavy taxes and a deliberate inflation. With flattering words he coddles your vanity, legalizes his fool's paradise where he has appointed himself the Grand Regulator. Yet, your greatest danger lies in none of those things, but in your failure to recognize the pattern he follows, for it is ancient; what he cannot accomplish by force and violence he will attempt by lure and deceit.

We are now engaged in a mighty conflict; a contest between freedom and "freeloading," between liberty and license, and between government by the people and government by the government: a struggle testing whether we can stand tall enough amidst the turmoil to see above the trappings of our proud affluence and catch the vision of our own Sons of Liberty a hundred years hence, moving as free beings in a world where free men can labor and draw themselves a portion of this world's blessings, and work and live in the safety and liberty of our own self-discipline; or whether our appetite and passion for the

transitory pleasures of our opulence will propel us on into the enslaving security of the oppressive government we are allowing to grow up around us as an angry bramble about the feet of the last free people on the planet.

We live in a day when selfishness is glorified, and the government enthroned as the patriarchal source of all blessings, the healer of all wounds, the savior of society, a singular entity to which one pays his share of his neighbor's goods. And there are many who promote the deception, unwittingly moved by a lazy conscience and a selfish habit. And all are partakers in the delusion; all are trained by the hypocrisy of public distribution of private production.

Those who seek to rule you promise to make you happy by capturing you in their private utopia; and while their desires may sometimes be honorable, their theory is wrong; and while they know it unjust for one to thrust his will upon another or to revel in the fruits of another's toil, they refuse to confess the immorality of their politics. Yet notwithstanding their false theories, they will succeed in your capture if you allow them to spoil you with promises of wealth without labor and security without honor: in your heart you know the right while the comforts of government welfare and the narcotic of a lazy morality woos you carelessly in the choice.

How high must the cost of freedom go before we appreciate its worth and determine to pay its price? Must each generation stumble in the same road? Must the cycles of history ever turn full round?

> When a man begins to think that the grass will not grow at night unless he lies awake to watch it, he generally ends either in an asylum or on the throne as an emperor.
>
> Robert Browning

There is no predetermined march of history. A common soldier, a child, a girl at the door of an inn, have changed the face of fortune, and almost of nature.

The world is ruled by imagination: so we were told by Napoleon Bonaparte, master of the big battalions. In our day the world appears to be ruled by what T.S. Eliot called the "diabolic imagination." The political imagination of the ferocious ideologue, the obscene imagination of the literary panderer, have brought us nearly to *finis*. The only weapon effective against the diabolic imagination is the moral imagination (a term we owe to Burke). So here let us turn to a diagnosis of the causes of our afflictions, public and private, and to conceivable remedies.

The most mischievous mover and shaker of the French revolutionary era was Rousseau – a moralist, as Burke acknowledged him to be. The most mischievous mover and shaker of the Russian revolutionary era was Marx – a moralist of the diabolic variety. (As Alexander Gray puts it, "To consider whether Marx was 'right' or 'wrong'; to dredge Volumes I and III of *Capital* for inconsistencies or logical flaws; to 'refute' the Marxian system is, in the last resort, sheer waste of time; for when we consort with Marx we are no longer in the world of reason or logic. He saw visions – clear visions of the passing of all things, much more nebulous visions of how all things may be made new.")

It was a principal error of the nineteenth-century Rationalists to fancy that most people are moved by enlightened self-interest. Certainly there is sufficient selfishness in all of us; but knowing where one's best interest lies in the long run is another matter. Instead, people are moved by visions of a sort, whether sublime visions or gross visions. How many people choose their spouses on the basis of enlightened self-interest – or have the opportunity to do so, even if they would? In affairs matrimonial, as in affairs public, the visionary imagination's part is much larger than that of either enlightened self-interest or pure reason.

People are moved by moral intentions – even when their intentions are to subvert the conventional morality. How many sincere Communists would there be if the avowed purpose of Marx was to slaughter; but those are incidental pleasures; the avowed motive is the redemption of humanity through the abolition of religion, property, and the old social order. You can't make an omelet without breaking eggs. The Bolsheviks who liquidated the Kulaks are said to have often gone about their task with tears in their eyes: they had convinced themselves that they were inflicting suffering for high moral purposes, not unlike many terrorists today: how little some things change.

This is an effort about an idea – the discovery of what kind of society man needs in order to function most efficiently and happily and how to achieve that society. It is an effort about freedom – what it really is and implies, why man needs it, what it can do for him, and how to build and maintain a truly free society.

Remember something: Slavery is the exact opposite of liberty; they cannot co-exist.

***Laissez faire* means "let people do as they choose." A *laissez-faire* society is a society of noninterference, a mind-your-own-business, live-and-let-live society. It means freedom for each individual to manage his own affairs in any way he pleases...** not just in the realm of economics but in every area of his life. **In a *laissez-faire* society, no man or group of men would dictate anyone's lifestyle, or force them to pay taxes to a State bureaucracy, or prohibit them from making any voluntary trades they wanted.**

Again, **A Remnant** speaks:

If a *laissez-faire* **society is attainable,** why haven't men established one before now? **The answer is** that essentially good people have prevented it by their unwitting support of slavery. **The majority of people throughout history have accepted the idea that it was both proper and necessary for some men to coercively rule over others. Most of these people weren't basically bad, and probably only a few of them have had a lust for power.**

The great conflict between freedom and slavery, though it has taken many forms, **finds its main expression in a conflict between two powerful and opposing human institutions** – the free market and government. **The establishment of a *laissez-faire* society depends on the outcome of the war between these two institutions** – a war whose most crucial battles are fought on the field of ideas.

Socialism is a system in which the government owns and controls the means of production (supposedly for "the good of the people," but, in actual practice, for the good of the few and the government).

Fascism is a system in which the government leaves nominal ownership of the means of production in the hands of the private individuals but exercises control by means of heavy taxation. In effect, fascism is simply a more subtle form of government ownership than is socialism. **Under fascism, producers are allowed to keep nominal title to their possessions and to bear all the risks involved in entrepreneurship, while the government has most of the actual control and gets a great deal of the profits** (and takes none of the risks). The U.S.A. is moving increasingly away from a free-market and toward fascist totalitarianism.

Because the weight of the government power has such influence on the structure and functioning of any society, ideas concerning social organization have typically centered on the structure of the proposed society's government. Most "social thinkers," however, have taken government as a giver. **They have debated over the particular form of government they wished their ideal societies to have but have seldom attempted to examine the nature of government itself.** But if one doesn't know clearly what government is, one can hardly determine what influences governments will have on society.

Government is a coercive monopoly which has assumed power over and certain responsibilities for every human being within the geographical area which it claims as its own. A coercive monopoly is an institution maintained by the threat and/or use of physical force – the initiation of force – to prohibit competitors from entering its field of endeavor. (A coercive monopoly may also use force to compel "customer loyalty," as, for example, a "protection" racket.)

Government has exclusive possession and control within its geographical area of whatever functions it is able to relegate to itself, and maintains control by force of its laws and its guns, both against other governments and against any private individuals who might object to its domination. To the extent that it controls any function, it either prohibits competition (as with the delivery of 39¢ mail) **or permits it on a limited basis only** (as with the American educational system). It compels the services or, if they do not want them, to pay for them anyway.

Government is unavoidably inefficient and expensive. If government did not compel its citizens to deal with it (by maintaining itself as a coercive monopoly), the free market could offer really effective services, efficiently and at lower prices, and the government would lose all its "customers."

Government is, and of necessity must be a coercive monopoly, for in order to exist it must deprive entrepreneurs of the right to go into business in competition with it, and it must compel all its citizens to deal with it exclusively in the areas it has pre-empted. Any attempt to devise a government which did not initiate force is an exercise in futility, because it is an attempt to make a contradiction work. Government is, by its very nature, an agency of initiated force. **If it ceased to initiate force, it would cease to be a government and become in simple fact another business firm in a competitive market. Nor can** there be any such thing as a government which is partially a free-market business, because there can be no compromise between freedom and brute force. Either an organization is a business, maintaining itself against competition by excellence in satisfying customer wants, or it is a gang of thieves, existing by brute force and preventing competition by force when it can do so. **It cannot be both.**

The belief that the people of a democracy rule themselves through their elected representatives, though sanctified by tradition and made venerable by multiple repetitions, is actually mystical nonsense. In any election, only a percentage of the people vote. **Those who cannot vote because of age or other disqualifications, and those who do not vote because of confusion, apathy or disgust at a tweedledum-tweedledummer choice can hardly be said to have any choice in the passage of laws which govern them.**

Nor can the individuals yet unborn, who will be ruled by those laws in the future. And, out of those who do "exercise their franchise," the large minority who voted for the loser are also deprived of a voice, at least during the term of the winner they voted against.

But even individuals who voted and who managed to pick a winner are not actually ruling themselves in any sense of the word, they voted for a man, not for specific laws which will govern them. **Even all those who had cast their ballots for the winning candidate would be hopelessly confused and divided if asked to vote on these actual laws. Nor would their representatives be bound to abide by their wishes, even if it could be decided what these "collective wishes" were.** And besides all of this, **a large percentage of the actual power of mature democracy, such as the U.S.A.,** is in the hands of the tens of thousands of faceless bureaucrats who are unresponsive to the will of any citizen without special pull.

Under a democratic form of government, a minority of the individuals governed select the winning candidate who then proceeds to decide issues largely on the basis of pressure from special-interest groups. What it actually amounts to is rule by those with political pull over those without it. Contrary to the brainwashing we have received in government-run schools, democracy as practiced – the rule of the people through their elected representatives – is a cruel hoax!

Not only is democracy mystical nonsense, it is also immoral. If one man has no right to impose his wishes on another, then ten

million men have no right to impose theirs on the one, since the initiation of force is wrong (and the assent of even the most overwhelming majority can never make it morally permissible). Opinions – even majority opinions – neither create truth nor alter facts. A lynch mob is democracy in action. So much for mob rule.

History seems to reflect that to advocate limited government is to put oneself in the ridiculous position of advocating limited slavery.

To put it simply, government is the rule of some men over others by initiated force, which is slavery, which is wrong.

I am suggesting that the real conflict in our age is between opposed types of imagination – or, to speak more accurately, among a variety of types of imagination. There are the idyllic imagination of Rousseau, the diabolic imagination of Sade (Comte Donatien Alphonse François de, "Marquis de Sade" 1740–1814, French author and libertine), the leveling imagination of Marx, the moral imagination of Burke, the Animal Farm imagination of the hedonists; and other species that might be distinguished.

So the great contest in these opening years of the twenty-first century is not for human economic interests, or for human political preferences, or even for human minds – not at the bottom. The true battle is being fought in the debatable land of the human imagination.

Ideas do rule the world!

PART III

And Today

It is a great paradox that we have in the American capitalist economic system (as mixed as it is) the most successful system in history. We need only remember that, at the birth of our nation, 97% of our citizens, by almost any definition, were poor. Yet this system has elevated us into the most powerful agricultural, industrial, and technological nation on earth. So successful is our system, so high the aspirations of the American people, that we in this country define poverty at an income level that is higher than the average income level of Russia and 800% above average world income. Yet this system, which has given us so much in terms of freedom and upward social mobility (utilitarianism if you will), is under attack at all levels of society and is being replaced by a system that historically has never worked and is working effectively nowhere in the world today.

We cannot fight *against* anything, unless we fight *for* something – and what we must fight for is the supremacy of reason, and a view of man as a rational being... (Most especially in education).[1]

...The battle of philosophers is a battle for man's mind. If you do not understand their theories, you are vulnerable to the worst among them.

Today's mawkish concern with and compassion for the feeble, the flawed, the suffering, the guilty, is a cover for the profound [...] hatred of the innocent, the strong, the able, the successful, the virtuous, the confident, the happy. A philosophy out to destroy man's mind is necessarily a philosophy of hatred for man, for man's life, and for every human value. Hatred of the good for being the good, was the hallmark of the twentieth century. *This* is the enemy you are facing.

A battle of this kind requires special weapons. It has to be fought with a full understanding of your cause, a full confidence in yourself, and the fullest certainty of the *moral* rightness of both. Only philosophy can provide you with these weapons.[2]

Philosophy brought to you or denied to you by education!

The symptoms of today's (educational) disease are: conformity, with nothing to conform to – timidity, expressed in a self-shrinking concern with trivia – a kind of obsequious anxiety to please the

[1] Ayn Rand

[2] Ayn Rand, "Philosophy: Who Needs It", An Address to the Graduating Class of the United States Military Academy at West Point, New York, March 6, 1974

unknown standards of some nonexistent authority – and a pall of fear without object. Psychologically, this is the cultural atmosphere of a society living under censorship [Editor's note: Fueled by an anesthetic].

As a mixed economy, we are chained by an enormous tangle of government controls; but, it is argued, they affect our incomes, not our minds. Such a distinction is not tenable; a chained aspect of a man's – or a nation's – activity will gradually and necessarily affect the rest. But it is true that the government, so far, has made no overt move to repress or control the intellectual life of this country. Anyone is still free to say, write and publish anything he pleases. Yet men keep silent – while their culture is perishing from an entrenched, institutionalized epidemic of mediocrity. It is not possible that mankind's intellectual stature has shrunk to this extent. And it is not possible that all talent has vanished suddenly from this country and this earth.

If you find it puzzling, the premise to check is the idea that governmental repression is the only way a government can destroy the intellectual life of a country. It is not. There is another way: *government encouragement.*[3]

> If ignorance paid dividends most Americans could make a fortune out of what they don't know about economics.
>
> Luther Hodges

I wonder because, as we get into the third millennium, we seem to be groping our way, confused and uncertain, along paths that appear to me increasingly forbidding and unpromising.

My concerns are many: The energy problem, and our fumbling and counter-productive attempts to deal with it. The uncontrolled power of privilege seeking pressure groups and the abuse of that power. The encroachment by government upon our personal and business lives. The conflict between social goals and individual rights. A foreign policy that I do not understand, and that I suspect its executors do not clearly understand.

But **what concerns me most**, because it affects everything else, **is an attitude**. An attitude that begins with condoning moral degeneration and fiscal irresponsibility and from there pervades all policies and all

[3] Ayn Rand

actions. Of all the dubious paths we are pursuing, **The Primrose Path of Fluff** – symbol of folly and recklessness – is the most perilous.

It is seldom that liberty of any kind is lost all at once. F. A. Hayek wrote:

> The most important change which extensive government control produces is a psychological change, an alteration in the character of the people. This is necessarily a slow affair, a process which extends not over a few years but perhaps over one or two generations. The important point is that the political ideals of a people and its attitude toward authority are as much the effect as the cause of the political institutions under which it lives. This means, among other things, that even a strong tradition of political liberty is no safeguard if the danger is precisely that new institutions and policies will gradually undermine and destroy that spirit.[4]

2,500 years ago, a troubled statesman said:

> This city of ours will never be destroyed by the planning of Zeus, or according to the wish of the immortal gods. But the citizens themselves in their wildness are bent on destruction. And money is the cause.

Solon was right. Athens accomplished her own destruction. And in the long record of history, the rule has prevailed. Except for those few cases where a strong and healthy nation has been overwhelmed by armed aggression, every collapse – of a regime, of a rule, of a political system of any kind – has been preceded and brought on by moral and financial bankruptcy. **Every failed society has accomplished its own destruction. And in most cases, morality and money – moral degeneracy and money wasted, squandered and become worthless – have been the prime causes.**

The rule still holds. Surveying the scene from Britain through Europe, to Africa, to Latin and South America, to Asia, every tottering or subdued democracy is threatened or has been defeated by moral and economic decay and financial chaos.

It is in this sense that I say that, except for the possible stupidity of blundering into nuclear war (terrorist or otherwise), **our nation stands in more danger from within than from without**. The most direct

[4] F. A. Hayek, The Road to Serfdom, Chicago, University of Chicago Press, 1994, p.xxxix.

road to destruction lies along **The Primrose Path of Fluff**. The alluring path that invites the indulgence of every desire and every demand, without care, without regard, without responsibility, without concern for costs or consequences. We are most immediately threatened in sum, by our own excesses – by our own endless demands, encouraged and abetted by many of our own leaders.

The threat is that the excess of demand will destroy the American system. First the economic system, and then, inevitably, the political system. And in the process destroy what we have come to know and cherish as the American way of life…

In his book, *The Theory of the Leisure Class*, Thorstein Veblen said it best:

> One's neighbors, mechanically speaking often are socially not one's neighbors, or even acquaintances; and still their transient good opinion has a high degree of utility. The only practicable means of impressing one's pecuniary ability on these unsympathetic observers of one's everyday life is an unremitting demonstration of ability to pay…[5] [**Editor's note: Or at least charge it!**]

If this hope is questioned, a simpler theory takes over. Which says, bluntly, what goes up must come down. Sooner, on our own heads – which would be bad – or later, on our children's heads – **which would be worse.**

The questions are growing. The idea that "it can't happen here" has received a serious setback. It has occurred to many. It does not appear to have occurred to Congress.

> To follow foolish precedents, and wink with both our eyes is easier than to think.
>
> William Cowper

Let me be clear. **There are those** who distrust and dislike the American economic system, and who would deliberately demolish it. But they are few. **The greater danger comes from those who believe in the system, but with more faith than understanding.** For those who believe, or take it for granted, that the system has an infinite capacity; that it is capable of providing, without limit and without end, whatever is demanded of it – if the demand is pressed with enough insistence; that

[5] Thorstein Veblen, *The Theory of the Leisure Class*, New York, Penguin Classics, 1994

it can withstand any strain, absorb any stress, endure any abuse, and keep on functioning, efficiently and uncomplainingly, world without end, amen.

So that it can fairly be said, we are not only in more danger from within than from without, we are also in more danger from our friends than from our enemies.

During the twentieth century a gradual but dramatic change occurred in the structure of our economy. The vast increases in the growth of services (personal, educational, medical, legal, etc.) and the enormous growth in government (federal, state, and local) have put a heavy strain on the productive base of our economy.

In a large measure the increased load on the productive base is directly attributable to the enormous growth in government at all levels. And this growth is in turn the result of a change in thought and attitude in our concept of the role of government and in our expectations.

The Primrose Path of Fluff, where there is no tomorrow, stands as the symbolic road to instant gratification of all desires and all expectations. It also stands as the avenue of escape for those responsible for satisfying or denying expectations, who seek to avoid their responsibility.

Upon the standard to which the wise and honest will now repair it is written:

> **You have lived the easy way; henceforth, you will live the hard way. You came into a great heritage made by the insight and the sweat and the blood of inspired and devoted and courageous men; thoughtlessly and in utmost self-indulgence you have all but squandered this inheritance. Now only by the heroic virtues which made this inheritance can you restore it again.**

It is written:

> You took the good things for granted. Now you must earn them again.

It is written:

> For every right you cherish you have a duty which you must fulfill. For every good that you wish to preserve you will have to sacrifice your comfort and your ease. There is nothing for nothing any longer.

Who was it who said:

> For years we the free peoples of the Western world have taken the easy way, ourselves more lightheartedly than any others. That is why the defenses of Western civilization are under attack. That is why we find ourselves knowing that we here in America may soon be the last stronghold of our civilization – the isolated and beleaguered citadel of law, of liberty, of mercy, of charity, of justice among men, and of love and of good will.

This message is addressed to Capitol Hill, because it is there that **The Primrose Path of Fluff** most conspicuously runs – a broad aisle, straight through the halls of Congress. A wide and welcoming thoroughfare, accommodating all men and all parties. And well used. For year after year thronged by a genial majority in annual procession, **scattering largesse by the wayside** and dancing its way to yet another centi-billion-dollar deficit. **By the way: Tax cuts do not cause deficits!**

According to the Office of Management and Budget, the economy's lackluster performance is responsible for more than half of the upward deficit revisions since 2001. Increased government spending is responsible for another 24%. The three tax cuts come in third, and are responsible for 23% of the upward deficit revisions. Indeed, even without the tax cuts, the deficit today would still be $278 billion.

Veblen, who coined the phrase "conspicuous consumption" again prophetically remarked with accuracy: "But the ways of heredity are devious, and not every gentleman's son is to the manor born..."

Asking myself why, I conclude that those who are elected representatives are in fact representative. As a politician, they are human, even as a citizen, I am human. But, it has been observed, some people are more human than others. And as many politicians seem to be human beings with common desires to be loved coupled with an uncommon, total, inability to say **no**, which leads to predictable consequences: **perpetual pregnancy, on the one hand, perennial deficits on the other.**

This suggests that the old-fashioned remedy for the one human weakness may provide an answer for the other. To state it plainly, and not at all facetiously, **there is nothing that Congress so sorely needs as the legal equivalent of a chastity belt**. A pay-as-we-go requirement that would compel us to live within our means, except in case of an extreme national emergency. (**Pay as you go is a vital, but immediate first step. Sunset laws a second, and zero-based budgeting a third.**)

I wonder what might happen if the Federal government showed as much care in giving as it does in taking. If, that is, the welfare agencies exercised half the vigilance in dispensing money that the I.R.S. shows in extracting money. If, to say it plainly, non-workers and non-contributors were subject to the same discipline and control as workers and contributors.

As an American citizen, I feel an urgent sense of responsibility for other citizens who are incapably lame, ill, too aged or too infirm to work. **But today there are far too many people riding in the wagon who are capable of pulling it.**

The growth of federal government control and regulation of education, business, and healthcare has greatly increased costs in the operating structure of our economy. The freedom to work at a job of one's own choosing has been a great freedom of choice for an American. The principle of choosing a neighborhood with a good school has also been one of America's great freedoms of choice. Now, however, our citizens no longer have these choices. Only with union sanction may the citizen work in many places. Only with judicial sanction may our children attend the neighborhood schools, and in growing instances these schools don't exist. I am reminded of the words of Dr. Laurence Peter; allow me to quote:

> **America has long pointed with great pride to its unparalleled economic growth and achievement. Now this achievement is under indictment by those who see it as preoccupation with bigness and economic power at the expense of the quality of life. Our recent environmental and social crises challenge our traditional and fundamental American assumption that economic growth is a good thing per se. Our traditional belief in the value of growth in all areas is based on the concept that bigger is better, and therefore we can measure our overall progress as a nation by our tabulation of our total production – GDP (gross domestic product). It is concerned only with quantity. Every plane that crashes raises the GDP and thereby, statistically, raises the standard of living. The cost of replacing the plane, investigating the crash, treating the survivors and burying the dead all help to escalate the GDP. And on a smaller scale, every auto crash contributes to the GDP, and so does the production of tobacco, the manufacture of cigarettes,**

the treatment of victims of cancer, and the building of caskets for those who succumb to the disease.

The increasing GDP represents more of something. It could be more production, a declining quality of goods and/or services, a grossly deteriorating environment, and escalation of the pathological side-effects of growth for growth's sake.

The GDP is not a measure of the quality of life but merely the total cost of goods and services. It is like a cost-plus contract that pays a bonus for inefficiency, delays, waste, redundancy, breakdowns, and short-lived, throwaway products. Every business conspiracy to raise prices, every employee strike, every product with built-in obsolescence, every war causes the GDP to go up.

The Gross Domestic Product does not account for love, beauty, nature's wonders, clean air, pure water, peace of mind, quiet, privacy, happiness, or many other aspects of the quality of life that cannot be totaled at the national checkout counter.

The government drains wetlands so farmers can grow more crops while it pays other farmers to let fertile cropland lie idle. If it were only money against money it would be the height of foolishness, but compounding this absurd, wasteful felony is the disturbing fact that it also destroys. Furthermore, draining the wetlands spoils the natural means of water retention, so that the project becomes counterproductive, causing a need for further flood control measures...

Politicians have been successful in persuading citizens that welfare is a major financial problem, but they fail to mention the fact that federal crop subsidy programs cost taxpayers more than all the federal, state, and local welfare programs combined...

Somewhere in our history we moved slowly from a government of the people to a government by vast bureaucracies. Within the mazes of the federal government there are huge empires removed as far from the processes of elective representative government as were the courts of Nero or Ivan the Terrible...

Our plea of innocence may be that we ordered none of this – but you cannot deny our inaction has permitted them! ...

The emphasis on government-guaranteed material possessions may now well be the "American way of life" (just as it has always been the collectivist way of life), but it most definitely is not freedom. That disappeared with the advent of the words "compulsory, coerced,

> forced, governmental decree," and so on. Freedom (choice) for the farmer really disappeared when he accepted those first **"free" seeds from government;** the present controls over what and how much he may grow followed automatically. Freedom (exemption from necessity) for employees disappeared with the Wagner Act (and its successors) that permits and encourages leaders to force them to join a union against their wishes. Freedom (choice in action) disappeared for all of us when the government first compelled us to pay tribute to its alleged insurance scheme whereby everybody is promised that he can live at the expense of everybody else. And so on and so on through the thousands of other material schemes that compel peaceful persons to participate against their wishes.[6]

> He who will not reason, is a bigot; he who cannot is a fool; and he who dares not is a slave.
>
> Sir William Drummond

Today we are trying to sell these compulsory material aspects of our society under the fraudulent label of freedom. The socialists will continue to beat us at this game for two reasons. **First, they can (and do) out-promise us in material benefits. Second, and by far the more important, the socialists understand that men prefer to fight for abstract ideals that appeal to their souls instead of their bellies.** Thus, though they have no intention whatever of fulfilling their promises, the socialists speak of the **abstract ideals** of brotherhood, peace, equality, justice, and so on. Meanwhile we Americans keep yapping about bathtubs, automobiles, soap, guaranteed jobs, the United Nations, compulsory social security, big screen TVs and federal aid to state and local governments. Can you find anything worth fighting and dying for in any of them?

We must learn to honor excellence in every socially accepted human activity, however humble the activity, and to scorn shoddiness, however exalted the activity. An excellent plumber is infinitely more admirable than an incompetent philosopher. The society that scorns excellence in plumbing because plumbing is a humble activity and tolerates shoddiness in philosophy because it is an exalted activity will have neither good plumbing nor good philosophy. **Neither its pipes nor its theories will hold water...**

In conclusion, may I as an American citizen commend those who

---

[6] Dr. Lawrence Peter

have labored long and hard to preserve our liberties and to build a better America. **I challenge, however, those who have taken the easy Primrose Path of Fluff.** You have tried to curry favor with your neighbor for your own self-gain. You have worked harder to be popular than you have worked to do your job. It is not too late to change, however – to review – to take a new look – a new direction to discover: **The Remnant.**

Two thousand years have passed since the founding of Christianity. During this time, civilization can boast of considerable progress. Yet in one respect, the world has moved backwards to a more primitive stage of development. For nowadays, the laws that govern human relationships in society have become increasingly dependent on might, rather than right. To be sure, the might of today takes the form of political, and/or financial instead of muscular, power, but its effect is, so to speak, to re-establish the muscle-man at the head of human society. Although today's Tarzan wears conventional clothing and emits smooth speech in place of guttural ejaculations, his power is productive of nothing but confusion and corruption and envy.

> You don't set a fox to watching the chickens just because he has a lot of experience in the hen house.
>
> Harry S. Truman

The checking of modern Tarzanism, therefore, depends on a rebirth of the qualitative concept of society. This renewal cannot come from the side of culture which has lost its influence, nor from an economy that is unwilling to abandon the special privileges already received at the hands of government. The strength to re-establish a government of limited powers can only come through a non-political movement or party that re-affirms the principles on which this country was founded. Its goal would be to restrict the use of power to the maintenance of common and equal rights. In this way, Tarzanism, the rule of a combination of power groups at the expense of others would be defeated and a qualitative society, where individual rights would have a real meaning, would be restored in the United States.

A new approach to the social problem would, first, define the area within which general laws are good and salutary, and second, it would indicate the issues that would have to be dealt with in some other way. **Whenever disputes arise today, the popular thought is that they must be settled by passing another law**. This view is seldom questioned. Yet, when the passing of law after law over a period of years fails to bring satisfactory results, the inescapable conclusion must be that something is wrong in our expectations of what the lawmaking process can do. **We must remember: To solve any problem, whether it be of "the body social" or "the body physical," three steps must be followed:**

1. **Proper diagnosis**, followed by
2. **Proper prescription**, followed by
3. **A willingness to take the medicine**.

Who was it who wrote:

> The proper function of government is limited only to those spheres of activity within which the individual citizen has the right to act. By deriving its just powers from the consent of the governed, government becomes primarily a mechanism for defense against bodily harm, theft, and involuntary servitude. It cannot claim the power to redistribute the wealth or force reluctant citizens to perform acts of charity against their will. Government is created by men. No man can delegate a power that he does not possess. The creation cannot exceed the creator...

The American Republic was to be a new kind of society, just as man, as a new kind of creature, was created above the animals. American citizens were to have both liberty and protection. Cultural opinion and choice of work were to be decentralized from political control. **The American Government had the task of safeguarding the rights of individuals against the interest of groups and against the government itself.**

Throughout history, government has proved to be the chief instrument for thwarting man's liberty. Government represents power in the hands of some men to control and regulate the lives of other men. And power, as Lord Acton said, corrupts men. "**Absolute power,**" he added, **"corrupts absolutely..."**

The framers of the Constitution had learned the lesson. They were not only students of history, but victims of it: they knew from vivid, personal experience that freedom depends on effective restraints against the accumulation of power in a single authority. And that is what the Constitution is: a **system of restraints against the natural tendency of government to expand in the direction of absolutism.** We all know the main components of the system. The first is the limitation of the federal government's authority to specific, delegated powers. The second, a corollary of the first, is the reservation to the States and the people of all power not delegated to the federal government. The third is a careful division of the federal government's power among three separate branches. The fourth is a prohibition against impetuous alteration of the system – namely, Article V's tortuous, but wise, amendment procedures.

Was it then a democracy the framers created? **Hardly.** The system of restraints, on the face of it, was directed not only against individual tyrants, but also against **a tyranny of the majority.** The framers were well aware of the danger posed by self-seeking demagogues – that they might persuade a majority of the people to confer on government vast powers in return for deceptive promises of economic gain. And so they forbade such a transfer of power – first by declaring, in effect, that certain activities are outside the natural and legitimate scope of the public authority, and secondly by dispensing public authority among several levels and branches of government in the hope that each seat of authority, jealous of its own prerogatives, would have a natural incentive to resist aggression by the others.

But the framers were not visionaries. They knew that rules of government, however brilliantly calculated to cope with the imperfect nature of man, however carefully designed to avoid the pitfalls of power, would be no match for men who were determined to disregard them. **In the last analysis** our system of government will prosper only if the governed are sufficiently determined that it should. "What have you given us?" a woman asked Ben Franklin toward the close of the Constitutional Convention. **"A Republic,"** he said, **"if you can keep it!"**

We have not kept it. The system of restraints has fallen into disrepair. Our federal government has moved into every field in which it believes its services are needed. The state governments are either excluded from their rightful functions by federal preemption, or they are allowed to act at the sufferance of the federal government. Inside the federal government both the executive and judicial branches have roamed far outside their constitutional boundary lines. And all of these things have come to pass without regard to the amendment procedures prescribed by Article V. **The result is a vast national authority out of touch with the people, and out of their control**. This monolith of power is bounded only by the will of those who sit in high places.

How did it happen? How did our national government grow from a servant with sharply limited powers into a master with virtually unlimited power?

In part, **we were swindled**. There are occasions when we have elevated men and political parties to power that promised to restore limited government and then proceeded, after their election, to expand the activities of government. **But let us be honest with ourselves. Broken promises are not the major causes of our trouble; kept promises are.** All too often we have put men and women in office who have suggested spending a little more on this, a little more on that, who have proposed a new entitlement program, who have thought of another reason to put off to another day the recapture of liberty and the restoration of our constitutional system. **We have gone the way of many a democratic society that has lost its freedom by persuading itself that if "the people" rule all is well.**

The Frenchman, Alexis de Tocqueville, probably the most clairvoyant political observer of modern times, saw the danger when he visited our country in the 1830s. Even then he foresaw decay for a society that tended to put more emphasis on its democracy than on its republicanism. He predicted that America would produce not tyrants, but "guardians." And that the American people would:

> **Console themselves for being in tutelage by the reflection that they have chosen their own guardians. Every man allows himself to be put in lead-strings, because he sees that it is not a person nor a class of persons, but the people at large that hold the end of his chain.**[7]

Our tendency to concentrate power in the hands of a few deeply concerns me. We can be conquered by bombs or by subversion; **but we can also be conquered by neglect** – by ignoring the Constitution and disregarding the principles of limited government. Our defenses against the accumulation of unlimited power in Washington are in poorer shape, I fear, than our defenses against the aggressive designs of terrorism. Like so many other nations before us, we may succumb through internal weakness rather than fall before a foreign foe.

I am convinced that most Americans now want to reverse the trend. I think that concern for our vanishing freedoms is genuine. I think that the people's uneasiness in the stifling omnipresence of government has turned into something approaching alarm. **But bemoaning the evil will not drive it back, and accusing fingers will not shrink government**.

---

[7] Alexis de Tocqueville, Democracy in America, Chicago, University of Chicago Press, 2000

Perhaps the most eloquent of all statements that Americans carry a divine mandate was Herman Melville's in *White-Jacket*, the book he wrote just before *Moby Dick*:

> **We Americans are the peculiar, chosen people... we bear the ark of the liberties of the world... We are pioneers of the world; the advance-guard, sent on through the wilderness of untried things, to break a new path in the New World that is ours. In our youth is our strength; in our inexperience, our wisdom. At a period when other nations have but lisped, our deep voice is heard afar. Long enough have we been skeptics with regard to ourselves, and doubted whether, indeed, the political Messiah has come. But he has come in *us* if we would but give utterance to his promptings. And let us always remember that with ourselves, almost for the first time in the history of earth, national selfishness is unbounded philanthropy; for we cannot do a good to America but we give alms to the world.[8]**

The time must come when we entrust the conduct of our affairs to men and women who understand that their first duty as public officials is to divest themselves of the power they have been given. It will come when Americans, in thousands of communities throughout the nation, decide to put individuals in office who are pledged to enforce the Constitution and restore the Republic. Who will proclaim in campaign speeches:

> I have little interest in stream-lining government or in making it more efficient, for I mean to reduce its size. I do not undertake to promote welfare, for I propose to extend freedom. My aim is not to pass laws, but to repeal them. It is not to inaugurate new programs, but to cancel old ones that do violence to the Constitution, or that have failed in their purpose, or that impose on the people an unwarranted financial burden. I will not attempt to discover whether legislation is "needed" before I have first determined whether it is constitutionally permissible. And if I should later be attacked for neglecting my constituents' "interests," I shall reply that I was informed your main interest is liberty and that in that cause I am doing the very best I can.

A momentous choice faces the people of this country today. Will we

---

[8] Melville, Herman, *White-jacket*, New York, Grove Press, 1956

choose a decentralist society in which the powers of government are limited to the equal protection of the individual rights of all, **or do we prefer a government by "liquidation" in a centralized society suited to the animals?**

More than eight decades ago an Austrian philosopher named Steiner wrote:

> **The impulse which would arouse those drowsing souls who will not see what is really happening, and which would transform the sleeping into waking souls. For it is a waking mankind that we need today; it is a waking mankind alone that can survey what is happening around it, which knows the tasks placed upon it by the course of human evolution; those tasks in regard to which humanity today is faced with severe tests and trials. It is the spirit, created by man out of himself, alone that can save us from this morass.**[9]

America needs statesmen! We so urgently need citizens dedicated morally and spiritually who will look to the future. We need men and women of character and integrity who will to the best of their ability take our country on the course that will preserve our freedoms and rededicate us to the most meaningful objective Americans can have – **to secure the blessings of liberty to ourselves and to our posterity**.

The author of *Common Sense* over two and a quarter centuries ago gave sage warning and advice:

> Every age and generation is, and must be (as a matter of right), as free to act for itself in all cases, as the age and generation that preceded it. The vanity and presumption of governing beyond the grave is the most ridiculous and insolent of all tyrannies. Man has no property in man, neither has one generation a property in the generation that is to follow... When we speak of rights we ought always to unite with it the idea of duties: rights become duties by reciprocity. The right which I enjoy becomes my duty to guarantee it to another, and he to me; and those who violate the duty justly incur a forfeiture of the right.
>
> Thomas Paine[10]

In Carroll's *Through the Looking Glass*, Humpty Dumpty made the

[9] Rudolf Steiner

[10] Thomas Paine, *Common Sense*, New York, Liberal Arts Press, 1953

statement: **"When I use a word, it means just what I choose it to mean – neither more nor less."** While this statement unfortunately may apply to a great many of the policies and practices of our modern day, never more would it appear to apply so neatly to the so-called definition of modern-day liberalism. From the authors that follow, the conversation begins with a darling of the "classical" liberal tradition, J.S. Mill, and follows with those who have witnessed this tradition's morphing into something entirely anew...

On Social Freedom

There is perhaps no question upon which it is possible to theorize to so little effect as upon the nature of human freedom; there is perhaps no range of thought in which we may so easily perplex ourselves with so little prospect of reaching a sound and serviceable result. On this field of thought, as perhaps on some others, it is possible, and in a sense easy, to arrive, by what appears to be a process of reasoning, at results which no mortal man can honestly and heartily accept as true – at results which are belied by the inviolable laws of human thought and feeling. I believe that it is not very difficult to set forth what will appear vastly like a demonstration of this proposition: That human freedom is altogether an illusion or a fiction, that every act of human creature is absolutely determined by unalterable laws. I will honestly confess that I am wholly unable to furnish anything like a satisfactory refutation of the arguments that may be urged against the existence of human individual freedom. At the same time I do not hesitate to affirm that there is no sane being who can adopt and consistently carry out this doctrine. It appears to me that every reasonable act of every sane man is a practical assertion of the existence of individual freedom.

But I am not at present concerned with arguments for or against the actual existence of human freedom. What I have now to say is exclusively addressed to those who admit the existence of human freedom, who believe, in fact, that they themselves can, within certain limits, *do what they please*, and that the same faculty of voluntary action is possessed by their human fellow-creatures. If any man does not know what we mean by *doing what we please*, I cannot now undertake to explain this meaning; if the phrase "voluntary action" conveys no distinct conception to the mind of the reader I cannot now undertake to furnish to him or to convey by any means to his mind, a distinct conception which shall answer to this phrase. Nor can I undertake to show *on what ground* men believe themselves to possess this faculty of voluntary action. It seems to me that this belief, like many others which have a wide influence upon the conduct and the well-being of mankind, is not based upon any process of logical argumentation, but upon some immediate or spontaneous sense, on some movement of consciousness. Men believe that they are free, or that freedom, or the power of voluntary action, is a natural feature in their being, in perhaps something the same way as they believe that they are *men*, and not mere locomotive vegetables, or two-legged beasts – mainly because they cannot help believing it.

I assume not only that men have the power of exercising freedom, but that this power is generally regarded by men as an object of desire. Even if human individual freedom, or the power of voluntary action, should actually prove to be a mere illusion, or should prove to be something totally different in its nature from what it is commonly supposed to be, still, while it is regarded as a reality by so large a portion of mankind, and while its possession is regarded so universally as an object of desire, it seems to me certain that the considerations set forth in this work are not wholly unworthy of attention. How far the desire of freedom is reasonable, how far the possession of freedom is really beneficial to all mankind, and under what special circumstances it may be more or less beneficial, are questions of which I shall not now attempt the *complete* solution. It seems to me very certain that, in this age and in this country, the desire of freedom, or of what is supposed to be freedom, is widely prevalent among all classes. The restrictions upon men's freedom – or what they regard as such restrictions – may not only occasion suffering or irritation to those who find themselves thus restricted, but may lead to ill-feeling and strife between men. If then it should prove that our freedom is necessarily limited – that there are limitations which arise inevitably out of the conditions under which we live, it must surely be important that we should know distinctly what are these limitations, and how they are connected with the circumstances and conditions of our lives. It is probable that men will often struggle vigorously, and sometimes with destructive violence, against those restraints upon their freedom which they believe to be imposed upon them by adventitious circumstances or by the arbitrary will of other men. It is possible that men may sometimes rebel against those restraints which are necessarily associated with the most valuable forms and modifications of our social life; and in their wild and undiscerning efforts after unlimited freedom, may overturn arrangements and institutions which are essential to the higher moral life of mankind. It is not even impossible that men, by their ill-directed efforts after unbounded freedom, may destroy those very features of our social life which tend to enlarge their freedom, and may thus bring themselves under a more degrading and oppressive bondage than that which they have cast off. Whatever may be our estimate of the absolute value of freedom, we cannot but profit by gaining a clear insight into the various causes of the limitations which restrict our freedom, by distinguishing those restraints which must be borne for the sake of our moral and social culture, from those which arise from abuses in our social system, and by accurately discerning those limits beyond which we cannot hope to extend our freedom without doing away with those conditions which render life valuable to us.

Whatever the special theory we may hold regarding the nature of human freedom, its source, or its foundation, it is certain that by freedom, if we mean anything at all, we must mean freedom *to act.* We cannot conceive of any exercise of freedom other than by *action.* A man who is free, is free to act; the man who is not free to act possesses no such freedom as we can form any conception of. Our notion of freedom is, therefore, based upon our notion of action. What is the precise connection or relation between these two notions, I leave for the determination of those who are more skillful in fashioning definitions than myself. Now, it is certain that no rational being will act without a motive; the motive will either *be* a desire or inclination, or will arise out of, or be connected with, some desire or inclination.

Now, there are two kinds of freedom, which perhaps have not yet been sufficiently distinguished, even by those eminent thinkers and writers who have given their attention to this subject. These are – the freedom to do what we wish to do – the freedom to do what we do *not* wish to do. If any sane man affirms that it is a matter of indifference to him *which* of these kinds of freedom he enjoys – that he does not care whether he is free to do *only* what he wishes to do, or free to do only what he does *not* wish to do, then I should certainly affirm without hesitation that he does not know what he is saying.

Now, if we should conclude that the freedom to do what one wishes to do, is in reality the only sort of freedom which any man seriously desires, or even the freedom which he *mainly* desires, it will be very manifest that the enfranchisement of the whole human race will be no simple problem. It will be manifest that this kind of freedom – the freedom to do what one wishes – will be different, to some extent, in the case of every human creature. For all men to be free, in this sense, supposes as many kinds of freedom as there are human beings in this world. It seems quite certain to me that the matter has not generally been looked at in anything like this light. I am almost sure that people have commonly supposed that Freedom is *one uniform thing*, and that the freedom which one may possess or may desire is, as a matter of course, the same sort of thing – differing only in degree – as the freedom which another man may possess or may desire.

It may seem an extravagant assertion that there are just a thousand million kinds of human freedom, but I am sure that any thoughtful person will soon convince himself that there are more kinds of freedom, which may be actually desired by human individuals, than can easily be thought of or examined in a brief space of time. One man would be free to get drunk, or to appear drunk in certain special places; another would be free to accost all passers-by with a certain familiarity or insolence; another, to hoot and jeer at persons obnoxious to him. One would be free to engage in brawls and riots in public places; another, to create public nuisances (a head which will comprise an almost infinite number of different kinds of freedom); some would be free to create obstructions in public thoroughfares, some to shut up such thoroughfares altogether, others to create thoroughfares for themselves, according to the caprice of the moment, regardless of any other consideration. One man would be free to use, according to his pleasure or caprice, any valuable property which he may chance to find in his way; another would be free to exclude all mankind from all use or enjoyment of any property upon which he can anyhow contrive to lay hands. One man's freedom would be exercised in tilling such a piece of ground; another man's freedom would require this land to remain untilled. One man would be free to build a house in a certain spot, another would find his freedom curtailed by such erection.

One man would be free to express his own opinions in his own way, at all times and under all circumstances; another would be free to prevent such expression of opinions, and to choose his own mode of prevention. One man would be free to teach the children of others, another to keep his children untaught. One man would be free to morally pervert, or cruelly treat, his own children; another would be free to beat his wife; another, to torture living creatures in general. One man would be free to have a multiplicity of wives, another to have no wife at all (and this latter kind of freedom is *not* so universally conceded to mankind, as a superficial observer of human affairs might imagine). One would be free to have as many children as he pleases, another to have as few (and this also is a kind of freedom which must not too hastily be assumed as the universal birthright of all mankind). Some would be free to utter obscene jokes or to sing obscene songs before miscellaneous company; some, to exhibit obscene pictures in public places; others, to exhibit their own persons without such covering as is demanded by the ordinary notions of decency. One man would be free to wear his hat while "God save the Queen" is being played or sung; another would be free to "bonnet" the person exhibiting such a mark of disloyalty. I should think that it can hardly be necessary to go on and fill five hundred pages with this catalogue; I should think the reader who has the least fertile invention could easily fill five hundred pages with such a catalogue without any help from me.

I believe that some persons have been disposed to regard each human individual as occupying, or as having a right to occupy, a certain "sphere of activity," in sole and exclusive possession. Within this sphere he is to exercise perfect freedom, unimpeded by the free action of any other human creature. To this sphere his activity is to be confined, so that he shall in no way encroach upon the spheres of activity which belong to other men, or impede their free action within their respective spheres. According to this theory, a state of perfect and universal freedom may be attained by merely assigning to each individual his own sphere of activity, by securing to him free and unimpeded action within this sphere, and by strictly and absolutely limiting his activity to this sphere. Every man will be perfectly free who has his sphere of action unencroached upon by others. If any man is deprived of his freedom, or his freedom is in any way curtailed, this must arise from his being expelled or excluded from his own sphere of activity, or from some encroachment being made upon this sphere. To do away with all forms of oppression, and to render all mankind perfectly free, all that we have to do, according to this theory, is to assign to each individual his own sphere of activity, and in some way to shut him up within this sphere.

I will not attempt to show just how far this theory of freedom – which I will take the liberty of calling the Individualist Theory – is now prevalent amongst men. I cannot help thinking, for my own part, that the ideas commonly prevalent amongst men concerning human freedom, and especially concerning practical modes of extending human freedom, are greatly muddled and confused. I have a strong conviction that, if men generally would reduce their ideas upon this question to something like order and clearness, it would be found that something like this theory of independent spheres of activity is at the basis of all attempts to attain a perfect state of human freedom, or even to effect a large extension of human freedom, by some means of mere legislative arrangements. So far as human freedom can be attained by the mere fencing off of human beings, each into his own sphere of activity, so far it is conceivable that men should look to the agency of civil governments for the enlargement of their freedom. Whatever step can be taken by civil governments towards the general enfranchisement of mankind, can only be effectual by more accurately ascertaining the sphere of activity of each individual, or by more securely guarding each person's sphere of activity from the encroachments of others.

But let us consider what sort of sphere of activity it is which can be assigned to each human individual for his exclusive occupation, and within which he is to exercise perfect freedom. I have referred to the necessary connection, in the case of every rational being, between action and some desire, inclination, or motive of action. If the action of a human being is to be limited to a certain sphere, he must find, within this sphere, desires, impulses, or motives of action, or the subjects which give rise to such desires, impulses, or motives.

Now, there is a certain class of human desires or impulses which have exclusive reference to the objects of inanimate or brute nature. Let us try and conceive this material universe, animate and inanimate, parceled out into provinces or districts, one of which shall be assigned to each voluntary agent as his *sphere of activity*, within which he shall exercise perfect freedom of action so long as he does not encroach upon the sphere of any other voluntary agent. We need not now inquire *precisely how* these provinces, districts, or spheres of activity shall be marked out or divided. Whether such a division would be barely possible in the nature of things, whether any rule or principle could be found which would guide us in carrying it out – whether any human ingenuity or sagacity would ever be sufficient accurately and justly to parcel out this universe of inanimate and brute nature into such districts or spheres of activity, to find a sphere for every rational or conscious being, and rigidly to pen up or confine each free agent within his own sphere – are questions upon which I am not now inclined to enter. But let us assume, for the sake of our present argument, that all this *would be* possible, that very human creature might be securely penned up within his own sphere of activity, and that he might have absolute and undisturbed possession of this sphere; our present question is, how far would such an arrangement afford men *Freedom* – that is to say, what they would feel to be freedom – such freedom they would in any way desire, or as any one would suppose to be desirable for them.

Let us look at those desires and impulses which most immediately and most exclusively relate to the external material world. These are clearly the animal appetites. Now, let us consider how far the province or sphere of activity which could be assigned to each human individual will comprise all those material objects to which a man is drawn by his animal appetites – how far, that is to say, supposing men to be mere animals, each human individual could be furnished with a "sphere of activity" within which he may exercise all the freedom which his animal appetites will lead him to desire.

There are but few objects in nature which in their crude or native condition are such as to satisfy any desire or inclination of man. We can pen up a tame ox upon a piece of pasture land, and if it be sufficiently large and sufficiently luxuriant, and if he be unmolested by tormenting insects or other causes of irritation, he will be, for a time at least, perfectly satisfied. But we cannot easily find a piece of pasture land upon which we can pen up *a man*, to his own perfect satisfaction, let him be ever so "bovine" in his tastes, disposition, or habits. We cannot now find, or even imagine, any Garden of Eden whose natural products will satisfy the wants of the most simple and unsophisticated of men. Whether there may be lands where the soil is so fertile, and the sky so genial, that the natural products will amply supply the wants of some small section of humanity, is not a question which we need now discuss. We may easily convince ourselves that the great mass of mankind have animal wants and desires which can only be satisfied by the *products of human labor*. Thus, supposing each human individual fenced off in his little district or "sphere of activity," supposing the most favorable state of circumstances, this province or district can only afford him satisfaction for his desires through the results of his own labor. Thus, if we could establish a perfect state of freedom by merely dividing the material universe into "spheres of activity," and by penning up each human individual (voluntary agent) in his own sphere, this freedom could only be enjoyed by any human creature, by means of a certain measure of toil. Whether this measure of toil would be such as most human beings, or as any human beings, would find agreeable – whether this toilsome freedom would not be more burdensome than a moderately easy servitude, is a question which we cannot undertake to settle on the present occasion to the satisfaction of all persons. If any one of my readers has any doubt upon the matter, I only wish he could try the experiment, and be fenced off for a year and a half in some "sphere of activity" where he should be unmolested, but *also unaided*, by any human creature, and where he should have no material means of enjoyment, or of satisfying any of his desires, save what might be the spontaneous production of nature or the exclusive result of his own toil.

I am certain that any thoughtful and observant reader of this work will easily convince himself, without actually making this experiment, that no such freedom as this would be any object of his desire. There are not many persons who are anxious to go back to the "state of nature," and to abandon all the benefits that civilization has conferred upon mankind. Those whose wants arise most exclusively from animal desires, require at every moment the *help of their fellow-men*. If we imagine the most equitable division of the material universe into "spheres of activity," and imagine each individual occupying his sphere under the circumstances most favorable for his comfort and enjoyment, I have not the slightest doubt that the life of each human individual, thus penned up in his own "sphere," would be a life of continual misery. His freedom would be practically limited, in most cases, to the freedom to *starve*.

But when we look at men as other than mere animals, we see still more plainly that their desires are not such as to find satisfaction in any such "sphere of activity" as we can imagine assigned exclusively to each rational and conscious being. Even the most brutal and sensual of men could not enjoy himself long grazing like an ox in his own little pasture, even if this pasture should comprise everything that could tempt the palate of an epicure. We cannot imagine a human creature, for any length of time, basking with perfect satisfaction insulated in a paradise of sensual bliss. Even the sot cannot always relish his cups in solitude; the most carnal of human enjoyments must sometimes be sweetened by companionship.

There will be few indeed amongst the readers of these pages whose actions are mainly determined by desires or impulses which relate exclusively to mere material objects. We are very liable to be misled, in reference to this question, by a superficial view of human conduct and human affairs. We see men earnestly engaged in what appears to be the pursuit of mere material objects, for the most part in the mere quest of gain. A large section of mankind seems to be exclusively occupied in the acquisition of money; may we thence conclude that money alone will satisfy every desire or inclination of these persons – that a person of this description, if penned up in a "sphere of activity" which should yield him an abundant harvest of coin, would enjoy the fullest freedom which he could desire? The miser may perhaps seem to hoard his gold for the mere sake of possessing it, with no thought of using it for any purpose, good or bad; yet even the miser, if he were perfectly isolated from all his fellow-beings – not only in regard to actual bodily presence, but in thought and in feeling – would perhaps find that his gold had lost its charm. Let us suppose the miser to become aware that every human being in the street or the parish where he lives has a hoard twice as large as his own – I think no miser would find his gold afford him any satisfaction after such a discovery. The miser's passion is a very subtle element of our nature, and one which it is not easy accurately to trace in all its workings, but the fact to which I have just alluded seems to me to indicate very plainly that, even in the just case of the miser, avarice is *not* mere love of gain *for its own sake,* but for the sake of some *social relation*, some relation, that is to say, with our fellow-men, which the possession of wealth enables us to maintain.

Every human being has, probably, a brute element in his nature – a set of desires and inclinations which can be satisfied by mere contact with the visible and tangible things of the material world, without regard to any *social relations* which may subsist between himself and any of his fellow-creatures.

But apart from all matters which admit of question, there cannot be the smallest doubt, in the mind of any thoughtful person, that, amongst all those classes who have any measure of cultivation, excepting a few eminently sensual persons, the far greater number of human desires are such as can only be satisfied through some kind of *social relation*, or relation between fellow-beings. To return to the love of gain, it is not for the sake of possessing so many thousands of circular plates of metal, or for the sake of having his name inscribed in some register with certain figures appended, that the worldly or avaricious man toils and hoards, but mainly for the sake, either of the power over other men, or of the eminence, distinction, or notoriety, amongst men, which this wealth will give him. Men do not desire merely to be *rich*, but to be *richer* than other men, or than certain other men. The avaricious or covetous man would feel little or no satisfaction in the possession of any amount of wealth if he were the *poorest* amongst all his neighbors or fellow-countrymen. A woman covets a pretty bonnet; you may perhaps fancy this is for the sake of the article itself. It is nothing of the kind; the bonnet would be just as pretty if every woman in the parish had just such a one; and yet in that case it would probably wholly cease to be an object of desire. There are some things which men desire because certain others possess things that are precisely similar; there are some things which men desire because *no* other persons can possess similar things. A coat of a particular material and make may be in request because of certain persons, or certain classes of persons, possess similar garments; a picture or a diamond may be an object of envy because there is no other in the world like it.

The Essential Nature of Freedom

There is clearly a certain kind or measure of freedom wherever a man chooses one course of action rather than another. In one case we say that a man *has* his choice, and in another case that he has *no* choice; and we feel that he has a freedom in the one case – which we feel to be wanting in the other case. But, at the same time it is no less certain that I may be, in some measure, *unfree* even where my course of action is determined by my choice. It will at least be admitted that, amongst a variety of cases in which I act according to my choice, I am more free in one case, and less free in another case. If the reader declines to admit an absolute want of freedom in some cases where a man selects his course of action from two or more courses which are offered him, he must at least admit a difference in such cases of choice – one action being *more* free, and another being *less* free. As my present object is practical utility, rather than scientific accuracy, this admission of a *comparative* unfreedom in cases of actions determined by choice, will suffer to render me in some measure intelligible to the reader. Thus, I have my choice – shall I take this valuable ring from the jeweler's counter, or shall I *not* take it? And yet, if the ring be not mine, no sane man would pretend to regard me as *so* free to take it as if it *were* mine. I am at least *comparatively un*free to take your property in that manner which the law would regard as felonious. Now, in what manner is my freedom circumscribed in a case where I have the opportunity of committing a theft, not indeed with the prospect of ultimate impunity, but without meeting with immediate opposition? We need say nothing, for the present, regarding the force of the moral law as limiting my freedom in such a case as this. The common mind unhesitatingly pronounces – I am not free to steal, because the law of the land forbids me.

Now in what way does the law of the land circumscribe my freedom? It leaves my limbs unrestrained; it leaves me in every case – or at least in nearly every case – the choice, to obey the law, or to disobey it. The law merely threatens me with a penalty, if I *choose* to disobey. If I have a desire or inclination urging me to disobey the law, I have to make my choice, between gratifying my desire or escaping the penalty of the law. It is clear that the law exercises upon me no kind of influence or restraint save by setting before me *a certain motive* for acting or forbearing to act.

It cannot be doubted that we have a certain notion of freedom which is based upon the nature of the motives which determine our actions. The man who acts from certain motives is *more* free, the man who acts from other motives is *less* free. The martyr or the patriot who defies bad or oppressive laws, and chooses to endure the penalty by which such laws are enforced rather than yield obedience to them, seems to us *more* free than the man who obeys these laws in opposition to the dictate of his conscience. Here are two men who, in the same circumstances, have, as we may suppose, the same motives urging them to action; the one man yields to one set of motives and is *free*, the other yields to another set of motives and is *unfree*. Certain citizens of a democratic republic will for the mere payment of a sum of money, vote for the appointment of one man as able, absolute, and hereditary dictator; certain other citizens of such a republic will suffer close and painful imprisonment for their unsuccessful resistance to a *coup de main*, and will *voluntarily choose* the continuance of their captivity rather than swear allegiance to the usurping tyrant. The latter act upon a certain class of motives, and are *free*, or comparatively free; the former act from another class of motives, and are *unfree*, or comparatively unfree. But, it may be asked, *what* are the motives which determine a free action, and what are the motives which determine an action which is *not* free or which is less free? This is not an easy question to answer fully, in general terms, and one to which I shall not in fact attempt to give a sufficient answer. I do not now aim at laying down a moral system which will give perfect satisfaction to all persons of deep thought and of extensive information. I believe that the science of morals is yet in its infancy, and I do not aspire to effect much by means of this work towards its final completion. I believe there are some persons who regard their feelings, in relation to some human interests, as having a more distinct and unquestionable reality than their intellectual conceptions. It is, perhaps, mainly to such that this work will commend itself, seeing that it is based rather upon the *sense* of freedom than upon any intellectual conception of freedom.

I may be wholly unable to demonstrate to the critical reader that the motives which influence our actions are, respectively, higher and lower; there may be those who will altogether decide the notion that one motive can be higher or nobler than another. The fact to which I would appeal is that we – meaning those persons to whom this work is mainly addressed – have a strong and unmistakable *feeling* that some motives are higher, and others lower. This feeling we who experience it are no more bound to explain or account for, in order to justify our acting upon it, than we are bound to account for the distinctions of color in order to justify our selecting our draperies according to their tints or patterns.

Indeed, with those who positively deny this distinction of human motives as higher or lower, I do not care much to argue. If a man really believes that the hog, in gobbling up his wash, is influenced by as high or as noble a motive as the philanthropist, who works unostentatiously early and late to relieve the destitute poor of his parish, I for my part do not care to discuss moral questions with him. If a man, who is ruled for the time being by mere appetite, pretends to have any higher or nobler motive than that of the pig, I am wholly unable to appreciate his view. If a man, when eating to satisfy his hunger, being conscious of nothing but his hunger and its satisfaction, yet professes, by virtue of his general excellence of character, or of his having fulfilled certain stated "religious observances," or by virtue of certain "latent principles," or of some mysterious knack of "doing everything to the glory of God," to convert his hunger into a high and noble motive, as high and noble as that of the philanthropist, I can only say that such subtleties are altogether out of the range of my intellectual powers.

I believe there are persons who resent, as a gross indignity, the charge of every being influenced by motives to which the term "low" or "lower" can be applied. They regard their persons and their actions as invested with that sort of sanctity or moral dignity that we cannot even, without doing them cruel wrong, pick out this or that action or feature in their conduct as worse or morally lower, or less noble, than another action or feature.

For my own part, having never seen fit to set myself up as a pattern of sanctity or moral excellence, I am quite certain that the motives which determine my actions are extremely variable in their degree of moral worth; and I am sufficiently certain that the same is true of those persons to whom this work is intended to appeal. Those persons whose actions are, all of them, already of the highest and noblest moral character possible to mortals, seem to me incapable of all such improvement as this work is designed to promote; in those whose actions are all of the lowest and most ignoble moral character I have but little hope of effecting any improvement. It is those who, being conscious of the need of improvement, are at the same time conscious of possessing those elements of character which render improvement possible, that I am anxious to aid or encourage in their strivings after a higher and noble state or moral being.

I would submit to the reader this view of human freedom, with all modesty, not knowing, in fact, how far I may claim for it the authority of noted writers upon moral questions, or how far I may claim the merit of originating it. That man seems to me to act with freedom who yields to the impulse of the *highest motive* which demands his obedience, or which presents itself to his consciousness, at the moment of determination. It is, perhaps, rarely that any action is determined upon by any human being under the *sole* impulse of *one* motive. I cannot help thinking that, when one solitary motive is present to a man's mind, he will certainly and inevitably act from this motive. Whether he is free or unfree in such an action, is a question which there is now no practical necessity for us to consider. I think there is at least some plausibility in the supposition that wherever a man clearly and manifestly exercises his freedom, there will be a variety of motives present to his mind. At any rate, it is quite certain that, in all such cases as we need now consider – that is to say, in those cases where it is a *practical* question whether a man shall be *more* free or *less* free – the action will be determined upon under the influence of a variety of motives – the action is, as it were, the final result of a conflict of motives. A new impulse or desire arising in a man's mind, where there is no positive force with which this new inclination has to contend, will, in nearly every case, find itself at least opposed by a certain mental inertia – the disinclination to action at all, or the charm or attraction of the previous condition or course of action. I should think there are few human actions which are not preceded by a state of mental indecision, however short, in which the agent asks – Shall I do this, or shall I do not?

It might possibly be a matter of no small difficulty to determine fully and completely which of all the motives that ever influence human actions are higher and which are lower – to arrange all motives of human action in a scale, showing their relative degrees of moral worthiness or unworthiness. This is a problem of which I shall not here attempt the complete solution, since it is not my present purpose to complete the extremely imperfect science of Ethics. But I am strongly convinced that, unless human motives can be thus arranged in a moral scale, there can never be any such science as Ethics at all, or any approach made to the construction of such a science.

I think that we may at least take one step towards the formation of such a scale of human motives, in placing the animal appetites at its lowest extremity, as being, of all the motives that can influence human conduct, and which are not actually vicious, the lowest and meanest.

Yet it is certain that we do not regard all actions as unfree which are performed under the mere impulse of bodily desire, or of some other low or base motive. The man who sits down to his meal with a hearty appetite and eats from pure hunger, uninfluenced by any other motive, is not necessarily regarded as unfree. There is no necessary want of freedom in drinking to quench one's thirst, or in falling asleep from weariness. It is not merely because an action is impelled by a low or base motive that it seems wanting in freedom, but because there is, *at the same time*, a higher and nobler motive which claims the obedience of the agent. In short, we regard an action as unfree when it is determined by some motive which is *not the highest* present to the mind of the agent, at the moment of determination.

Let us take a variety of those most ordinary cases in which men act in a manner which is commonly regarded as wanting in freedom – the elector who votes with his landlord or his wealthy customer lest he should lose his farm or injure his trade; the man of position in society who conceals his religious, social, or political views lest he should forfeit his social standing; the political leader who attaches himself to a party whose policy he does not approve of in order to gain a lucrative place; the clergyman who belies his most solemn convictions in order to retain or to obtain a benefice; the author who publishes sentiments which are not his own in order to win favor from the public or from some section of the public; the lady who wears a dress which she feels in her heart to be grossly indecent in order to be fashionable; the villager who forsakes his conventicler and attends the parish church, contrary to his convictions of duty, lest he should offend the squire's lady and lose his Christmas soup and coals, or who sends his child to the "National" school rather than to the "British," in spite of his convictions as to their respective merits, from dread of the clergyman's influence; the shopkeeper who is ruled in all matters connected with political, parochial, or municipal interests by the dictation of those wealthy persons from whose custom a considerable part of his income is derived. Now, in all these cases it is manifest that the agent *chooses* his course of action, and yet in every one of these cases we feel that there is a want of freedom. In each of these cases we can imagine the agent *choosing to act* in a contrary manner, and in a manner which we should feel to be at least *more* free. In each of the cases cited above the agent acts in violation or in disregard of some serious conviction, for the sake of some low and selfish object; in each of such cases we feel that the agent is ruled by a lower motive, to the suppression or the disregard of a higher motive, of which he may be more or less clearly conscious.

It is not, of course, easy in all cases to discern clearly and accurately the whole of the motives which influence, or which ought to influence, those persons whom we see acting around us, and the relative strength of each of the various motives which may influence them; yet I am convinced that, the more closely we look at men's actions, the more frequently shall we find them acting under the impulsion of a variety of motives, some of which we feel to be higher and more worthy to rule men's actions than others.

I am convinced that a careful scrutiny of human actions will show that where, in actual life, men act with unfreedom – where we feel them to be in any way enslaved or deprived of their freedom, their actions are nevertheless determined by *choice* – that the free action differs from the action which is less free, in the *different orders of motives which prompt them.*

Whatever theory we may adopt, guided either by philosophy or by common-sense, regarding the actual nature of human freedom, we cannot but regard our freedom as limited, or as liable to be limited. Whatever kind of freedom we may enjoy, or however numerous the different kinds of freedom we may enjoy, it is certain that we can have no clear conception of freedom without having a conception of some kind of restraint, or other circumstance which either does limit, or may limit, this freedom. Whatever questions may be raised in reference to this subject which we may be unable to solve to our own satisfaction, we may at least feel – those of us, that is to say, who will give any serious attention to the matter – that this department of our subject, the nature of those restraints or other circumstances which circumscribe our freedom, is a topic upon which we can reflect with some hope of attaining a useful result.

I think there can be little doubt that this negative view of human freedom – the view of those features and circumstances in our lives which limit our freedom or tend to render us *unfree* – is that aspect of the subject which minds of the ordinary stamp are best to realize. And yet I think it can as little be doubted that the ideas commonly prevalent amongst men upon this point are far from clear or consistent. First of all we meet with the notion that the main limitations upon men's freedom are owing to oppressive or unjust laws, enforced by civil governments. I believe most firmly that his is a fallacy which is as mischievous as it is absurd. I think that any intelligent man who will try and picture to himself the restraints upon his freedom to which he is likely to submit, or the sacrifice of freedom which he is likely to make, during an ordinary day of his life, he will see at once that civil or judicial coercion has a very small share in laying down those limits which actually circumscribe his freedom. I am not alluding, of course, to persons of singularly vicious or lawless character, or in either respects exceptional in their dispositions or habits. A person of ordinary decency and respectability will, at least in this country, rarely find himself checked in the carrying out of his desires, by the restraints and prohibitions of law. A person of ordinary decency and good repute, in ordinary circumstances, who should wish, many times during a year, to do an act which is forbidden by the law, will be the subject of some kind of thonomania or idiosyncrasy.

I have already referred to the force of habit and the embarrassment which it may occasion us in our treatment of this subject. So far as a man is absolutely ruled by habit, so far our inquiries concerning human freedom can have no more reference to his case than to the case of an ordinary vegetable. It is useless to make arrangements for the freedom of such a one; it is useless to refer to the case of such a one for any illustration of our principles or our conclusions. We can therefore learn nothing from the case of a man who, if left to himself, would, from the mere force of habit, under all conceivable circumstances, rise every morning at the same hour, take his meals, day after day, precisely at the same hour and, as far as possible, in the same manner, and who will go on throughout the day fulfilling precisely the same routine of action. We should rather try and imagine circumstances which might render a man desirous of breaking through his habitual routine. Let us imagine a man to have some strong inducement to spend the day, or some considerable portion of the day, in some occupation altogether remote from his ordinary engagements – in some pleasure excursion, in some scientific, literary, or artistic pursuit, or in the advancement of some benevolent object, or in response to some demand of friendship. Or imagine him to have found some special inducement for economy in some detail of household or personal expenditure, in some case where a considerable saving could be effected, without any sensible diminution of comfort or enjoyment, by taking a course unusual with persons in his position of life. Or imagine him to have found some person whose society is singularly agreeable to him, or promises to be highly beneficial, but whose occupation, social position, or "ungenteel" appearance is far removed from that of those persons with whom he has been accustomed to associate. Or imagine him to have undergone some change in opinion, on either a theological or a political question, which would lead him to adopt a course of action widely different from any which he has ever followed, or which has ever been followed by any of those persons who form the social circle in which he has moved. Or imagine him to feel a strong impulse to devote a large portion, either of his time or of his property, to the improvement of his fellow-creatures, or to the carrying out of some favorite theory or project for the advancement of human society. Or imagine him to feel impelled, either by taste or caprice, to adopt an occupation or profession totally different from that which he has hitherto followed, and which will be either far less profitable than his old pursuit, or will command far less consideration in society. None of these suppositions is altogether extravagant; they are most of them conceivable in the case of a man whose mental and moral structures differ widely in no feature from the ordinary type of mankind.

Now it is quite certain that, with the great majority of mankind, in well-ordered societies, the restraining influence which will check such impulses as these and force the man back into the old track of use and wont, will *not* be the force of judicial coercion. This at least we may conclude without hesitation, although we may find it difficult to determine what *will* be the actual restraining force in all or any of these cases. Assuming that the force of habit does not operate – and if we do *not* assume this, I think all considerations regarding a man's freedom are futile – in the case of a man who is engaged in a lucrative occupation, out of ten cases in which he will feel an inclination to break through his general routine of customary actions, in nine cases he will be forced back into the habitual track through the desire of pecuniary gain, or through the fear of loss. In a great variety of matters he will be absolutely governed by public opinion, the opinion, that is to say, of the class or section of the public whose opinion he most regards. In matters of social etiquette, or those observances which have special relation to the distinctions of social rank, he will probably be mainly ruled by the desire to appear as "genteel" in the eyes of his neighbors as his circumstances will admit. In many matters a man will be wholly controlled by the opinion of some particular person, some leader of fashion, or great man in his neighborhood or amongst his party, or even of his own ward. If he be an employer, and desirous of offering some concession to his discontented workmen, he will probably be deterred by the fear of some sort of social ostracism amongst his fellow-employers, especially if he be one of the least considerable amongst them. If he be disposed to make some unusual effort or sacrifice for a benevolent object – to give a larger sum of money than would generally be thought reasonable or becoming in his position of life – or to spend some considerable portion of his time in some practical effort for the good of others, such as a ragged or adult school, he would probably be restrained from the indulgence of such inclinations by the fear of ridicule. If he should be tempted to throw himself earnestly into some project or scheme for the general improvement of mankind, or of some section of mankind, it would be the fear of being called "Utopian" that would drive him back into the tramway of conventional self-seeking. If he should hold some extreme or exceptional view on a theological or a political question, or regarding the relations of social ranks or classes and their relative duties, it will probably be a very complex feeling that will induce him to conceal this opinion, or at least to refrain from that course of action to which it would most naturally lead – partly the fear of losing caste or of becoming "ungenteel," the fear of forfeiting the respect or good-will of his associates, and of losing, in some measure, his social connection, the fear of losing the influence which he now holds amongst his neighbors, or the fear of injuring his business – all these fears being, perhaps, aggravated by his dread of the displeasure or disfavor of some particular class, as the clergy or the gentry, or the wealthier class amongst his neighbors.

And, in general, there is a vast, vague, mysterious authority which casts its shadow over all human affairs, and which governs men's actions with a far more stringent rule than that exercised by the civil governor – the authority of Conventionalism or Conventional Propriety. There is a strange and vague dread of doing what no one else ever does, of being altogether singular, which far more frequently restrains men – excepting the lowest or poorest classes in society, and perhaps *not* excepting these – from the indulgence of their personal fancies and caprices, than the prohibitions of civil law.

If it should here be said, regarding all these influences, that a man yields to them voluntarily, and that they are no restraint upon his freedom, and if it be asked – How can a man be unfree in a matter where he himself makes choice of his course of action? I will refer the reader to what has been said in reference to certain aspects in which freedom seems to consist, *in some measure*, in the subordination of a lower order of motives to a higher. In case the reader should have forgotten the remarks alluded to, or should have failed to find convincing force in arguments, which to me, I say with all humility, seemed quite unanswerable, I will here so far repeat myself as to remark that if a man yields voluntary obedience to the dictates of fashion, of public opinion, of the "genteel" circle in which he moves, or in which he aspires to move, of his employer, of his customers, he as truly yields voluntary obedience to the injustices of the law. Whatever *sense* of unfreedom a man may experience in paying assessed taxes or parish rates, in filling up a census paper, or even in putting in an appearance to a writ of summons, I am quite sure that a man will often feel quite as oppressive a sense of unfreedom in "cutting" a shabby relative for fear of his "genteel" neighbor, in appearing at a social gathering which is wholly devoid of cordiality or friendly warmth, and which comprises only persons disagreeable to him, in attending a religious service which is altogether wearisome to him, in complimenting a lady upon her musical performance or in listening to the conversation of a noted *bore*.[11]

Return of the "L" Word

To put it bluntly, in the years after 1965 liberals badly mishandled conflicts surrounding race, class, war, peace, and ideology. As long as civil rights meant ending the legal foundations of segregation in the South, liberalism surged ahead; but once the movement's agenda focused on subtler processes of racial discrimination that were well-entrenched in the North as well as the South, progress was no longer easy and the movement faltered.

In the end, liberal elites failed to appreciate the sacrifices being asked of middle- and working-class Americans to remedy the nation's sorry legacy of racial inequality; and rather than reaching a political accommodation to offset the real costs with concrete benefits, they sought to use executive and judicial power to force change upon an apprehensive and fearful public while decrying all opponents as narrow-minded bigots. As a result, the segregation of schools and neighborhoods has continued despite successive civil rights acts, and conservatives were able to use the issue of race to break apart the New Deal coalition.

The liberals who sought to use executive and judicial power to extend civil rights were generally affluent, well-educated, and effectively insulated from the consequences of social change by their privileged class position. In contrast, the people affected by their policies had less education and income, thus opening a class divide into which Republicans quickly plunged a dagger. Rather than recognizing the tenuousness of working-class achievements, liberals

[11] J.S. Mill, "On Social Freedom", reprinted from the *Oxford and Cambridge Review*, June 1907

more often looked with contempt upon middlebrow Americans who were threatened by change and resisted the liberal policies of the 1960s and 1970s...

Although liberals must recognize their own complicity in the conservative resurgence of the late twentieth century and learn from their past mistakes, *mea culpas* will not win elections or convince voters to return liberal politicians to power. A second reason for the demise of liberalism over the past thirty years was the lack of a coherent program to offer voters. Until liberals can unite around a sensible political philosophy that can be explained to voters in straightforward terms, they cannot expect to win elections. In addition to *opposing* the radical conservative policies of today's Republicans, liberals must themselves *stand for* something – a set of consistent principles that can be communicated widely and translated into concrete public policies...

Although it has become popular in some liberal political circles to view globalization as the great Satan of our era, a truly liberal viewpoint recognizes that the expansion of markets through international trade and global finance are essential to world peace and prosperity. The negative results of globalization to date have come less from the expansion of trade and markets per se than from the rules and conditions under which this expansion has occurred...

In addition to admitting past mistakes, setting forth a defensible political philosophy, and translating this philosophy into a practical agenda for domestic and international politics, liberals must accurately appraise the formidable array of conservative forces lined up against them. Based on this knowledge, they must work to develop effective political strategies to counter conservative influence. To date, liberals have been outclassed by the ideological ingenuity and organization capabilities of the conservative right...[12]

The Liberal Arts and Money

It is the *liberal arts* that I wish to speak about.

The point I wish to make is that we pay lip-service to the liberal arts – largely because we don't know what we're talking about.

The agenda illustrates the problem I have in mind when it lists "Disciplinary Approaches" to Philanthropy. The term "disciplinary" is offensive in its own right because it confirms *specialization* as the measure of learning. These are the disciplines mentioned:

[12] Douglas S. Massey, *Return of the L Word: A Liberal Vision for the New Century*, Princeton, Princeton University Press, 2005

Economics, Religion, Philosophy, Sociology, Anthropology, Politics, and History. As presently understood, these subjects have little of nothing to do with the liberal arts. For one thing, they are or want to be sciences, even "human sciences," and for another they are specialized rather than general subjects.

Is Philanthropic Studies a "discipline"?

More to the point: *Are the liberal arts* "disciplines" or *something else? Have they become* "liberal sciences"?

Let me list the "liberal arts" as Cicero knew them as the core of liberal education:

The first was *grammar*: the art of written expression, emotion, and ideas. **The second was *rhetoric*: the art of persuasion,** especially in the courts and other public forums. **The third was *logic* or *dialectic***: the arts **and methods of reason** and demonstrative proof. We then seem to forget that when the liberal arts first emerged, education was primarily intended to prepare citizens for public life. It was a largely verbal society and so knowing how to think and compose one's thoughts and opinions for public expression was practical training in writing and arguing.

[*Incidentally, teachers called Sophists came to Athens from Syracuse in the fourth century* B.C. *and brought their oratorical skills with them. The young Athenians were dazzled by their oratory and wanted to learn how to be eloquent themselves. The Sophists not only offered to teach the young Athenians oratory – for a fee – but also to teach them virtue and the way to the good life. It was probably Plato who took the various notions of argument and public discourse and training in oratory and brought them together under a new term that he invented: Rhetoric.*]

There was in fact a fourth liberal art: ***poetic:* the art of poetry** as also expressed in the visual and performing arts.

By Cicero's time he was able to add two other methods of thought or "disciplinary approaches" of the liberal arts: **history** and **moral philosophy.** When the liberal arts were at their most influential in public life, when their practice had to do with matters of life and death, there were therefore ***six* rather** than three liberal arts.

Our obsession with classification also obscures the ancient practice: in practice the **liberal arts were integrated,** not separate and distinct as they came to be in teaching. Cicero writes in his first book on rhetoric about personal appearance and projecting the voice as well as about how to seize the case to be argued or the points to be made. He always used illustrative examples in his speeches; there were always heroes drawn from Greek and Roman mythology and history.

I have to confess that I know a great deal less about my own traditions than Cicero knew about his. Were I to follow Cicero's example more closely, I would mention James Madison's understanding of the idea of *faction* and its influence on the text of the First Amendment. To make my point here I would mention John Adams's understanding of the concept of a *republic* and of the rule of law as he read about them in Cicero. To give a hint of what studies in the liberal arts meant to the Founders, I might mention John Quincy Adams's two-volume textbook on the art of rhetoric. The Founders were steeped in the classics, especially Cicero; they knew Latin and sometimes Greek and they knew Greek and Roman history. That knowledge and historical perspective permeates our Constitution.

Alongside grammar, rhetoric, logic, poetic, and history I would also have to follow Cicero and make a case for *moral philosophy*. Cicero was much concerned about personal and public morals. The political life around him was becoming more corrupt year-by-year, and survival in politics often meant compromise or death. In the end, **when Cicero refused to compromise and join those who would overthrow the republic, his head and hands were chopped off and nailed to the wall of the Forum to make the point that speaking and writing could be fatal. The liberal arts can be poetically neutral but adding history and moral philosophy to them makes them politically dangerous.**

The educational challenge to our age seems far more complex and difficult than the challenge faced by the Greeks and Romans. The most important influence is, of course, technology. It isn't necessary to call technology *mindless* to make the point that technology seems to have a mind of its own. Technology seems not to care wither we're ready to handle it or not.

Cicero is said, by some historians, to be the most influential voice in the history of Western civilization – that is, until the past fifty years, when he seems simply to have disappeared from the public scene. I've discovered that some of the best students in the Master of Arts Program in Philanthropic Studies know little or nothing about Cicero, and know little more about Roman history (I leave it to your imagination to speculate on the present [incumbent's] knowledge of ancient history, or Cicero and the origins of the rule of law, of Greek ideas about freedom and democracy and Roman ideas about law and government and how those ideas shaped the United States of America. We have instead a self-proclaimed born-again Christian who reads the Bible every day and whose favorite philosopher is Jesus. Cicero, too, knew how to draw on religion when he needed it, how to appeal to the gods in times of stress, and how to appeal to the popular ignorance and fear when necessary. Of course, Cicero knew what he was up to).

[***The Sophists were also criticized by people like Socrates for being the first relativists, teaching people how to win an argument without being concerned about whether the right view won out.***]

I am a generation older than most of you. It was my generation that is at fault for these failures of liberal arts education more than any other. It was my generation that stood by in the late 1960s while angry undergraduates successfully revolted against the requirements of general education. It was my generation that was beguiled by pop psychology and pop sociology and all of those other mutations of social and behavioral science. Pop textbooks about the ideas of B.F. Skinner and Carl Rogers displaced original texts of the ideas of William James and John Dewey and even of Freud himself. **Most seriously, abandoning the undergraduate requirement of a year or two in history has left us with a generation with no knowledge of the past, no sense of tradition, no respect for ancestors or founders or heritage. No acquaintance with Cicero.**

One of the reasons I insist on the importance of **Cicero** to us is that he gave us a concept that draws on philanthropy, liberal education, and public service: **the ideal he invented and named the *humanitas.*** Cicero began with a broad and generous attitude of **good will toward others,** including strangers; it was an idea he drew from the Greeks and he used the Greek word for it: **philanthropia.** Cicero realized that although an attitude of good will is one of the things that makes humans humane, he knew that philanthropy must be more than an attitude or emotion. The worldview he called philanthropy should be grounded in complex understanding of human nature and the human condition. He believed that such an understanding could only be gained from an education such as the Greeks had developed; he used the **Greek word** *paideia*, or what we would call ***liberal education.*** To put the point in the terms that I urge upon my students: *the only justification for an elite education is a life of service.*

We indulged in much emotional rhetoric about compassion and generosity, a good deal of which is phony as well as self-serving. It is phony because it is uncritical and self-serving because it is amoral. Our rhetoric is phony and self-serving because it is not grounded, as

Cicero insisted, in the liberal arts amplified by a knowledge of history and self-examination through the lens of moral philosophy. All of this knowledge and skill and wisdom was to be brought to bear on public life, every education in the liberal arts was to become manifest in public service.

In my old age I have come to be very skeptical about what passes as knowledge and expertise and the so-called wisdom of popular culture. There are two reasons for my skepticism: the first is that knowledge is ephemeral and unreliable; the second is that I am an elitist: understanding and wisdom require a level of thought and discipline of reflection that few people achieve. That was true in the early days of the Republic and it is true now. Madison and Adams and Jefferson and Paine and their peers were educated in the liberal arts and by Cicero himself. Theirs was an elite education; their sense of tradition and history and moral philosophy led them to a higher level of social and political understanding than most of their fellow citizens.

[*The rapid rise of a young Bill Gates to become the wealthiest American might be put in perspective by remembering that James Madison was 36 when he wrote the* Federalist Papers – *and Hamilton was only 33.*]

An education in grammar, rhetoric, logic, poetry, history, and moral philosophy remains the best of the tradition we have inherited from Greece and Rome. We have come to realize that there are comparable education philosophies in Confucianism and Buddhism; I have found nothing comparable elsewhere but I rightly consider myself ignorant and uninformed.

What I most feel the need for is an open and accessible discussion and debate about education everywhere – liberal education, general education, education of the public, education in democracy, education in the face of a windstorm of technology and a dense fog of specialization. We seem to be **producing a great many people who are very, very *smart* but not many who are very, very *wise*.**

Cicero admired the Greeks; as a young man in his twenties he went to Athens to study philosophy. He came to the conclusion that Romans were good at government but the Greeks were not. The Greeks were too theoretical and the Romans too practical. They needed each other. We have been given both traditions. We are much more like the Romans in our practicality, except that we have reduced all of our complex values to only one: the economic. **If historians a couple of thousand years from now study our civilization and its traditions, they will say that the Greeks knew about ideas and the Romans knew about institutions**

and the Americans knew about buying and selling. And about little else.

I am an angry old man because it has taken me a lifetime to begin to understand what a good education might be and to realize that it has been there in front of me all along. But along with most of my friends and colleagues I have been preoccupied with the fads and fashions and simply too *contemporary* to realize how shallow and facile and *ignorant* we are behind a façade of expertise and statistics and formulas and slogans.

I am frustrated, too, because I have a sense that not many other people give a damn about these things – about the liberal arts and what they mean, about *philanthropia* and *paideia* and *humanitas*, and other ancient understandings of how one becomes more human, more honest, more responsible.[13]

Liberal Education on the Ropes

The association of colleges and universities currently defines liberal education as: "a philosophy of education that empowers individuals, liberates the mind from ignorance, and cultivates social responsibility. Characterized by challenging encounters with important issues, and more a way of studying than specific content, liberal education can occur at all types of colleges and universities."...

Through most of the 20th century, liberal education was more or less exclusively identified with the four-year liberal-arts colleges and a handful of elite universities. Both the institutions and its advocates were avowed educational elitists. But times have changed – hence the attempt of the association of colleges and universities to universalize liberal education across all types of institutions. But liberal education is being asked to carry more freight than it did a century ago, and it is not clear that it can succeed.

As it has expanded throughout higher education, it has suffered inevitable losses and unresolved tensions. As it spread from what were once primarily church-related colleges, for example, it lost its focus on moral values. But even the surviving emphasis on an orientation that stresses general values has been an uncomfortable fit in the modern research university, which has increasingly stressed the production of scientific knowledge over the transmission of culture.

Many of the attempts to package liberal education in the modern university have centered on "general education." The idea of general

[13] Robert Payton, *The Liberal Arts and Money*

education derives from Matthew Arnold, and it was picked up and Americanized in the United States early in the 20th century. Although we seldom recognize the fact, there were actually three streams in American thinking at the time.

The first stream is perhaps one of the oldest, but still continues. It has been the self-conscious rejection of specific courses in favor of a vague notion of enforced diversity of subject matter, to be provided by regular disciplinary departments. Here the pre-eminent example is, alas, my own university, Princeton. Under the leadership of James McCosh in the late 1880s, Princeton developed the "distribution" system that is still all we have to provide structured liberal education at Old Nassau.

At Princeton it was not necessary to offer special courses or designate faculty members to provide the content of liberal education – just to ensure that students did not concentrate too narrowly by requiring a variety of what McCosh called "obligatory and disciplinary" courses. With the exception of a sequence of humanities courses and a large program of freshman seminars, present-day Princeton still has neither non-departmental general-education courses nor any structured mechanism for thinking about the broader contours of undergraduate liberal education. We review the program periodically, but we seem always to conclude that McCosh had it right. Well, perhaps.

The most obvious and most highly publicized example of the next stream began at Columbia University as the United States was entering World War I. This was an attempt to ensure that undergraduates in an increasingly scientific university would be broadly educated across the fields of the liberal arts and to integrate their increasingly fragmented selection of courses into some coherent form. (Admittedly, it was also fueled by a felt need to promote Western civilization in the face of German barbarism.) Combining new synthetic courses outside the disciplinary-obsessed department structure with the inculcation of a notion of democratic citizenship, the curriculum was organized around surveys of "Contemporary Civilization." In essence, the Columbia sequence humanized the now-secular university curriculum by broadly historicizing it. As time passed, most other elite institutions did the same.

In the 1930s Robert Maynard Hutchins and Mortimer J. Adler at the University of Chicago launched an important experiment in this approach. It was complex and somewhat inwardly self-contradictory, but the bottom line was an insistence on the centrality of the Greek classics and other Great Books to undergraduate education, later supplemented by the construction of a "core curriculum" to educate undergraduates across the liberal-arts subjects and to force them to think through and across traditional disciplinary approaches.

In 1945 Harvard, under James Bryant Conant, issued *General Education in a Free Society*, commonly known as the *Harvard Red Book*. I still have my copy, for it was the basis of my undergraduate education at Harvard beginning in 1951, when as a freshman I took a "Natural Sciences" course in the general-education sequence taught by President Conant, a stunning chemistry professor named Leonard Nash, and an obscure assistant professor of physics named Thomas S. Kuhn. I never had a better undergraduate course. The political rationale for the *Red Book* was grander than Columbia's or Chicago's, but the basic principles of general education were not that different, based on sweepingly synthetic historical approaches to classically great ideas. The attempt to give all undergraduates at least a taste of different disciplines is now one of the unchallenged principles of general education.

The third stream, which in some ways has had a more profound influence on our actual educational practices, was that championed by John Dewey and Arthur O. Lovejoy. This effort focused on cognitive development and individual student growth, and its key was the idea of reflective thinking as a goal of liberal education. That concept was institutionalized at Columbia under the leadership of Dewey and at the Johns Hopkins University under Lovejoy. This approach was entirely cognitive, lacking in specific education content. To this day it forms the basis of the stress on process at the heart of approaches to liberal education.

To be sure, there have been many other approaches to liberal education over the years. Until recently, many liberal-arts colleges used both sophisticated distribution systems and a variety of innovative course designs. Many still continue to innovate. As Ernest L. Boyer forcefully noted in *College: The Undergraduate Experience in America*, first published in 1987, some such colleges have become university wannabes or citadels of pre-professional education. In any case, in most of the major four-year institutions that are educating a larger and larger proportion of undergraduates, the challenge has seemed to be modifying the historical principles of general education in order to bring them up to date.

In the humanities, the focus moved from studies of Europe (especially classical Europe) and America to contemplation of the rest of the world. We discovered world literature, philosophy, history, and music. New subdisciplines developed (the history of everything in the social sciences and humanities, for instance), new languages were studied, new techniques were employed. And the relevance of the humanities to politics became a problem and an opportunity.

For undergraduate education, the center simply could not hold. There were many attempts to identify an essential core of knowledge, and many new attempts will undoubtedly be made. I think them unlikely to succeed given the breadth and complexity of the intellectual content students now confront.

Nor do we seem to have the educational leaders capable of defining new content. Let me say that I do not think the blame should fall on university presidents and deans. It should be assigned to research faculties for whom thoughtful consideration of undergraduate education is simply not on the agenda. They are dominated by scholars committed to disciplinary approaches, who would mostly prefer to teach graduate students and, increasingly, postgrads. The professional schools at least claim to prefer to admit generally educated students, but what about graduate departments? Can we simply presume that the products of American secondary education are already liberally educated? To ask the question is to answer it.

The changing structure of the university is the place we may need to start the discussion. A great deal is at stake for undergraduate education, and for the country. If we believe, as so many of the founders of liberal education did, that the vitality of American democracy depends upon the kind of liberal education undergraduates receive, we need to put the reimagination of liberal education near the top of our agenda for education in our research universities.[14]

Today's College Students and Yesteryear's High School Grads

America has led the world in democratizing access to higher education. Between 1947 and 1995 the number of high school graduates entering college (including community college) rose from 2,338,226[15] to 14,261,800[16] – a rate of growth three times faster than that of the population.[17] Spending on campuses and faculties expanded even faster, overall public and private outlays for higher education going from $12.6 billion[18] in 1947–48 to $190 billion[19] in

[14] Stanley Katz, "Liberal Education on the Ropes", *Chronicle of Higher Education*, April 1, 2005, Vol. 51, Iss. 30, p.6

[15] *Digest of Education Statistics*, 1995, U.S. Department of Education, p.176

[16] *Almanac Issue*, *The Chronicle of Higher Education*, September 1, 2000, p.24

[17] Based on a population of 144,126,071 in 1947 and 262,764,948 in 1995. *U.S. Population From 1900*, Demographia.com, November 13, 2002. Source: U.S. Census Bureau.

[18] *Digest of Education Statistics*, 1995, U.S. Department of Education, p.346

[19] *Almanac Issue*, *The Chronicle of Higher Education*, September 1, 2000, p.42

1995–96 (measured in constant 1995–96 dollars). But a key question – too often taken for granted – remains unanswered: has this vast increase in expenditure of student time and national wealth actually led to commensurate increase in knowledge?

It is clear that college graduates have an earnings potential substantially greater than those who proceed no further than high school, and that this, in some part, is a result of the acquisition in college of profession-related skills. But evidence that the extension of the average length of the academic experience has had any impact on the acquisition of general cultural knowledge, or upon the desire to attain it (both major goals of liberal education), is scant…

It is, of course, common today for educators to denigrate the importance of factual knowledge, giving emphasis instead to what they usually call "thinking skills." While this is not the place to enter into this debate at length, it seems to us that learning "how to think" about matters pertaining to culture and society has at least as much to do with having a fund of reliable information "to think about" as it does to possessing special thinking skills (other than common sense) or some body of abstruse theoretical understandings…

If an important part of a liberal education consists in opening the mind to the peak achievements of human genius and developing an appropriate respect for them, the time and treasure we've been showering on education's prolongation may not be getting us materially closer to these goals…[20]

More Americans than ever before are attending institutions of higher education. The percentage of the population pursuing college studies has grown steadily since the end of World War II. Today, almost 70% of high school graduates attend some postsecondary institution. If the quality of students enrolled were all that mattered, we would undoubtedly regard our higher education system as a stunning success.

But quantity is certainly not all that matters. Educational *quality* is at least as important if not more so, and many observers have documented a serious decline in the quality of the instruction and programs at many of our colleges and universities. Part of that decline stems from the abandonment of the idea that a college education should be built around a sound core curriculum.

At one time, most college students received a broad, general education that pushed their frontiers of knowledge and thinning ability far past those who had only a high school education. Today,

[20] The National Association of Scholars press release, December 2002

> however, many students graduate from college with less knowledge about the world and fewer useful skills than high-schoolers of fifty years ago. Whether the subject is history, science, mathematics, English, or any other, both surveys and anecdotal evidence demonstrate that many recipients of college diplomas these days have a thin and patchy education, rather than the strong, general education that used to be the hallmark of college graduates.

Many colleges and universities have permitted the formerly rigorous, sequential curriculum that gave students a broad, general education to be replaced with a curriculum that does not guarantee students any particular learning experience. At many schools, students now determine the course of study largely on their own, as they choose among a vast array of classes. Often, they avoid courses that used to be regarded as the pillars of a college education. The problem of the vanishing core curriculum was recently noted by the Wingspread Group on Higher Education, which reported that:

> 26.2 percent of recent bachelor's degree recipients earned not a single undergraduate credit in history; 30.8 percent did not study mathematics of any kind; 39.6 percent earned no credits in either English or American literature; and 58.4 percent left college without any exposure to a foreign language. Much too frequently, American higher education now offers a smorgasbord of fanciful courses in a fragmented curriculum that accords as much credit for "Introduction to Tennis" and for courses in pop culture as it does for "Principles of English Composition," history or physics, thereby trivializing education – indeed, misleading students by implying that they are receiving the education they need for life when they are not.

Similarly, the authors of *Integrity in the College Curriculum*, a report done under the auspices of the Association of American Colleges, wrote:

> As for what passes as a college curriculum, almost anything goes. We have reached a point at which we are more confident about the length of a college education than its content and purpose.

Evidence that American college students are poorly served by the scattered, ill-defined curriculum that so many of them find in college is abundant. One continuing source of criticism is from the business community, which now has to spend large amounts on remedial programs to teach college graduates such elementary skills as clear writing. John Chambers, CEO of Cisco Systems, has written that:

> If universities don't reinvent their curriculum and how they deliver them [...] many students [...] will "go to school" online. Many big firms – Cisco, G.E., I.B.M., and AT&T – are starting on-line academies to train new employees and to constantly upgrade the skills of existing ones.

But poor preparation for the world of work is only a part of the damage done by a weak college curriculum. Equally harmful is the fact that students miss out on their best opportunity to partake of the life-enriching elements of our civilization – literature, philosophy, art, music. Of course, it is possible for people to get that exposure after college, but it is much less likely that they will do so. The college years are the ideal time for young adults to expand their intellectual horizons. As Professor David Mulroy of the University of Wisconsin-Milwaukee has written:

> The time is brief that students spend in college under pressure to read what their teachers assign. Why should we ever assign anything other than the best books of all time? In four years, even the best students will read only a small fraction of those, but they could at least get started. Why *require* them to watch sitcoms and movies?
>
> The college curriculum is the *design* for what an educated person should know. It should, to the greatest extent possible, ensure that students finely hone their basic skills and learn about the most important aspects of our heritage, our culture, and our world.
>
> Unfortunately, students are often tempted to take the path of least resistance in the quest for their college degree; many will choose to get the number of course credits they need by taking easy, entertaining courses if they are given the opportunity. **It is the educational equivalent of a steady diet of junk food. Schools that have abandoned the idea of a core curriculum are allowing their students to earn degrees without taking the important coursework that used to be the hallmark of a college education.**
>
> Many colleges and universities give the *appearance* that they provide a good general education because they require students to take a certain number of credits in several departments other than their major. "Distribution requirements" is the term for this approach, and, while it is preferable to giving students complete *carte blanche* to

direct their college studies, this cafeteria-style approach is a poor substitute for a true, carefully designed core curriculum.

Some schools' "distribution requirements" are stronger than others. The best are those that restrict students to choosing among a limited number of rigorous, broad-based courses that introduce them to basic areas of learning, e.g., "Principles of Economics," or "American History," or "Masterworks of Western Literature." It is possible for students to receive exposure to the critical areas of knowledge under the "distribution requirements" approach if it is structured so that students have no choice but to take a range of key foundational courses. Allowing students to have some choice is not necessarily objectionable, so long as the choices allowed are all consistent with the goal of giving the student a sound, general education.

But there are two inherent weaknesses in the "distribution requirements" approach. The first is a tendency for the administration gradually to allow more and more courses to be added, often in response to pleading by deans and influential professors that more of their courses be included on the list of those that will satisfy a distribution requirement. As a result, at many schools, the number of courses that satisfy general education requirements is mind boggling. At one major state university, for instance, students can choose from almost 200 different courses in meeting the distribution requirements. Very few of those courses offer the student knowledge that is integral to a strong general education. The great majority are narrow and trendy.

Once the distribution requirements begin to loosen, students can take an odd list of random, unconnected, and sometimes academically dubious courses that fail to give them a well-rounded education. The humanities requirement might be satisfied with a course on "Vampire Fiction." The history requirement might be satisfied with a course on "History of College Football." The science requirement might be satisfied with a course on "Personal Fitness." When such courses can supplant the fundamental courses, students fail to obtain any grounding in the major scholarly disciplines. They may earn a degree, but haven't received an education.

College students are usually neither well prepared nor motivated to select a rigorous, coherent course of study. A student who has not read any great books may have no idea why some books are great and why they merit study. As a student from a university with a strong core curriculum commented, **"They made me read the books I didn't know I wanted to read."** That statement shows precisely why a core curriculum is beneficial. It can make students read books they didn't know they wanted to read. It broadens their horizons in ways they could never imagine.

The second reason why the distribution requirement approach is flawed is that even an assortment of sound introductory courses – English 101, Philosophy 101, etc. – is not a good substitute for a series of courses designed to give students a broad educational foundation. Introductory departmental courses are usually designed to be the first step in specialization and do not necessarily give the kind of overview that all students should have...

Rather than compelling students to choose among an assortment of introductory departmental courses – or, worse, to choose among a vast array of departmental offerings – educational leaders should "determine the essentials of a liberal education and ... devise an integrated system of courses to provide them."

It is the responsibility of colleges and universities to structure a curriculum that will serve their students well for a lifetime.

Professors and university leaders will debate at great length precisely what courses should go into a school's core curriculum, but most would agree that it must ensure a full and broad educational experience for students. We believe that all students should derive from their college years the following experiences and attributes:

First, they should learn crucial habits of mind: inquiry, logical thinking, and critical analysis. Those aren't taught in any one class; rather, they are built up and refined over time as the student sees how great minds have wrestled with questions in many different fields of knowledge.

Second, they should become *literate* – proficient in their reading, writing, and speaking. Literacy is a vital and increasingly overlooked component of education that should not be regarded as the exclusive province of the English department.

Third, students should become familiar with quantitative reasoning. In a world filled with numbers and statistics, responsible citizenship calls for an understanding of the correct, and incorrect, uses of numerical data.

Fourth, they should have the perspective on human life that only history can give. People with a grasp of Western civilization, world history, and American history are much better able to see the complexity of uncertainty, and limitations inherent in the human condition. They understand the long struggle to create free and civilized societies. Knowing how we have gotten to our present situation is valuable in comprehending where society may, and can, go in the future.

Fifth, every culture has contributed to the rich repository of human experience. In an interconnected world, it is important to study cultures that may be very different from our own.

Sixth, students should have an understanding of the natural world and of the methods the sciences use to explore that world. They also need to appreciate what sorts of questions are susceptible of scientific inquiry and which are not.

Seventh, to prepare themselves to become citizens, they should study the American political system and principles articulated in the country's great founding documents.

Eighth, to prepare themselves to participate successfully in a dynamic economy, they should study economics and such basic principles as the law of supply and demand.

Ninth, they should learn something about art, music, and aesthetics. Besides adding greatly to the enjoyment of life, a study of the arts shows the importance of disciplined creativity.

Tenth, in an increasingly interdependent world, students should learn a *foreign language*.

Many colleges and universities seem to have forgotten that their purpose is to provide each student with an *education* – not just to process through as many paying bodies as they can.

College students need guidance from scholars in what they should learn in college. If they already knew what books and ideas were the most important, they wouldn't need to go to college.

The prevalent smorgasbord approach to the curriculum, allowing students to select almost any combination of courses, results in patchwork education that reflects youthful interests, but at the expense of life-long educational needs.[21]

It is for those who care about the future of our young people – and the future of our nation – to become forceful advocates for an education that gives students a true education that will equip them to lead fuller, richer lives after they have completed their college years, rather than simply be credentialed into a world of fat, fantasy – and fluff.

Truth always passes through three stages. First, there is **RIDICULE.** Then there is **OPPOSITION.** Finally, it is **SELF-EVIDENT** or so wrote Plato.

[21] Professor David Mulroy, University of Wisconsin-Milwaukee

We are drowning in information, while starving for knowledge.

May I suggest a life preserver?

Before summation, read a postscript from three great minds.
A thought from Descartes, 1637:

"Cogito ergo sum."[22]

Another from Albert Schweitzer:

> A new public opinion must be created privately and unobtrusively. The existing one is maintained by the press, by propaganda, by organization, and by financial and other influences which are at its disposal. This unnatural way of spreading ideas must be opposed by the natural one, which goes from man to man and relies solely on the truth of our thoughts and the hearer's receptiveness for new truth. Unarmed, and following the human spirit's primitive and natural fighting method, it must attack the other, which faces it, as Goliath faced David, in the mighty armor of the age.
>
> About the struggle which must ensue no historical analogy can tell us much. The past has, no doubt, seen the struggle of the free-thinking individual against the fettered spirit of a whole society, but the problem has never presented itself on the scale on which it does today, because the fettering of the collective spirit as it is fettered today by modern organizations, modern unreflectiveness, and modern popular passions, is a phenomenon without precedent in history.
>
> Will the man of today have strength to carry out what the spirit demands from him, and what the age would like to make impossible?
>
> In the over-organized societies which in a hundred ways have him in their power, he must somehow become once more an independent personality and so exert influence back upon them. They will use every means to keep him in that condition of impersonality which suits them. They fear personality because the spirit and the truth, which they would like to muzzle, find in it a means of expressing themselves. And their power is, unfortunately, as great as their fear.
>
> There is a tragic alliance between society as a whole and its economic conditions. With a grim relentlessness those conditions tend to ring up the man of today as a being without freedom, without self-collectedness, without independence, in short as a human being so full of deficiencies that he lacks the qualities of humanity. And they are the

[22] "I think therefore I am."

last things that we can change. Even if it should be granted us that the spirit should begin its work, we shall only slowly and incompletely gain power over these forces. There is, in fact, being demanded from the will that which our conditions of life refuse to allow.

And how heavy the tasks that the spirit has to take in hand! It has to create the power of understanding the truth that is really true where at present nothing is current but propagandist truth. It has to depose ignoble patriotism, and enthrone the noble kind of patriotism which aims at ends that are worthy of the whole of mankind, in circles where the hopeless issues of past and present political activities keep nationalist passions aglow even among those who in their hearts would fain be free from them. It has to get the fact that civilization is an interest of all men... It has to maintain our faith in the civilized State, even though our modern States, spiritually and economically ruined by the war, have no time to think about the tasks of civilization, and dare not devote their attention to anything but how to use every possible means, even those which undermine the conception of justice, to collect money with which to prolong their own existence. It has to unite us by giving us a single ideal of civilized men, and this in a world where one nation has robbed its neighbor of all faith in humanity, idealism, righteousness, reasonableness, and truthfulness, and all alike have come under the domination of powers which are plunging us ever deeper into barbarism. It has to get attention concentrated on civilization while the growing difficulty of making a living absorbs the masses more and more in material cares, and makes all other things seem to them to be mere shadows. It has to give us faith in the possibility of progress while the reaction of the economic on the spiritual becomes more pernicious every day and contributes to an ever growing demoralization. It has to provide us with reasons for hope at a time when not only secular and religious institutions and associations, but the men, too, who are looked upon as leaders, continually fail us, when artists and men of learning show themselves as supporters of barbarism, and notabilities who pass for thinkers, and behave outwardly as such, are revealed, when crises come, as being nothing more than writers and members of academies.

All these hindrances stand in the path of the will to civilization. A dull despair hovers about us. How well we now understand the men of the Greco-Roman decadence, who stood before events incapable of resistance, and, leaving the world to its fate, withdrew upon their inner selves! Like them, we are bewildered by our experience of life. Like them, we hear enticing voices which say to us that the one thing which can still make life tolerable is to live for the day. We must, we

> are told, renounce every wish to think or hope about anything beyond our own fate. We must find rest in resignation.
>
> The recognition that civilization is founded on some sort of theory of the universe, can be restored only through a spiritual awakening, and a will for ethical good in the mass of mankind, compels us to make clear to ourselves those difficulties in the way of a rebirth of civilization which ordinary reflection would overlook. But at the same time it raises us above all considerations of possibility or impossibility. If the ethical spirit provides a sufficient standing ground in the sphere of events for making civilization a reality, then we shall get back to civilization if we return to a suitable theory of the universe and the convictions to which this properly gives birth.[23]

And a third: in a short article, "Why Socialism", Albert Einstein wrote:

> I have now reached the point where I may indicate briefly what to me constitutes the essence of the crisis of our time. **It concerns the relationship of the individual to society**. The individual has become more conscious than ever of his dependence upon society. But he does not experience this dependence as a positive asset, as an organic tie, as a protective force, but rather as a threat to his natural rights, or even to his economic existence. Moreover, his position in society is such that the egotistical drives of his make-up are constantly being accentuated, while his social drives, which are by nature weaker, progressively deteriorate. All human beings, whatever their position in society, are suffering from this process of deterioration. Unknowingly prisoners of their own egotism, they feel insecure, lonely, and deprived of the naïve, simple, and unsophisticated enjoyment of life. Man can find meaning in life, short and perilous as it is, only through devoting himself to society.[24]

...And so **The Remnant**, first mentioned in Isaiah, proceeds!

---

[23] Albert Schweitzer, *The Philosophy of Civilization*, New York, The Macmillan Company, 1949

[24] Albert Einstein, "Why Socialism", *Monthly Review*, Vol. I, I, 1949, pp.9–15

FINIS

A great duel is underway in the world today. Its issue will determine the basic character and quality of human civilization on this planet for centuries to come. In our own country it has been at the core of the political and economic turmoil of the last eight decades.

I refer to the fateful duel between two conceptions of human existence, two ways of life, that may be summed up in the oversimplified formula: *individualism versus statism*.

The contest cannot be identified in terms of party labels or regions, because it cuts across political and geographical lines. I mean that it is not being fought out *between* nations, but *within* nations.

The United States is without doubt the outstanding example of individualism in practice, as well as the greatest champion of the principle, yet there are millions in our midst who yearn for the "planned society" under an all-powerful State.

The age-old struggle between authority and liberty seems to have come to a head. In country after country the principle of at least partial liberty is triumphing while here in America we continue to move toward statism.

> Everywhere, an answer is being sought to the riddle whether the people own The State or The State owns the people; whether the fullest dignity of man or the glory and power of The State is the paramount purpose of existence.

The clichés of American tradition are as good an indication as any of the essence of individualism. All men are created free and equal. Life, liberty, the pursuit of happiness. Government of the people, by the people, and for the people. The centralized, dictated nations use some of these words, but in a sense so remote from ours that there is not even a point of contact. When they speak of equality, for instance, they really mean uniformity, sameness – the equality of men in an army accepting the identical discipline, or of men in prison subjected to the identical regulations.

For the individualist, by contrast, equality means identical freedom to be different, to make of his or her life and abilities such use as he or she deems best. He is not a cog in a machine, but a self-sufficient machine in himself. The primary assumption is that the individual has inherited God-given rights which not even society can take away. In a time of supreme crisis, such as war, one may voluntarily suspend some of those rights, but even then one surrenders as little as possible and remains vigilant to restore those rights as soon as the crisis is ended.

Let me venture a prediction which, I hope, may also strike the reader as a timely warning. If recent tendencies toward state domination of business in our nation should go unchecked much longer, we must expect to see business moving in on government. The process is already underway in our country.

If the rewards of business risks are to be limited almost to the vanishing point, while the risks and losses remain as great as ever, why continue at all? In that case why not allow and even encourage government to take the headaches along with the profits? If bureaucracy is permitted to rule the roost, will not the great executives and administrators be tempted to take over the bureaucracy as the only outlet for superior organizing and business talent? They need only to adjust themselves – as so many in collectivized societies have done – to hoarding power instead of making money to become perfect bureaucrats themselves.

The very thing feared – concentration of both political and economic authority in the same hands – is being achieved under beguilingly "progressive" labels.

In building up the State we are playing with dynamite. Statism is more menacing today then ever in the past because modern technology has equipped government with mechanical means for enforcing its arbitrary will that absolutist tyrannies in the past did not dream of. What is more, by control of radio, printing presses, schools, television, can it also hold the minds of its population in subjection?

We have urgent cause to hold tight to the most basic idea in American political philosophy and tradition – the idea that government is a tool of the people, never the other way around. In our economic life government must be kept to its role as an arbitrator, not as a competitor or dictator.

The State, of course, denies free will of the individual. All will is monopolized by the government. If we Americans are to remain free, we must practice that man is a worthy object in himself and not merely an infinitesimal and contemptible cog in a great machine; that he has a conscience to which he must be true and a soul to be saved.

The duel between Individualism and Statism is the most

decisive fact in this period. America indubitably belongs on the side of Individualism. We must not lose by default.

The conflict affects every aspect of our life: family vs. government; private vs. communal property; free vs. fair in speech, employment, trade; free choice as consumers vs. government protection of ourselves from ourselves.

The outcome is by no means certain: once government's grasp has extended as far as it has, it is not easily loosened.

The key issue in the early 2000s is whether we shall be able to do so, and thereby reinvigorate the human freedom and economic freedom that together have made the U.S. a magnet for the poor and oppressed peoples of the world – or whether we shall succumb to creeping collectivism and become a controlled welfarist society.

So here we are. We, in too many cases, have become a nation of abdicators – abdicating the education of our children to an army of social reformers; abdicating the incredible productivity of the free market to redistributionist zealots; abdicating our hopes for old age to a computer that spits out government checks worth less and less in real dollars with each passing decade. Weary of vigilance, we are abdicating our very right to govern. And thus we leave a terrible vacuum in which government grows and grows and grows.

Unless we reverse ourselves – unless we eliminate that vacuum – we will lose everything. Do we have the guts to put our own government in its place?

A Magnificent Challenge

Decades ago an old friend, Benjamin Rogge, wrote, and I now adjust to fit:

> **The question before us is this: Has the [American Communications Network – The Brian Bex Report, Inc. –] in its [four decades] succeeded in its mission? Most [individuals] on such occasions are capable of supplying only one answer to such a question. I intend to give you [three] answers to this question. They are in order:** Yes; [I don't know; and absolutely!]
>
> **The reason I can give you [three answers to this] … question is that the phrase** "succeeded in its mission" **is capable of at least [three] meaningful interpretations, each calling for its own answer.**

One possible interpretation is that the mission of any organization at first ... is quite simply to survive. That [ACN] has survived is testified to [by not only the writing of this document, but your reading the same.] Nor should any of us think lightly of this accomplishment. Given the general, social, and economic climate [today] the survival chances of any organization committed to individual [liberty] and limited government could well be described as two in number: slim and none.

While most organizations have their "beginning" with some type of background, the organization in question began with no "background" as merely an idea. It has in fact not only survived, but has grown and prospered.

[The corporate motto – "Eagles don't flock – you have to find them one at a time" **– has definitely been implemented by the founder and through boundless effort, others of like philosophy and character have in fact been found (The Remnant).] ...survival is not as "mere" as you might think. [One should] never underestimate the significance of the simple fact of the continuing existence of [the]** island of sanity **in what seems an increasingly insane world. Whether this sanity can eventually turn the battle is still moot [and I will touch on that later], but its simple existence is a very present help in time of trouble.**

I am reminded of Tolstoy's description of the role of the Russian commander, Prince Bagration, in the battle of Schon Grabern. Although himself in doubt of the outcome and aware of how little he really knew of the battle's progress, the prince stood serene and confident in the view of all, answering each report of the action, whether encouraging or discouraging, with a ... "Very good!" – as though even the local defeats were part of an overall pattern of events that foretold ultimate victory ... **As with the soldiers [in Tolstoy's battle], we grow more cheerful in the presence of [those with whom we are associated] and, more anxious to display our own limited courage. Believe me, this is something, even though the battle itself seems at times to be already lost,** as it may well be, **[we have here] the island of sanity to which we repair for warmth and comfort, which may still be counted a great and significant success...**

We [now turn] to a [second] possible interpretation of success as it relates to [this work]. Has [The Brian Bex Report, Inc.] succeeded in its mission in the sense of being a part of

> **[the] action that promises to actually turn the tide of battle in the direction of [individual] freedom? My answer to this, [while certainly it is something to be determined by history, my best guess is** "I just don't know."]
>
> **I offer this not as a criticism of [our work,] but as what seems to me the only realistic appraisal of where the current of events is tending in this [country]. The situation in this [nation] as it relates to [individual freedom] is almost certain to become worse before, and if, it ever becomes any better. Why must I adopt this [potentially] defeatist line...?**[1]

In the preface to the second edition of his great work, *Capitalism, Socialism, and Democracy*, **a work in which he sees the current of events moving the Western world from capitalism to socialism, Joseph Schumpeter answers those who have charged him with defeatism as follows:**

> This finally leads to the charge of defeatism, I deny entirely that this term is applicable to a piece of analysis. Defeatism denotes a certain psychic state that has meaning only in reference to action. The facts in themselves and inferences from them can never be defeatist, or the opposite, whatever that might be. The report that a given ship is sinking is not defeatist. Only the spirit in which this report is received can be defeatist: the crew can sit down and drink, but it can also rush to the pumps. If the men merely deny the report, though it may be carefully substantiated, then they are escapists.
>
> Frank presentation of ominous facts was never more necessary than it is today because we seem to have developed escapism into a system of thought. This is my motive as it is my apology for writing the new chapter. The facts and inferences there presented are certainly not pleasant or comfortable, but they are not defeatist. Defeatist is he who, while giving lip service to Christianity, and all the other values of our civilization yet refuses to rise to their defense – no matter whether he accepts their defeat as a foregone conclusion or deludes himself with futile hopes against hope. For this is one of those situations in which optimism is nothing but a form of defection.[2]

My none-too-original analysis of the trend of events tends to bring me into agreement with [Schumpeter and the many

[1] Paraphrase of Rogge, *Can Capitalism Survive?*

[2] Joseph Schumpeter, *Capitalism, Socialism and Democracy*, New York, Harper, 1950

others,] friends and foes of capitalism alike, who believe that the odds are very much against the survival of [classical] capitalism in the decades immediately ahead of us. [Moreover, believing as we all do that economic freedom is a necessary condition for the continued existence of the so-called non-economic freedoms, we must be equally questioning the survival chances of the truly liberal society, in the traditional sense of that term.]

This is not the time or the place for a detailed [and hopefully convincing] presentation of the analysis that leads me to these conclusions ... I offer only the following...:

Nowhere is this denial of reason of rational choice more clearly revealed than in the approach of the more demented environmentalists ... One of the best critiques of this approach I know [was an article by one Larry Ruff written when American Communications Network was founded called "The Economic Common Sense of Pollution". The author wrote in part:]

> Those who call for immediate action and damn the cost, merely because the spiny starfish and the furry crab population are shrinking are putting an infinite marginal value on these creatures. This strikes a disinterested observer as an over-estimate."

But the voice of reason is rarely raised and is shouted down by the new romantics (the new barbarians) as soon as it is raised.

Lady Chatterley's lover, once a hero of the young and the teachers of English literature for his sexual acrobatics, is now their hero as the man who said, "It's a shame what's been done to people these last hundred years: men turned into nothing but labor insects and all their manhood taken away... I'd wipe the machines off the face of the earth and end the industrial epic absolutely like a black mistake." [A quote from the television soap, *The Young and the Restless* – or was it said on Oprah?]

It is symptomatic of the times that a call like this for over 90% of those now living in the Western world to be wiped out (for such would be the effect of such a proposal) is hailed as a voice of humanitarianism and love, while those who dare to offer even gentle [ideas of industrial gain] are derided as gross and disgusting materialists.

So much for the treason of the intellectuals, a treason that a few forewarned us of and is now largely a fact. If [ACN] is to be judged by its success in swinging the intellectual vote, then it has failed, indeed. [But the intellectual vote was really never our mission.]

What of the businessman? Surely [American Communications Network – The Brian Bex Report, Inc.,] has been able to make secure for freedom this section of the American Public! At this point, it is difficult to know whether to laugh or cry. **[Remember Joseph Schumpeter?] There is not one piece of lunacy put on paper by some academic scribbler or spoken by some public demagogue that is not to be found in at least one, if not more, of the published statements of the self-designated spokesmen for the business community. For reasons I don't have time to develop here, it is also clear that the larger the firm, the more certain is its leader's commitment, or at least lip service, to the philosophy of statism. Study of the changing character of the business firms that have contributed to [this organization] over [three and one-half decades shows: In the beginning, most contributors came from organizations where ownership and management were synonymous. As a matter of fact, many of those in positions of power in those contributing businesses were in fact the founders of those businesses. But during the life of ACN up to the present time, the entrepreneurial spirit has to a large degree given way to the professional manager non-spirit. Organizations have been sold, been merged, or in fact gone out of business as the founder either retires or reaches toward the stars. The new are (there are exceptions to this rule) primarily risk-aversive. Irving Krystol in the *Wall Street Journal* described many moons ago the actual attitude of those in pin-striped suits at private clubs for lunch – they call themselves conservatives – they pay lip service to the free enterprise system, as well as pay lip service to the ideology that government is too big, but:]**

> [Too many American business people equate conservative with a desperate, defensive commitment to the status quo, not with staking a claim on the world's future. Too many of us in business today are risk-aversive, in both temperament and policy. And *in an era of ideological warfare, the risk-aversive most emphatically do not inherit the earth.]*

[The tragedy is that the large percentage of American

businessmen operating in positions of power and influence today have never operated within a free enterprise system.] Yes, even the businessman is more likely to be a part of the problem than a part of the solution, and [ACN's] failure, so judged, could not be more obvious or complete. But, of course, contrary to the popular impression, there is no reason to expect the businessman to be more committed to the system of economic freedom than anyone else. Not only is he not the greatest beneficiary of that system – he is not even the *principal* **beneficiary. Again,** contrary to popular impression, it is the ["average working American,"] the member of the masses, [not the leisure class,] who far from being the exploited victim of capitalism, is precisely its principal beneficiary. **Under all other arrangements, those possessed of intelligence, high energy, and a strong desire to achieve (i.e., precisely those who tend to become the entrepreneurs, the businessmen under capitalism, [the founders]) get ahead by using their positions in the political, or caste or religious hierarchy to exploit the masses. Only under capitalism can the stronger get ahead only by serving the weaker – and the weaker wish to be served...!**

The strong tend to survive and prosper under any system, and strength does not necessarily carry with it a sophisticated understanding of systems. The American businessman has probably been on balance (wittingly or unwittingly) the most important single force working against the survival of the capitalist system. [**Oh sure, there are a few crusty, cantankerous characters from the business world (still left) who still think well of unfettered capitalism and ill of all forms and degrees of socialism and some of the best of them support this crusade, but they are no more typical of the community of American businessmen than Thomas Jefferson was typical of the community of American politicians, two plus centuries ago.**]

This brings us to another of the straws in the wind. If further evidence of where we seem to be headed is needed, I offer you [any administration in Washington D.C. for the past eight decades: These administrations of the past have been] manned by a number of intelligent, capable public servants of roughly [American, or sometimes in fact] conservative [outlook, and headed by an intelligent, enormously well-meaning man of varying political instincts] ... Yet I am prepared to wager that history will reveal that [the accumulated effect of the last eighty years' administration in

Washington – i.e., the modern times –] did more to move this country away from freedom and toward socialism and authoritarianism than [any single element in history. People are interested in reducing government only so long as the services and privileges of government cut are those affecting someone else, not themselves.]

In other words, whenever we look to the intellectuals, to the businessmen, the political leaders, we find the score to be: Lions – 100... [Remnants] – 0. If [ACN – The Brian Bex Report, Inc.'s] mission has been to win such games in the here and now, then it is indeed a 100-carat failure...

Am I predicting that we are inevitably headed for a great, all-encompassing crisis sometime in the next few decades? I am not. In the first place, nothing is inevitable. What has happened has happened because of decisions made by human beings ... I am simply saying that if things continue to go as they have been going, we are going to move further and further away from reasonable prosperity and substantial freedom, and [travel] toward stagnation and authoritarianism...

[Nor do I believe that our world as we have known it will end with a bang; it is far more likely to end with a whimper. I believe our situation today is very similar to that in Great Britain a number of decades ago – as one British journalist wrote, "Britain is now sinking slowly into the sea, giggling as she goes down." **Or as I have put it on other occasions,** America's fate may be that of the worker in the lanolin factory, who fell into a tub of lanolin and softened to death.]

[But] let us be frank with each other. [I do not really know the precise shape of things to come – I could be wrong on the precise form and timing of our fate, nor should we ever underestimate the enormous survival strength of a once largely-free and even now partly-free economy and society. **In the words of Adam Smith, such a society viewed as patient may well survive not only its disease,** "but the absurd prescriptions of the doctor as well." **At the same time, I am absolutely convinced that with Archie the Cockroach, "there is more reason to be optimistic about the past than about the future...** if we look for success by traditional methods and thoughts." **(More on that later.) If any of you have seen ACN – The Brian Bex Report, Inc.'s, mission as that of winning now and winning big, then you have no choice but to label it a failure. But as I have communicated many times I have always believed that our mission is something**

quite different from (and quite superior to) that of winning tomorrow's election, or next week's TV popularity poll. I am to this day little interested in triumphs as spectacular and as short-lived as the go-cart, the hula-hoop, or video games or consumer electronics.]

[I have never] promise[d] us a win in the near future. [**On many occasions my] unmitigated gall [has surfaced] to tell [you] that we still don't even fully understand the game or how to recognize a win when we see one. [I have on many occasions stated that if you're looking for a guarantee, help someone else. The total mission of ACN – The Brian Bex Report, Inc., is what might be called** a magnificent challenge.] ... **a magnificent challenge where the odds-makers have installed the Lions as a [three touchdowns] favorite ... [We have been told:]** "It is the effort, not the outcome, that counts in the life of human beings."

Cervantes' "The road is better than the inn", should serve to remind aspiring men that there isn't any inn for them, but only the road, now and forever. It is the effort along the trail that matters."

And now the final interpretation of the phrase "succeeded in its mission." [The real question, the real purpose, the real evaluation of mission:] Does [the effort, in all its forms, in all its varieties,] induce in others what Aristotle once termed "activity of soul?" **[Does the effort get through to some and motivate others?] It is to this question that the final, unqualified and** significant "yes" **can be given. Throughout this country, throughout the world, there is** "activity of soul" **underway, that would never have been undertaken but for the work and the inspiration of [people like you through this organization.]**[3]

A good example rests within the attitudes of American youth. Many have turned 180° from the ideals that prevailed in the late 1960s and early 1970s – from anti-capitalist to pro-capitalist, anti-work to pro-work, anti-business to pro-business, anti-future to pro-future. They are beginning to actually care. Activity of soul is surely underway. As proof of same read the following singular example from a graduate student enrolled in current Remnant Trust class at Indiana University:

[3] Paraphrase of Rogge, *Can Capitalism Survive?* pp.307–318

Recently I have had the privilege of visiting the headquarters of The Remnant Trust with Professor Bex. I am excited by the mission that this organization has taken in providing a hands-on exposure to original writings and translations of the classical ideals in an effort to raise consciousness and elevate educational standards. I have discussed with Professor Bex possibilities of involving myself in the organization. With the permission of the SPEA department, I would like to pursue this in the form of an internship beginning next semester.

After completing my undergraduate studies in political science and now pursuing a concentration in policy analysis at the graduate level, I am constantly being presented with the ever-increasing problems of society. It is my belief that many, if not all of these problems could be lessened and eventually eliminated through the process of education – teaching others how to think for themselves. Unfortunately, in today's academic world, educating seems to have become synonymous with certifying. Many university administrators and professors are lowering their academic standards and cutting core curriculum in an effort to make the obtainment of a college degree accessible to more individuals. Their attempts are a success – more individuals are obtaining college degrees; however, very few of these students could profess to be truly obtaining a college education.

Working within The Remnant Trust, I would be provided with a unique opportunity to help remedy this situation in a way that no other organization in the country provides. The Remnant Trust looks to reinstall within the academic arenas those conversations on the principles and ideals of man and thinking that have weathered the ages by making available original texts – not the textbook versions, not edited or updated accounts – but original documents and original translations. I would be a part of a process of lighting a fire – inspiring students and educators with a direct provision of a hands-on exposure to history. They can see, smell, and touch the compilations of the original ideas that continue to inspire the quest for truth, justice, liberty and education in their truest sense.

The benefits that this experience could provide are numerous. It is rare when an opportunity comes available that would allow an individual the ability to pursue something that they are excited and passionate about and benefit others in the process – yet this is what I am presented with. I am presented with the opportunity of continuing my exposure to these classic ideas, and focusing my passion and knowledge in a practical application of helping to inspire and educate others.

As a student of a university, I believe I can provide a particular asset with my perspective and familiarity of present academic settings. I can easily relate to the "customers" that this organization targets and provide insight on what situations might motivate them to take advantage of this unique product. This experience might even afford me the opportunity to expand the scope of their influence by presenting to administrators and faculty of various academic institutions the benefit that can result from capitalizing on the loan of The Remnant Trust's acquisitions.

As a student and representative of the SPEA program of IUPUI, I believe that being provided with the opportunity to pursue an internship with The Remnant Trust offers an advantage to all involved. If granted, I would be taking my continuing education that this university is providing me and combining it with a one-of-a-kind opportunity to encourage a higher learning and continuing education for others.

I look forward to hearing your thoughts on the possibility of this internship opportunity. Feel free to contact me at any time, and if desired, I would look forward to meeting with you at your earliest convenience to discuss the matter personally.[4]

Sincerely,
Amy Weismiller

The greater part ... is totally unknown as yet to any of us ... and will come to light only in the decades ... ahead, and much of it will be done by people who will never have heard of this [organization,] and will have no awareness that the activity of soul **in which they are involved is the last link in a long chain that goes back to something that was started by this [organization three and one-half decades ago. We are heirs of a tremendous heritage:** Are we worthy? **Some heirs are not. The youth of America are receptive to the point of duty – an opportunity is now afforded not previously offered. If we fail to accept this** "magnificent challenge" **we fail not only ourselves but generations yet unknown, in fact we fail the cause of all mankind.]**

[It seems to me most relevant that] I close with [two pieces of verse] that seem to me to capture what I have been trying to say. [This first] is ... a remarkable poem by [one]

[4] For additional effectiveness measurement see appendix.

W.H. Auden [written in the latter part of 1939,] at a dark moment in the history of the Western world, [the second is one written by a former editor of *Fortune Magazine*, Russell Davenport. They both spell out clearly the mission of American Communications Network – The Brian Bex Report, Inc., and now The Remnant Trust, Inc. Only you and history will decide whether that mission is meritful of success.]

Defenseless under the night
Our world in stupor lies;
Yet, dotted everywhere,
Ironic points of light
Flash out wherever the Just
Exchange their messages:
May I, composed like them
Of Aros and of dust,
Beleaguered by the same
Negation and despair,
Show an affirming flame.[5]

A Prayer For America's Tomorrow[6]

Spirit of Man: Founder of Liberty:
Great Light for which Democracy exists!
America is the land that You have loved:
On us the burden falls to lead the nations
Out of this frightful wilderness of steel:
On Us depends the course of that which is
To come hereafter – whether freedom was
A stolen dream from Heaven, or is the truth
On which to found the future of mankind.
Brother of all races and all creeds!
If there is anything we can do,
Now let us do it! If there is any price
That will repurchase from the hungry past
The honor of our dead, let us pay it now!
If, by resolution, we who live
Can reinspire the faint and mongled truths
Of human liberty, let us henceforth

[5] Paraphrase of Rogge; W.H. Auden, "September 1, 1939", *Another Time*, Random House, London, 1940, cited in Rogge, *Can Capitalism Survive?* p.319
[6] Russell Davenport, "A Prayer for America's Tomorrow"

Be as resolved and desperate in our course
As the immense and undeflected stars
That travel down the channels of Your Will!
And if, within the ancient universe,
There yet remains one spark of charity,
Brother, give us that spark, that by its light
We may reread the chapter of our time,
And from this flickering chronicle relearn
The truths that might have been self-evident.

"If I have seen farther, it is by standing on the shoulders of giants," said Fulbert of Chartres. To overthrow a giant, it is necessary either to be a giant oneself, or else a David favored of the Lord; and few of us are either. Therefore we yield to the seers – the prophets and poets and philosophers of the Great Tradition – as authorities, because without their guidance we would wander hungry in a dark wood. Government is not made in virtue of natural rights, which may and do exist in total independence of it; and exist in much greater clearness, and in a much greater degree of abstract perfection. Government, by perceiving a right to everything, wants everything and Americans being so enamored of equality seemingly would rather be equal in slavery than unequal in freedom.

The idea we have to spread is very easy to understand – *it is simply that government, as it is today, is an unnecessary evil and that freedom is the best and most practical way of life.*

For it is not inevitable **that we submit ourselves to a social life-in-death of boring uniformity and equality**. It is not inevitable **that we indulge all our appetites to fatigued satiety**. It is not inevitable **that we reduce our schooling to the lowest common denominator**. It is not inevitable **that obsession with creature-comforts should sweep away belief in a transcendent order**.

Yet the sands run swiftly through the waist of Father Time's hour-glass. Efforts like ours alone will not redeem us: for the most part, they will fall upon deaf ears. **If we are to give the lie to those wicked things written on the sky, there must appear among us men and women endowed with the sort of imaginative power that transforms the spirit of an age. Conceivably that power may come somehow from without – as it seems to have come to the poetic imagination of Albert Einstein: more probably it shall come from within. Adversity may strengthen**

character, grim circumstances may quicken wits. Providence operates ordinarily through human agents, whose thoughts and actions may reverse the whole drift of their times.

Let us seek our redemption from outside the ranks of the Knowledge Class. Let us remember that even a common soldier, a child or a girl at the door of an inn may change the face of fortune. **Our personal and our public future may be determined by the sort of imagination that this effort reflects**. *Think and act, for ideas rule your future.* Nothing is inevitable save physical death and taxes.

It is not too late to write some good things in the sky.
As we plant trees the shade under which we will never sit.

APPENDIX I

Message from the Publisher

Jonathan Swift wrote in *Gulliver's Travels* about three centuries ago (1726):

> The reader may be disposed to wonder how I could prevail on myself to give so free a representation of my own species among a race of mortals who are already too apt to conceive the vilest opinion of humankind from that entire congruity betwixt me and their Yahoos. But I must freely confess that the many virtues of those excellent quadrupeds, placed in opposite view to human corruptions, had so far opened my eyes and enlarged my understanding that I began to view the actions and passions of man in a very different light, and to think the honor of my own kind not worth managing; which, besides, it was impossible for me to do before a person of so acute a judgment as my master, who daily convinced me of a thousand faults in myself, whereof I had the least perception before, and which among us would never be numbered even among human infirmities. I had likewise learned from his example an utter detestation of all falsehood or disguise; the truth appeared so amiable to me that I determined upon sacrificing everything to it.[1]

Now, if you can't understand that, continue in simpler language:

The Paradox of Our Time

> The paradox of our time in history is that we have taller buildings, but shorter tempers; wider freeways, but narrower viewpoints; we spend more, but have less; we buy more, but enjoy it less.
>
> We have bigger houses and smaller families; more conveniences, but less time; we have more degrees, but less sense; more knowledge, but less judgment; more experts, but more problems; more medicine, but less wellness.

[1] Jonathan Swift, *Gulliver's Travels*, London, Puffin, 1997

We drink too much, smoke too much, spend too recklessly, laugh too little, drive too fast, get angry too quickly, stay up too late, get up too tired, read too seldom, watch TV too much, and pray too seldom.

We have multiplied our possessions, but reduced our values. We talk too much, love too seldom, and hate too often. We've learned how to make a living, but not a life; we've added years to life, not life to years.

We've been all the way to the moon and back, but have trouble crossing the street to meet the new neighbor. We've conquered outer space, but not inner space; we've done larger things, but not better things.

We've cleaned up the air, but polluted the soul; we've split the atom, but not our prejudice.

We write more, but learn less; we plan more, but accomplish less. We've learned to rush, but not to wait; we have higher incomes, but lower morals; we have more food, but less appeasement; we build more computers to hold more information to produce more copies than ever, but have less communication; we've become long on quantity, but short on quality.

These are the times of fast foods and slow digestion; tall men, and short character; steep profits, and shallow relationships. These are the times of world peace, but domestic warfare; more leisure, but less fun; more kinds of food, but less nutrition.

These are days of two incomes, but more divorce; of fancier houses, but broken homes. These are days of quick trips, disposable diapers, throw away morality, one-night stands, overweight bodies, and pills that do everything from cheer to quiet to kill.

Ours is a time when there is much in the show window and little in the stockroom; a time when technology has brought these ramblings to you, and a time when you can choose either to make a difference, or to just hit "Delete"...[2]

Why not find out about... then join... ***The Remnant Trust***? Great ideas belong to everyone... **share them**... put some substance in your brain.

[2] Dr. Bob Moorehead, "The Paradox of Age", *Words Aptly Spoken*, Overlake Christian Press, Kirkland, W.A., 1995

Acknowledgement

For these reasons and others it appears to me that Isaiah's job was not only excellent but also extremely interesting; and especially so at the present time when few are doing it. If I were young and had the notion of embarking on a career, I would certainly take up this freedom as vocation business; therefore, I have no hesitation about recommending it as a career for anyone with interest. It offers an open field, with little competition; our civilization so completely neglects and disallows **The Remnant** that anyone going in with focus and energy might pretty well count on success.

What a refuge, what a marvelous retreat, at certain periods, to live with the great thinkers and their works – choosing them as we will!

A six-word formula guaranteeing success: **Find a need and fill it.**

Do not reproach me with being a prophet of the past, thereby enervating your activities. The sentiment I describe is not very infectious and imperils nothing. Be reassured; there will always be enough to live in the present, to build there, firmly or not, to invade the future, and proclaim its magnificence for good or for evil. So long as the masses are taking up the tabernacle of the MTV, Madonna, Britney and Paris, their images, and following the star of their words, we will have no lack of prophets to point the way that leadeth to the "more abundant life"; and hence a few of those who feel the prophetic magnetic pull might do better to apply themselves to serving **The Remnant...** merely a suggestion.

For only by understanding the past can man constructively build the future – only by understanding from whence we came can we progressively proceed where we will.

A sincere **thank you** to Amy Weismiller for her eternal patience throughout the entire process of research, editing and creation. There are some cases that cannot be overdone by language and this is one of those cases.

When there is no wind... row!

Brian Bex

APPENDIX II

1886 Campaign, Henry George & Abram S. Hewitt for Mayor of New York City

A Conversation

It reminds me of an old fable I used to read. There was a terrible pestilence among the animals once upon a time. The lion made proclamation and called all the beasts together. They were suffering for their sins, he said, and ought to investigate who it was that provoked the wrath of Heaven, and then offer him up as a sacrifice. And so all the animals met. They elected the fox as chairman. The lion said he was a great sinner; that he had eaten many flocks of sheep, and even once eaten a shepherd. The fox said to the lion that the sheep ought to feel complimented to be eaten by his majesty, and as for the shepherd, it served him right, "for evidently," went on the fox, "he had been throwing stones at your majesty." And then the wolf and the hyena and the tiger and so on confessed their several sins, until it came to the fox, who said he had eaten a great many chickens, but they crowed so in the morning that they disturbed him very much. Lastly came the donkey, who said that as he was carrying a load of hay to the market for his master he turned around and took a mouthful. "Wicked monster," cried the fox. "But I was hungry," continued the ass; "he had forgotten to give me my breakfast." "That makes no difference," cried the fox, and it was unanimously decided that it was the sin of the ass that brought the pestilence, and all the animals fell on him and tore him to pieces by way of sacrifice...

"Thou shalt earn thy bread by the sweat of thy brow?" Nature gives to man nothing. Without work nothing can be produced. Work is the producer of all wealth...

An English writer has divided all men into three classes – working-men, beggar-men, and thieves – and this is correct. There are only three ways of getting the product of labor – by working for it, by having it given to you, and by stealing it...

The experience of the world has shown that social improvement, by which I mean the physical, mental, and moral growth of the mass of mankind, is only achieved by slow and patient steps. Evils are not

> corrected until they are acknowledged to be evils by the majority, and it is the chief merit of government by the majority that the remedy for grievances is prompt and effective. While the present century has witnessed a rapid improvement in society, no one denies that great evils remain to be overcome. In the discussion of the rights of man the pretence that vested rights may arrest the just claims of society has received a fatal blow. Privilege can no longer be pleaded successfully against the demands of progress. In this day it only remains for the majority to formulate remedies for admitted wrong and put them into operation through the machinery of legislation. But when one class in the community undertakes to usurp the functions of the majority, a direct attack is made upon social order, which is the foundation of all progress and prosperity…
>
> All means of throwing greater light upon the situation, so that the law, which is the parent of progress, may be wisely amended, should be encouraged…
>
> We do not need to be told that national prosperity and liberty rest upon the security of property. There is no liberty where there is no property, and the man who attacks the sacred foundations of private property attacks the liberty of the citizen, the freedom of the country, and the Constitution of the United States. He is untrue to the memories of the patriots who founded this Government by untold sacrifices. He is recreant to the spirit that is so nobly typified by that magnificent statue which stands bearing the torch of liberty – the hope of the future, the glory of the past…

Again Mr. George:

> All such talk in a campaign reminds me of a story, that I used to read when I was a boy, in an old English classic – "***Addison's Spectator***." A young Frenchwoman married an old man. Her husband lay very sick; a number of friends were in the sick-room. She threw herself down on her knees, sobbing and crying, "Oh, Death! Death! Death! Come and take me, but spare my dear husband." All of a sudden there came a rap at the door, and the door flew open, and there stood Death. "Who called?" said Death. The lady covered herself up, saying, "The gentleman in the next room."…

In support of his position Mr. George presents, in "**Progress and Poverty**," a complete examination of the entire subject in all its bearings. That book has excited more attention and comment over the world than any other American book, and yet has called forth no reply.

It is simply unanswerable. Every step in the argument is proved, and the conclusion is inevitable. The principles of the work were introduced into the politics of this country at the late election; and now, as with all principles founded in truth, they cannot be stamped out, nor can their advocates be silenced, for "truth is tough, and will not break like a bubble at a touch."

A Conversation with Thomas Paine and Ayn Rand

It has all been said before and since, but never better: Let's listen in:

> Perhaps the sentiments contained in the following pages are not yet sufficiently fashionable to procure them general favor; a long habit of not thinking a thing wrong, gives it a superficial appearance of being right, and raises at first a formidable outcry in defense of custom. But the tumult soon subsides. **Time makes more converts than reason.**
>
> In the following sheets, the author has studiously avoided every thing which is personal among ourselves. Compliments as well as censure to individuals make no part thereof. The wise and the worthy need not the triumph of a pamphlet; and those whose sentiments are injudicious or unfriendly will cease of themselves, unless too much pain is bestowed upon their conversions.
>
> The cause of America is in a great measure the cause of all mankind. Many circumstances have, and will arise, which are not local, but universal, and through which the principles of all lovers of mankind are affected, and in the event of which their affections are interested...
>
> Some writers have so confounded society with government, as to leave little or no distinction between them; whereas they are not only different, but have different origins. Society is produced by our wants and government by our wickedness; the former promotes our happiness positively by uniting our affections, the latter negatively by restraining our vices. The other creates distinctions. The first is a patron, the last a punisher.
>
> **Society in every state is a blessing, but government, even in its best state, is but a necessary evil; in its worst state an intolerable one: for when we suffer, or are exposed to the same miseries by a government, which we might expect in a country without government, our calamity is heightened by reflecting that we furnish the means by which we suffer.** Government, like dress, is the badge of lost innocence; the palaces of kings are built upon the ruins of the bowers of paradise. For were the

impulses of conscience clear, uniform and irresistibly obeyed, man would need no other law-giver; but that not being the case, he finds it necessary to surrender up a part of his property to furnish means for the protection of the rest; and this he is induced to do by the same prudence which in every other case advises him, out of two evils to choose the least. Wherefore, security being the true design and end of government, it unanswerably follows that whatever form thereof appears most likely to ensure it to us, with the least expense and greatest benefit, is preferable to all others.

Here then is the origin and rise of government; namely, a mode rendered necessary by the inability of moral virtue to govern the world; here too is the design and end of government, viz. freedom and security. And however our eyes may be dazzled with show, or our ears deceived by sound; however prejudice may warp our wills, or interest darken our understanding, the simple voice of nature and reason will say, 'tis right…

As parents, we can have no joy, knowing that this government is not sufficiently lasting to insure any thing which we may bequeath to posterity. And by a plain method of argument, as we are running the next generation into debt, we ought to do the work of it, otherwise we use them meanly and pitifully. In order to discover the line of our duty rightly, we should take our children in our hand, and fix our station a few years farther into life; that imminence will present a prospect which a few present fears and prejudices conceal from our sight…

Interested men, who are not to be trusted, weak men who cannot see, prejudiced men who will not see, and a certain set of moderate men who think better of the world than it deserves; and this last class, by an ill-judged deliberation, will be the cause of more calamities to this continent than all the other three…

When William the Conqueror subdued England, he gave them law at the point of the sword; and, until we consent that the seat of government in America be legally and authoritatively occupied, we shall be in danger of having it filled by some fortunate ruffian, who may treat us in the same manner, and then, where will be our freedom? where our property? …

The present state of America is truly alarming to every man who is capable of reflection. Without law, without government, without any other mode of power than what is founded on, and granted by, courtesy. Held together by an unexampled occurrence of sentiment, which is nevertheless subject to change, and which every secret enemy is endeavoring to dissolve. **Our present condition is, legislation without law; wisdom without a plan; a constitution without a name; and, what is strangely astonishing, perfect independence contending for dependence. The instance is without a precedent, the case never existed before, and who can tell what may be the event? The property of no man is secure in the present unbraced system of things.** The mind of the multitude is left at random, and seeing no fixed object before them, they pursue such as fancy or opinion presents. **Nothing is criminal; there is no such thing as treason; wherefore, every one thinks himself at liberty to act as he pleases...**

These are the times that try men's souls. The summer soldier and the sunshine patriot will, in this crisis, shrink from the service of their country; but **he that stands it now, deserves the love and thanks of man and woman.** Tyranny, like hell, is not easily conquered; yet we have this consolation with us, that the harder the conflict, the more glorious the triumph. What we obtain too cheap, we esteem too lightly: it is dearness only that gives every thing its value. Heaven knows how to put a proper price upon its goods; and it would be strange indeed if so celestial an article as **FREEDOM** should not be highly rated.

...Wisdom is not the purchase of a day...

...It matters not where you live, or what rank of life you hold, the evil or the blessing will reach you all. The far and the near, the home counties and the back, the rich and the poor, will suffer or rejoice alike. The heart that feels not now is dead; the blood of his children will curse his cowardice, who shrinks back at a time when a little might have saved the whole, and made them happy. **I love the man that can smile in trouble, that can gather strength from distress, and grow brave by reflection. 'Tis the business of little minds to shrink; but he whose heart is firm, and whose conscience approves his conduct, will pursue his principles unto death. My own line of reasoning is to myself as straight and clear as a ray of light.** Not all the treasures of the world, so far as I believe, could have induced me to support an offensive war, for I think it murder; **but** if a thief breaks into my house, burns and destroys my property, and kills or threatens to kill me, or those that are in it, and to "bind men in all cases whatsoever" to his absolute will, am I to suffer it? What signifies it to me, whether he who does it is a king or a common man; my countryman or not my countryman; whether it be done by an individual villain, or an army of them? If we reason to the root of things we shall find no difference; neither can any just cause be assigned why we should punish in the one case and pardon in the other. **Let them call me rebel and welcome, I feel no concern from it; but I should suffer the misery of devils, were I to make a whore of my soul by swearing allegiance to one whose character is that of a sottish, stupid, stubborn, worthless, brutish man.** I conceive likewise a horrid idea in receiving mercy from a being, who at the last day shall be shrieking to the rocks and mountains to cover him, and fleeing with terror from the orphan, the widow, and the slain of America.

There are cases which cannot be overdone by language, and this is one. There are persons, too, who see not the full extent of the evil which threatens them; they solace themselves with hopes that the enemy, if he succeed, will be merciful. It is the madness of folly, to expect mercy from those who have refused to do justice; and even mercy, where conquest is the object, is only a trick of war; the cunning of the fox is as against both...

This is our situation, and who will may know it. By perseverance and fortitude we have the prospect of a glorious issue; by cowardice and submission, the sad choice of a variety of evils...

Those who expect to reap the blessing of freedom, must, like men, undergo the fatigues of supporting it... It is not a field of a few acres of ground, but a cause, that we are defending, and whether we defeat the enemy in one battle, or by degrees, the consequences will be the same.

...We have always been masters at the last push, and always shall be while we do our duty...

Men who are sincere in defending their freedom, will always feel concern at every circumstance which seems to make against them; it is the natural and honest consequence of all affectionate attachments, and the want of it is a vice. But the dejection lasts only for a moment; they soon rise out of it with additional vigor; the glow of hope, courage and fortitude, will, in a little time, supply the place of every inferior passion, and kindle the whole heart into heroism.

...The nearer any disease approaches to a crisis, the nearer it is to a cure. Danger and deliverance make their advances together, and it is only the last push, in which one or the other takes the lead.

To argue with a man who has renounced the use and authority of reason, and whose philosophy consists in holding humanity in contempt, is like administering medicine to the dead, or endeavoring to convert an atheist by scripture. Enjoy,

sir, your insensibility of feeling and reflecting. It is the prerogative of animals. And no man will envy you these honors, in which a savage only can be your rival and a bear your master...

To the Inhabitants of America

...The wisdom, civil governments, and sense of honor of the states of Greece and Rome, are frequently held up as objects of excellence and imitation. Mankind have lived to very little purpose, if, at this period of the world, they must go two or three thousand years back for lessons and examples. We do great injustice to ourselves by placing them in such a superior line. We have no just authority for it, neither can we tell why it is that we should suppose ourselves inferior.

Could the mist of antiquity be cleared away, and men and things be viewed as they really were, it is more than probable that they would admire a greater variety and combination of difficulties, than, I believe, ever fell to the share of any one people, in the same space of time, and has replenished the world with more useful knowledge and sounder maxims of civil government than were ever produced in any age before. **Had it not been for America, there had been no such thing as freedom left throughout the whole universe...**

A good opinion of ourselves is exceedingly necessary in private life, but absolutely necessary in public life, and of the utmost importance in supporting national character. I have no notion of yielding the palm of the United States to any Grecians or Romans that were ever born. We have equaled the bravest in times of danger, and excelled the wisest in construction of civil governments...

That in which every man is interested, is ever man's duty to support. And any burden which falls equally on all men, and from which every man is to receive an equal benefit, is consistent with the most perfect ideas of liberty. I would wish to revive something of that virtuous ambition which first called America into the field...

When information is withheld, ignorance becomes a reasonable excuse...

To see it in our power to make a world happy – to teach mankind the art of being so – to exhibit, on the theatre of the universe a character hitherto unknown – and to have, as it were, a new creation entrusted to our hands, are honors that command reflection, and can neither be too highly estimated, nor too gratefully received.

In this pause then of recollection – while the storm is ceasing, and the long agitated mind vibrating to a rest, let us look back on the scenes we have passed, and learn from experience what is yet to be done…

So far as my endeavors could go, they have all been directed to conciliate the affections, unite the interests, and draw and keep the mind of the country together; and the better to assist in this foundation work of the revolution, I have avoided all places of profit or office, either in the state I live in, or in the United States; kept myself at a distance from all parties and party connections, and even disregarded all private and inferior concerns: and when we take into view the great work which we have gone through, and feel, as we ought to feel, the just importance of it, we shall then see, that the little wranglings and indecent contentions of personal parley, are as dishonorable to our characters, as they are injurious to our repose.

It was the cause of America that made me an author. The force with which it struck my mind, and the dangerous condition the country appeared to me in, by courting an impossible and an unnatural reconciliation with those who were determined to reduce her, instead of striking out into the only line that could cement and save her, A DECLARATION OF INDEPENDENCE, made it impossible for me, feeling as I did, to be silent: and if, in the course of more than seven years, I have rendered her any service, I have likewise added something to the reputation of literature, by freely and disinterestedly employing it in the great cause of mankind, and showing that there may be genius without prostitution…

Every age and generation must be as free to act for itself, in all cases, as the ages and generation which preceded it. **The vanity and presumption of governing beyond the grave, is the most ridiculous and insolent of all tyrannies.**

Man has no property in man; neither has any generation a property in the generations which are to follow…

Every generation is, and must be, competent to all the purposes which its occasions require…

Those who have quitted the world, and those who are not yet arrived in it, are as remote from each other, as the utmost stretch of moral imagination can conceive. What possible obligation, then, can exist between them; what rule or principle can be laid down, that two nonentities, the one out of existence, and the other not in, and who never can meet in this world, that the one should control the other to the end of time?

The circumstances of the world are continually changing, and the opinions of men change also; and **as government is for the living, and not for the dead, it is the living only that has any right in it.** That which may be thought right and found convenient in one age, may be thought wrong and found inconvenient in another. **In such cases, who is to decide, the living, or the dead?...**

It has been thought a considerable advance toward establishing the principles of freedom to say, that government is a compact between those who govern and those who are governed: but this cannot be true, because it is putting the effect before the cause; for as a man must have existed before governments existed, there necessarily was a time when governments did not exist, and consequently there could originally exist no governors to form such a compact with.

The fact therefore must be, that the individuals themselves, each in his own personal and sovereign right, entered into a compact with each other to produce a government: and this is the only mode in which governments have a right to arise, and the only principle on which they have a right to exist.

To possess ourselves of a clear idea of what government is, or ought to be, we must trace it to its origin. In doing this, we shall easily discover that governments must have arisen, either out of the people, or over the people...

Reason and Ignorance, the opposites of each other, influence the great bulk of mankind. If either of these can be rendered sufficiently extensive in a country, the machinery of government goes easily on. Reason obeys itself; and Ignorance submits to whatever is dictated to it...

...Freedom had been hunted round the globe; reason was considered as rebellion; and the slavery of fear had made men afraid to think.

...Reason, like time, will make its own way, and prejudice will fall in a combat with interest...

Government is no farther necessary than to supply the few cases to which society and civilization are not conveniently competent; and instances are not wanting to show, that every thing which government can usefully add thereto, has been performed by the common consent of society, without government.

The more perfect civilization is, the less occasion has it for government, because the more does it regulate its own affairs, and govern itself; but so contrary is the practice of old governments to the reason of the case, that the expenses of them increase in the proportion they ought to diminish...

Government is not a trade which any man or body of men has a right to set up and exercise for his own emolument, but is altogether a trust, in right of those by whom that trust is delegated, and by whom it is always resumable. It has of itself no rights; they are altogether duties...

When extraordinary power and extraordinary pay are allotted to any individual in a government, he becomes the center, round which every kind of corruption generates and forms. **Give to any man a million a year, and add thereto the power of creating and disposing of places, at the expense of a country, and the liberties of that country are no longer secure. What is called the splendor of a throne, is no other than the corruption of the state. It is made up of a band of parasites, living in luxurious indolence, out of the public taxes.**

When once such a vicious system is established, it becomes the guard and protection of all inferior abuses. The man who is in the receipt of a million a year is the last person to promote a spirit of reform, lest, in the event, it should reach to himself. It is always his interest to defend inferior abuses, as so many outworks to protect the citadel, and in this species of political fortification, all the parts have such a common dependence, that it is never to be expected they will attack each other...

...Infidelity does not consist in believing, or in disbelieving; it consists in professing to believe what he does not believe. It is impossible to calculate the moral mischief, if I may so express it, that mental lying has produced in society. When a man has so far corrupted and prostituted the chastity of his mind as to subscribe his professional belief to things he does not believe he has prepared himself for the commission of every other crime.

The lady replied: My dear Mr. Paine...

When a country begins to use such expressions as "seeking a bigger share of the pie," it is accepting a tenet of pure collectivism: the notion that the goods produced in a country do not belong to the producers, but belong to everybody, and that the government is the distributor. If so, what chance does an individual have of getting a slice of that pie? No chance at all, not even a few crumbs. An individual becomes "fair game" for every sort of organized predator.

Thus people are pushed to surrender their independence in exchange for tribal protection.

The government of a mixed economy manufactures pressure groups – and, specifically, manufactures "ethnicity." The profiteers are those group leaders who discover suddenly that they can exploit the helplessness, the fear, the frustration of their "ethnic" brothers, organize them into a group, present demands to the government – and deliver the vote. The result is political jobs, subsidies, influence, and prestige for the leaders of the ethnic groups...

To give you an example: **If a building were threatened with collapse and you declared that the crumbling foundation has to be rebuilt, a pragmatist would answer that your solution is too abstract, extreme, unprovable, and that immediate priority must be given to the need of putting ornaments on the balcony railings, because it would make the tenants feel better...**

The basic philosophic credo of the United States was eloquently stated two centuries ago by Elihu Palmer, a spokesman of the revolutionary era. "The strength of the human understanding," he wrote, "**is incalculable, its keenness of discernment would ultimately penetrate into every part of nature, were it permitted to operate with uncontrolled and unqualified freedom.**" At last, he says, men have escaped from the mind-destroying ideas of the Middle Ages; they have grasped "**the unlimited power of human reason,**" "**reason, which is the glory of our nature.**" Now, he says, men should feel "an unqualified confidence" in their mental powers and energy, and they should proceed to remake the world accordingly...

What is the solution? The only answer to a corrupt philosophy is a rational philosophy, and the only way to spread a rational philosophy is through the universities. The universities today – not the churches any longer, and not the press or TV – are the main transmitters of philosophy; they are what set the tone and direction of a culture. To those of you of college age, therefore, those who do not subscribe to Kant's philosophy, I want to say that the moral of my remarks is not: quit college. On the contrary, if you are considering college or are already enrolled in one, **I urge you to enter or stay, stay and fight the system, by trying to gain a hearing for some other ideas**, some pro-American ideas. The colleges pretend to be open to all viewpoints, even though they are not. The only hope is to make them live up to their pretense. If you give up the colleges, you give up any role in the decisive battle for the world, the intellectual battle.

I am not suggesting that you become a martyr, or enter into arguments with professors who will penalize you for your ideas. Not all of them will, however, and I am speaking within the context and limits of rational self-interest. Within that context, I say: speak up when appropriate, let your voice be heard on campus, try to stick it out and obtain your degree, come back to teach if you can get in the door and if that is the lifework you want; and if you are an alumnus, be careful what kind of academic programs you support financially. In this battle, every word, man, and penny counts.

...Let me remind you – as I have said many times before – that there is no such thing as historical determinism. The world does not have to continue moving toward disaster. But unless men change their philosophical direction – which they still have time to do – the collapse will come. And if you want to know the specific process that will bring it about, that process – the beginning of the end – is visible today...

The fundamental principle of capitalism is the separation of State and Economics – that is: The liberation of men's economic activities, of production and trade, from any form of intervention, coercion, compulsion, regulation, or control by the government. This is the essence of capitalism, which is implicit in its theory and in the operation of a free market – but this is not the way most of its advocates saw it, and it is not the way it was translated into practice. The term "*laissez-faire* capitalism," which one has to use today in order to be understood, is actually a redundancy: Only an economy of total "*laissez faire*" is capitalism; anything else is a "mixed economy," that is, a mixture, in varying degrees, of freedom and controls, of voluntary choice and government compulsion, of individualism and collectivism.

A full, perfect system of capitalism has never yet existed in history. Various degrees of government intervention and control remained in all the mixed, semi-free economies of the nineteenth century, undercutting, hampering, distorting, and ultimately destroying the operations of a free market. But **during the nineteenth century, mankind came close to economic freedom, for the first and only time in history. Observe the results. Observe also that the degree of a country's freedom from government control was the degree of its progress. America was the freest and achieved the most.**

When two opposite principles are operating in any issue, the scientific approach to their evaluation is to study their respective performances, trace their consequences in full, precise detail, and then pronounce judgment on their respective merits. In the case of a mixed economy, **the first duty of any thinker or scholar is to study the historical record and to discover which developments were caused by the free enterprise of private individuals, by free production and trade in a free market – and which developments were caused by government intervention into the economy.** It might shock you to hear that no such study has ever been made. To my knowledge, no book dealing with this issue is available. If one wants to study this question, one has to gather information from random passages and references in books on other subjects, or from the unstated implications of known but unanalyzed facts.

Those who undertake such a study will discover that all the economic evils popularly ascribed to capitalism were caused, necessitated, and made possible not by private enterprise, not by free trade on a free market, but by government intervention into the economy, by government controls, favors, subsidies, franchises, and special privileges.

The villains were not the private businessmen who made fortunes by productive ability and free trade, but the bureaucrats and their friends, the men who made fortunes by political pull and government favor. Yet it is the private businessmen, the victims, who took the blame, while the bureaucrats and their intellectual spokesmen used their own guilt as an argument for the extension of their power. Those of you who have read *Atlas Shrugged* will recognize the difference between a businessman such as Hank Rearden, the representative of capitalism, and a businessman such as Orren Boyle, the typical product of a mixed economy. If you want an historical example, consider the career of James Jerome Hill, who built the Great Northern Railroad without a penny of federal help, who was responsible, practically single-handedly, for the development of the entire American Northwest, and who was persecuted by the government all his life, under the Sherman Act, for allegedly being a monopolist. Consider it, then compare it to the career of the famous California businessmen known as "The Big Four," who built the Central Pacific Railroad on federal subsidies, causing disastrous consequences and dislocations in the country's economy, and who held a thirty-year monopoly on railroad transportation in California, by means of special privileges granted by the state legislature which made it legally impossible for any competing railroad to exist in the state.

The difference between these two types of business career has never been identified in the generally accepted view of capitalism. By imperceptible degrees – first, through the default of capitalism's alleged defenders, then through the deliberate misrepresentations and falsifications of its enemies – **the gradual rewriting of our economic history has brought us to the stage where people believe that all the economic evils of the last two centuries were caused by the free-enterprise element, the so-called "private sector," of our mixed economy, while the economic progress of these two centuries was the result of the government's actions and interventions.** People are now told that America's spectacular industrial achievements, unmatched in any period of history or in any part of the globe, were due not to the productive genius of free men, but to the special privileges handed to them by a paternalistic government. The fact that much more autocratic governments, with much wider privilege-dispensing powers and policies, did not achieve the same results anywhere else on earth is blanked out by the proponents of this theory...

No politico-economic system in history had proved its value so eloquently or had benefited mankind so greatly as capitalism – and none has ever been attacked so savagely and blindly. Why did the majority of the intellectuals turn against capitalism from the start? Why did their victims, the businessmen, bear their attacks in silence. The cause of it is that primordial evil which, to this day, men are afraid to challenge: **the morality of [coerced – editor] altruism.**

Altruism has been men's ruling moral code through most of mankind's history. It has had many forms and variations, but its essence has always remained the same: altruism holds that man has no right to exist for his own sake, that service to others is the only justification of his existence, and that self-sacrifice is his highest moral duty, virtue, and value.

The philosophical conflict which, since the Renaissance, has been tearing Western civilization and which has reached its ultimate climax in our age is the conflict between capitalism and the altruist morality. Capitalism and [coerced – editor] altruism are philosophical opposites; they cannot coexist in the same man or in the same society.

The moral code which is implicit in capitalism had never been formulated explicitly. The basic premise of that code is that man –

every man – is an end in himself, not the means to the ends of others, that man must exist for his own sake, neither sacrificing himself to others nor sacrificing others to himself, and that men must deal with one another as traders, by voluntary choice to mutual benefit. This, in essence, is the moral premise on which the **United States of America was based: the principle of man's right to his own life, to his own liberty, to the pursuit of his own happiness**.

This is what the philosophers and the intellectuals of the nineteenth century did not and could not choose to identify, so long as they remained committed to the mystics' morality of [coerced – editor] altruism. If the good, the virtuous, the morally ideal is suffering and self-sacrifice – then, by that standard, capitalism had to be damned as evil. Capitalism does not tell men to suffer, but to pursue enjoyment and achievement, here, on earth – capitalism does not tell men to serve and sacrifice, but to produce and profit – **capitalism does not preach passivity, humility, resignation, but independence, self-confidence, self-reliance – and, above all, capitalism does not permit anyone to expect or demand, to give or to take the unearned**. In all human relationships – private or public, spiritual or material, social or political or economic or moral – capitalism requires that men be guided by a principle which is the antithesis of [coerced – editor] altruism: **the principle of justice...**

There were two crucial errors – or evasions – in the liberals' view of capitalism, from which all the rest of their debacle proceeded. One was their attitude toward the businessman; the other, their attitude toward the use of physical force.

Since wealth, throughout all the centuries of stagnation preceding the birth of capitalism, had been gained by conquest, by physical force, by political power, the intellectuals took it as their axiom that wealth can be acquired only by force – and refused to break up their mental package deal, to differentiate between a businessman and a feudal baron.

I quote from my book, ***For the New Intellectual***: "Evading the difference between production and looting, they called the businessman a robber. Evading the difference between freedom and compulsion, they called him a slave driver. Evading the difference between reward and terror, they called him an exploiter. Evading the difference between paychecks and guns, they called him an autocrat. Evading the difference between trade and force, they called him a tyrant. **The most crucial issue they had to evade was the difference between the earned and the unearned.**"

The intellectuals refused to identify the fact that the source of industrial wealth is man's mind, that the fortunes made in a free economy are the product of intelligence, of ability. This led them to the modern version of the ancient soul–body dichotomy: to the contradiction of upholding the freedom of the mind, while denying it to the most active exponents of creative intelligence, the businessmen – the contradiction of promising to liberate man's mind by enslaving his body. It led them to regard the businessman as a "vulgar materialist" or a brute or a Babbitt [this is a reference to Sinclair Lewis's novel – editor], as some sort of inferior species born to serve them – and to regard themselves as some sort of elite born to rule him, to control his life, and dispose of his product. **The shabby monument to this premise was the idea of divorcing production from distribution, of assuming the right to distribute that which one has not produced.** The only way to implement an idea of that kind, the next step in their moral descent, was the intellectuals' alliance with the thug, with the advocate of rule by brute force: the totalitarian collectivist.

The intellectuals' second error – their attitude toward the use of force – is a corollary of the first. So long as they refused to identify the nature of free trade and of a social system based on voluntary, uncoerced, unforced, non-sacrificial relationships among men, so long as the moral cannibalism of the altruist code permitted them to believe that it is virtuous and right to sacrifice some men for the sake of others – the intellectuals had to embrace the political creed of collectivism, the dream of establishing a perfect altruist society at the point of a gun. They projected a society where all would be sacrificed to that conveniently indefinable idol **"the public good," with themselves in the role of judges of what that "good" might be** and of who would be "the public" at any given moment – and ideal society to be achieved by means of physical force; that is, by means of the political power of the state, by means of a totalitarian dictatorship...

In the early years of American capitalism, the government's intervention into the country's economy was minimal; the government's role was predominantly confined to its proper function: that of a policeman and arbiter charged with the task of protecting the individual citizen's rights and property. (The most notorious exception to that rule existed only in the agrarian, non-industrial, non-capitalist states of the South, where the state governments upheld the institution of slavery.)

The attempts to obtain special economic privileges from the government were begun by businessmen, not by workers, but by businessmen who shared the intellectuals' view of **the State** as an instrument of "positive" power, serving "the public good," and who invoked it to claim that the public good demanded canals or railroads or subsidies or protective tariffs. It is not the great industrialists of America, who ran to government for special favors, but random adventurers with political pull or, later, those pretentious types, indoctrinated by the intellectuals, who dreamed of statism as a "manifest destiny."

It was not the businessmen or the industrialists or the workers or the labor unions that began the revolt against freedom, the demand for greater and greater government power and, ultimately, for the return to an absolute, totalitarian state; it was the intellectuals. For a detailed history of the steps by which the intellectuals of Germany led it toward totalitarianism, culminating in the establishment of the Nazi dictatorship, I will refer you to a brilliant book entitled ***Omnipotent Government*** by Professor Ludwig von Mises...

Promises? "Don't remind us of promises, that was yesterday, it's too late." Results? "Don't expect results, it's too soon." Costs? "Don't think in terms of old-fashioned economics – the more we spend, the richer we'll get." Principles? "Don't think in terms of old-fashioned labels – we've got a consensus." **The future? "Don't think."**

A widespread ignorance of a crucial economic issue is apparent in most discussions of today's problems: it is ignorance on the part of the public, evasion on the part of most economists, and crude demagoguery on the part of certain politicians. The issue is the function of wealth in an industrial economy.

Most people seem to believe that wealth is primarily an object of consumption – that the rich spend all or most of their money on personal luxury. Even if this were true, it would be their inalienable right – **but it does not happen to be true.** The percentage of income which men spend on consumption stands in inverse ratio to the amount of their wealth. The percentage is of no significance to a country's economy. The money of the rich is invested in production; it is an indispensable part of the stock seed that makes production possible.

Mr. Paine, I ask you: Who is John Galt?

Mr. Paine replies: My dear Ms. Rand, I have already answered.

One must view with profound respect the infinite capacity of the human mind to resist the inroad of useful knowledge.

I hope that doesn't describe me… does it describe you?

SELECT BIBLIOGRAPHY

Auden, W.H., "September 1, 1939", *Another Time*, Random House, London, 1940

Aurelius, Marcus, *Meditations*, New York, Penguin Books, 1964

Birkerts, Sven, *The Gutenberg Elegies*, Boston, Faber & Faber, 1994

Bloom, Allan, *The Closing of the American Mind*, New York, Simon and Schuster, 1987

Boyle, Leonard, *The Summa Theologiae of Saint Thomas Aquinas; Latin Text and English Translation,* Vol. I, New York, McGraw Hill, 1904

Brogan, D.W., *The American Character*, New York, Alfred A Knopf, 1944

Burke, Edmund, *Reflections on the Revolution in France*, New Rochelle, NY, Arlington House, 1966

Butler, Nicholas Murray, *Why Should We Change Our Form of Government?*, New York, Columbia University, 1912

Carlyle, Thomas, *The French Revolution: A History*, Everyman's Library, 1931

Conant, James Bryant, "Introduction", *General Education in Free Society: A Report of the Harvard Committee*, Cambridge, Mass., Harvard University Press, 1945

De Tocqueville, Alexis, *Democracy in America*, Chicago, University of Chicago Press, 2000

De Voto, Bernard, "Invocation", *The Year of Decision 1846*, New York, St. Martin's Press, 2000

Durant, Will, *Life of Greece*, New York, Simon and Schuster, 1939

Einstein, Albert, "Why Socialism", *Monthly Review*, Vol. I, I, New York, 1949,

Emerson, Ralph Waldo, "The American Scholar", *The Complete Works of Ralph Waldo Emerson*, Boston, New York, Houghton Mifflin Co., 1903–18

Hayek, F. A., *The Road to Serfdom*, Chicago, University of Chicago Press, 1994

Hutchins, Robert Maynard, "The Great Conversation", *Encyclopaedia*

Britannica, Chicago, 1955

—, Robert Maynard, *The Higher Learning In America,* New Haven, Yale University Press, 1936

Katz, Stanley, "Liberal Education on the Ropes", *Chronicle of Higher Education*, April 1, 2005, Vol. 51, Iss. 30

Kirk, Dr. Russell, *The American Cause*, Chicago, H. Regnery Co., 1957

Lippmann, Walter, address given at the annual meeting of The American Association for the Advancement of Science, December 29, 1940

Mansfield, Harvey C., "A More Demanding Curriculum", *Claremont Review of Books*, Winter 2004

Massey, Douglas S., *Return of the L Word: A Liberal Vision for the New Century*, Princeton, Princeton University Press, 2005

Melville, Herman, *Moby Dick*, New York, The Modern Library, 1930

Melville, Herman, *White-jacket*, New York, Grove Press, 1956

Mill, John Stuart, "On Social Freedom", reprinted from the *Oxford and Cambridge Review*, June 1907

Moorehead, Dr. Bob, "The Paradox of Age", *Words Aptly Spoken*, Overlake Christian Press, Kirkland, W.A., 1995

Nock, Albert Jay, *Isaiah's Job*, Irvington-on-Hudson, New York, Foundation for Economic Education, 1962

Paine, Thomas, *Common Sense*, New York, Liberal Arts Press, 1953

Plato, *Republic*, Book IX, New York, Basic Books, 1968

Postman, Neil, *Amusing Ourselves to Death: Public Discourse in the Age of Show Business*, New York, Penguin Group, 1986

Quigley, Carroll, *The World Since 1939: A History*, New York, Collier Books, 1968

Rand, Ayn, *Atlas Shrugged*, New York, Dutton, 1992

Rogge, Benjamin, *Can Capitalism Survive?*, Indianapolis, The Liberty Fund, 1979

Schumpeter, Joseph, *Capitalism, Socialism and Democracy*, New York, Harper, 1950

Schweitzer, Albert, *The Philosophy of Civilization*, New York, The Macmillan Company, 1949

Spencer, Herbert, *The Man Versus the State*, Caldwell, Id., The Caxton Printers Ltd, 1940

Steinbeck, John, *America and Americans*, New York, Viking Penguin, 2002

Swift, Jonathan, *Gulliver's Travels*, London, Puffin, 1997

Thucydides, *Peloponnesian War*, Book II, Ch. 36–39, Chicago, University of Chicago Press, 1989

Veblen, Thorstein, *The Theory of the Leisure Class*, New York, Penguin Classics, 1994

Printed in the United States
79163LV00003B/100-435

9 781844 016990